DISCOURSES OF DIFFERENCE

DISCOURSES OF DIFFERENCE

An analysis of women's travel
writing and colonialism

Sara Mills

London and New York

First published 1991
First published in paperback 1993
by Routledge
11 New Fetter Lane, London EC4P 4EE

Simultaneously published in the USA and Canada
by Routledge Inc.
29 West 35th Street, New York, NY 10001

Typeset in 10/12pt Baskerville by
Ponting-Green Publishing Services, London
Printed in Great Britain by
TJ Press (Padstow) Ltd, Padstow, Cornwall

British Library Cataloguing in Publication Data
Mills, Sara
Discourses of Difference: Analysis of
Women's Travel Writing and Colonialism.
New ed
I. Title
828.8080932

Library of Congress Cataloging in Publication Data
Mills, Sara
Discourses of difference: an analysis of women's travel
writing and colonialism / Sara Mills
p.   cm.
1. English prose literature —Women authors—History and
criticism. 2. Women travelers in literature. 3. English
prose literature—19th century—History and criticism.
4. English prose literature—20th century—History and
criticism. 5. Feminism and literature—Great Britain—
History. 7. Great Britain—Colonies—Historiography.
8. Discourse analysis, Literary. 9. Authorship—Sex
differences. 10. Imperialism in literature. 11. Colonies
in literature. 12. Travel in literature.
I. Title
PR788.T72M5   1991
828'.80809'9287—dc20   93—15720
ISBN 0–415–09664–2

To my Nan, Great Granny Anny and
my mother, Barbara

The World is surfeited with Male travels, all in the same Tone and stuft with the same trifles, a *Lady* has the skill to strike out a New Path and to embellish a worn-out Subject with a variety of fresh and elegant Entertainment.

(Mary Astells, in her Introduction to *Lady Wortley Montague*, 1724)

The thing you always suspected about yourself the minute you become a tourist is true: a tourist is an ugly human being . . . pausing here and there to gaze at this and taste that, and it will never occur to you that the people who inhabit the place in which you have just paused cannot stand you, that behind their closed doors they laugh at your strangeness.

(Jamaica Kincaid, *A Small Place*, 1988)

CONTENTS

ACKNOWLEDGEMENTS

Patrick Williams has, as always, been tremendously supportive, encouraging and insightful in the comments he made on drafts of this book, and the discussions we have had on the ideas of this book and colonial discourse in general have been exceptionally useful. Lynne Pearce has been very generous with her time in commenting on drafts, as has Tony Brown. Deirdre Burton was the instigator, in many ways, of interest in this and many other fields of study. I would like to thank Network members, especially Shirley Foster and Margaret Beetham, for their very helpful comments on early versions of the book and for discussion sessions on women's writing. I am grateful to both of my parents for their encouragement.

The staff at the National Library of Scotland and the Andersonian Library, at Strathclyde University, have always been very willing to help. Thanks are due to students and staff in the Programme in Literary Linguistics for an openness to interdisciplinary work and for providing a motivating research environment, and also to students and staff in English and Drama at the University of Loughborough.

INTRODUCTION

This book is concerned with the analysis of women's travel writing in the period of what James Morris calls 'high imperialism', roughly demarcated here as the mid-nineteenth century to early twentieth century. (Morris, 1979c: 23). In this period, a new colonial relationship emerged, where formal conquest, annexation and administration became the most common relation between Britain and certain other countries, and Britain declared itself to be an imperial nation (Hobsbawm, 1987). I will be concentrating mainly on the writings of British women travel writers who describe their travels to colonised countries, which I am taking to mean broadly those countries which were under British economic, religious or political control, however loosely that may be defined.[1] Rather than viewing colonialism as a unified phenomenon, I concentrate on the differences of discursive frameworks which the changes in the colonial situation entailed. Critics such as Peter Hulme and Dennis Porter have analysed the heterogeneity in discourse structures within the colonial period, but they have not considered the way that women writers had to negotiate different textual constraints (Hulme, 1986; D. Porter, 1982).

The period of 1850–1930 is the one where British colonial interests in other nations were made most apparent; but how was this colonial strength negotiated in texts by women who were conventionally seen not to be part of the colonial expansion? When I first started studying women's travel writing, I was surprised at the sheer volume of writing, especially since critics like Worley suggest that 'very few women broke out of the domestic circle in the nineteenth century to venture into the wider world as self-acknowledged travellers' (Worley, 1986: 40).

1

In contrast to Worley's view, my study revealed many hundreds of women travellers, a fact which Shirley Foster, also working on this area, has confirmed (Foster, 1988 and 1990).

In recent years there has been a revival of interest in the analysis of travel writing: firstly, from those who read travel writing from a fairly uncritical political position, and, secondly, from those who analyse it as part of the critical study of colonial discourse. We might see the former group as belonging to a larger-scale 'Raj revival' which permeates cultural production in Britain at present, with images and ideological positions of the colonial period being transposed onto British cultural forms of the 1980s and 1990s. Reading travel writing from Britain's colonial past may be part of an attempt to distract attention away from the present historical situation. Within this view, travel writing is approached less in terms of its subject-matter than in terms of its literary qualities. There are now many travel books and anthologies of travel writing published, and there are travel writing competitions with prestigious prizes. This compares quite markedly to the view of travel writing twenty years ago, when Paul Fussell's question 'Is there not perhaps something in the genre that attracts second-rate talents?' was a common one (Fussell, 1980: 212).

With this resurgence of interest in contemporary travel writing and the reissuing of earlier examples, has also come the critical study of the genre within colonial discourse, that is, the analysis of texts written by westerners about colonised countries. This work began with Edward Said's book *Orientalism* (1978a), which traced the similarities in rhetorical and informational structure of a wide range of seemingly objective writings about the Orient. Said's work has been continued by many others, most notably Mary Louise Pratt, Peter Hulme, Homi Bhabha, Rana Kabbani and Gayatri Spivak.[2] For them, along with more clearly 'literary' texts, travel writing is essentially an instrument within colonial expansion and served to reinforce colonial rule once in place. These critics study travel texts using the kind of careful analysis of tropes and structures which would normally be undertaken on 'literary' texts. It was not until the advent of colonial discourse as a legitimate field of research in the 1970s that travel writing began to be considered worthy of academic study.

This book considers the ways in which women's writing in the colonial period might demand different theoretical tools to those developed within colonial discourse. This is the first book to set women travellers within the colonial context; most writers on this subject have represented them as individuals struggling against the social conventions of the Victorian period, who were exceptional in managing to escape the system of chaperonage. Their role within the colonial period is often strenuously avoided, as if, in order to read the texts as accounts of individual women's lives, the colonial material, i.e., that which links their accounts to larger discursive structures, has to be ignored. In the colonial context, British women were only allowed to figure as symbols of home and purity; women as active participants can barely be conceived of. This is because of social conventions for conceptualising imperialism, which seem to be as much about constructing *masculine* British identity as constructing a national identity *per se*. For this reason, women as individuals and as writers are always seen to be marginal to the process of colonialism. A further reason why the colonial context is not considered by critics is that women's writing and their involvement in colonialism was markedly different from men's; their work was informed by different discursive frameworks and pressures. It is these frameworks which I shall map out. Because of the way that discourses of femininity circulated within the late nineteenth and early twentieth centuries, women travel writers were unable to adopt the imperialist voice with the ease with which male writers did. The writing which they produced tended to be more tentative than male writing, less able to assert the 'truths' of British rule without qualification. Because of their oppressive socialisation and marginal position in relation to imperialism, despite their generally privileged class position, women writers tended to concentrate on descriptions of people as individuals, rather than on statements about the race as a whole. It is in their struggle with the discourses of imperialism and femininity, neither of which they could wholeheartedly adopt, and which pulled them in different textual directions, that their writing exposes the unsteady foundations on which it is based. Their textual unease is labelled as 'bad writing'; for example, Paul Fussell explicitly refuses to consider women travel writers within his account of literary travel, as he states that they are not sufficiently concerned either with travel or with writing itself (Fussell, 1980). However, these tensions reveal some of the contradictions and silences implicit in writing of the period.

3

Women's travel writing is problematic because, although it was widely read at the time of its publication, and many of the texts present a slightly different view of colonialism to male counterparts, in general it is not considered within critical studies of colonial discourse. Instead, the books which are written about women travellers tend to come in the form of coffee table books, with lavish illustrations of these eccentric creatures.[3] Certain women's travel writing within the late nineteenth and early twentieth centuries has been reprinted, but it has been almost exclusively by the feminist presses, such as Virago. The way these texts have been read has been primarily 'realist', that is, they are not analysed as textual artefacts, but rather as simple autobiographies. The only critics who have concerned themselves with women's travel writing have been women critics, who have usually situated themselves, at least implicitly, within a feminist framework.

The relatively unexplored nature of the subject-matter seemed to me curious, since these texts, in their various ways, are very challenging theoretically – a strange mixture of the stereotypically colonial in content, style and trope, presenting the colonised country as naturally a part of the British Empire, whilst at the same time being unable to adopt a straightforwardly colonial voice. For a feminist reader in the 1990s, the texts are a mixture of the thoroughly enjoyable (adventure narratives depicting strong, resourceful, women characters in situations rarely found in literature of the period) and the almost impossible (the racism, the concern to present the narrator as feminine, and the lengthy descriptions of the domestic). It is precisely this difficulty of interpretation which I find of interest. As a feminist, one easy option is to read the texts as proto-feminist, a strategy encouraged by the fact that many of them have been reissued by Virago. By judicious quotation and selective reference to their authors' lives, it is possible to depict these writers and their narrative figures as proto-feminists who live up to the titles 'indomitable' and 'eccentric'. However, that would entail ignoring many women's texts which do not fit that mould. Much of the analysis done by women critics so far falls into this category of proto-feminist reading, yet it is possible to 'prove', by selective reading, that these writers were proto-feminist, anti-feminist, colonial and anti-colonial. As Gillian Beer notes:

We shall read as readers in 1987 or 1988, or with luck, 1998, but we need not do so helplessly, merely hauling, without noticing, our own cultural baggage. That is likely to happen if we read past texts solely for their grateful 'relevance' to our expectation and to those of our circumstances.

(Beer, 1989: 67)

In the desire to produce a coherent reading of the texts, many critics impose a schema of reading, whereby many parts of the text have to be left out of the account. Beer suggests that our task when reading texts from the past is to:

receive the same fullness of resource from past texts as from present . . . respect their difference . . . revive those shifty significations which do not pay court to our concerns, but are full of meaning of that past present . . . . The past is past only to us.

(Beer, 1989: 68)

The reading strategy which I adopt in this book will be less concerned with proving a point (arguing, for example, that women's travel writing is better or worse than men's), but rather with exploring the possibilities of interpreting this writing within its period and its discursive constraints. I will be analysing travel writing in its complexity, and paradoxically, despite its superficial readability, in its indecipherability.

Because of the problems of reading the texts from a realist position, I have tried to find alternative strategies. One of the most obvious choices is colonial discourse analysis, but it is not possible to transpose the work which has been done on colonial discourse on to these texts. Although this work is theoretically more attractive than some of the biographical readings of the texts, the way that the writing of the colonial period is described is often in masculinist terms, to the extent that it seemed impossible to fit women's writing into such frameworks. This study aims to discover the specificity of women's travel writing, and also, at the same time, the elements which it shares with men's writing. I shall argue that even when women's writing seems to consist of similar elements to men's, it is judged and categorised differently. Thus, the difference is not a simplistic textual distinction between men's writing on the one hand and women's writing on the other, but rather a series of discursive pressures on production and reception which female writers have to negotiate, in very different ways to males. It is this attempt to both view women's travel writing in this period in relation to men's writing, but also in its own terms which makes this study so complex. Certain discursive elements are shared by both male- and female-authored texts, but they are nevertheless received, commented upon and marketed differently. I will certainly not be arguing that women's travel writing is generically distinct from men's. Rather I will be arguing that women's travel texts are produced and received within a context which shares similarities with the discursive construction and reception of male texts, whilst at the same time, because of the discursive frameworks which exert pressure on female writers, there may be negotiations in women's texts which result in differences which seem to be due to gender.

I want to take these texts seriously, not simply to reduce them to biographical studies of exceptional spinsters, as some critics have done.[4] What I intend to do has more in common with Peter Hulme's work on colonial discourse: 'The venture . . . is archaeological; no smooth history emerges, but rather a series of fragments which, read speculatively, hint at a story that can never be fully recovered' (Hulme, 1986: 12). In constructing an archaeology of these texts, we, as readers in the 1990s, will never really know what discursive elements acted on women travellers when they wrote, but this book is an attempt at an avowedly partial account. This archaeological analysis exists in a contrastive, as well as in a complementary relation with much of the criticism there is in this field, both by colonial discourse theorists and feminists.[5] For this purpose I have blended together the work of Michel Foucault and feminist theory, but not in the seamless way that perhaps the term 'blend' suggests; rather I am interested in the way that Foucault's theories, colonial discourse and feminist theories can interact to produce an analytical framework.

FOUCAULT AND THE STUDY OF COLONIAL DISCOURSE

In writing a book, it has become a convention to frame one's work under the aegis of a particular theorist or group of theorists. It is important to ask what explanatory advantages the use of

Michel Foucault's work has. This question is especially pertinent in the case of Foucault, who does not seem a particularly straightforward theorist to choose: a philosopher who studied the history of medical practice, the development of the prison and the discourses of sexuality and madness; in Clifford Geertz's words, 'a non-historical historian, an anti-humanist human scientist, a counter-structuralist structuralist' (cited in Dreyfus and Rabinow (eds), 1982: iii). At first sight, it would be difficult to understand what relevance Foucault might have for a feminist analysis of women's travel writing since he rarely addresses the question of gender, and he certainly does not produce 'readings' of texts.[6] However, Foucault's work poses questions which are of relevance to any study that involves an analysis of discourses and power. And furthermore, Foucauldian analyses embody a certain productive scepticism which is useful for readings of all kinds: it is essential to look at all types of writing in just as critical and suspicious a way as one would a literary text.

For many, the notion of using the work of Michel Foucault is theoretically problematic; as Meaghan Morris and Paul Patton say: 'Foucault's work does not form a system', it is 'not a consistent theory' and 'it is a patchwork of studies which . . . may produce something resembling a pattern, but in which no single rule governs the move from one piece to the next' (Morris and Patton (eds), 1979: 8). Although the theoretical status of Foucault's work is problematic, that does not therefore invalidate my intention to put his theories to work.

Throughout his career, Foucault remained an iconoclast, refusing to be limited to the position of his last text, or to be classified as belonging to a school of thought, whether Marxism, structuralism or post-structuralism. For this reason, it is difficult to talk about Foucault in the singular, since there are several positions which Foucault occupies. As Diane Macdonell comments:

> there is little to gain from a fully unified survey of Foucault's work . . . a survey which places the writing under the control of whatever is taken to be the author's final meaning. Authorism of this kind is idealist, and to cover the early writings with a fictitious coherence, fabricating from some end their total sense, would be rather an ironic gesture.
>
> (Macdonell, 1986: 83)

For this reason, I will be using Foucault's work very much in the manner that he suggests that readers do, as a 'tool-box' and not as totalising theory, able to explain everything, but rather as a fragmentary theory which is descriptive of changing contexts, and therefore subject itself to change and re-evaluation.[7]

His work has been used by many theorists within the study of colonial discourse, but usually as an addition to Marxist theorising: for example, Said uses his work in conjunction with Gramsci (Said, 1978a) and Peter Hulme uses his work in conjunction with Althusser and Macherey (Hulme, 1986). Although Marxist theory allows the critic to be explicit about her political motivation, I have chosen to use the work of Foucault instead. Although I would identify myself as Marxist feminist, there are three aspects of Foucault's work which are of particular use in the analysis of colonial writing: the notion of discourse, a concern with the surface of discourse and a critique of claims to scientificity.

Firstly, the notion of discourse plays an important role in much work on colonial writing. With such texts, it is especially important to formulate the notion of a general group of shared characteristics. Edward Said, drawing on Foucault's work, uses the term discourse to refer to all texts, literary and non-literary, which are written about the Orient, because, for him, they have a similar intent, and a similar effect. He says about the discourse he terms 'Orientalism', i.e., works written by westerners about the Orient:

> My contention is that without examining Orientalism as discourse one cannot possibly understand the enormously systematic discipline by which European culture was able to manage – even to produce – the Orient politically, sociologically, militarily, ideologically, scientifically, and imaginatively during the post-Enlightenment period.
>
> (Said, 1978a: 3)

Many critics have worked within the field of discourse theory and have developed different definitions of the term. Foucault himself has several. Discourse is used to mean: firstly, all language and the system of rules whereby utterances/texts are produced; secondly, all texts and utterances produced by those rules, regardless of their literary or factual status; thirdly, groupings of texts/utterances. Perhaps it is best to follow Macdonell in describing discourse in the following way: 'Whatever signifies or has meaning can be considered part of discourse' (Macdonell, 1986: 4). Discourse is not, however, a homogeneous term which subsumes all distinctions. As Macdonell says: 'Discourses differ with the kinds of institutions and social practices in which they take shape, and with the positions of those who speak and those whom they address' (ibid.: 1).

One of the important elements which defines a discourse is its relation to other discourses, rather than its role in expressing an individual's 'feelings' or 'opinions'. To quote Macdonell again:

> A 'discourse', as a particular area of language use, may be identified by the institutions to which it relates and by the position from which it comes and which it marks out for the speaker. The position does not exist by itself, however. Indeed, it may be understood as a standpoint taken up by the discourse through its relation to another, ultimately an opposing discourse.
>
> (Macdonell, 1986: 3)

Colin Gordon reinforces this idea of discourse as heterogeneous, since he sees it as 'irreducible either to the history of the careers, thought and intentions of individual agents (the authors of utterances) or to a supra-individual teleology of discovery and intellectual evolution (the truth of utterances)' (C. Gordon, 1979: 34). Thus, it is not necessary to read travel writing as expressing the truth of the author's life, but rather, it is the result of a configuration of discursive structures with which the author negotiates.

Within the study of colonial discourse, which poses itself as referring to 'reality', as telling the 'truth' about other countries, the notion of discourse can be useful. In discussing the way we can describe 'reality' Foucault says:

> We must not imagine that the world turns towards us a legible face which we would only have to decipher. The world is not the accomplice of our knowledge; there is no pre-discursive providence which disposes the world in our favour.
>
> (Foucault, 1981b: 67)

This remark is clearly aimed at dismissing the idea that the 'world' has an order which we simply have to transcribe in writing. It thus, in some measure, distinguishes the 'world' from the act of knowing the 'world'. The distinctions we make when we 'read' the world are those which society has constructed and instilled in us through representations, and they do not depend on structures *in* the world. This is particularly true of the colonial and post-colonial period where what the writer 'knows' and 'sees' is determined through large-scale discursive constructs. In *The Archæology of Knowledge*, Foucault shows that when one analyses signifying practices, the relation between words and objects becomes problematic:

> I would like to show with precise examples, in analysing discourses themselves one can see the loosening of the embrace, apparently so tight, of words and things, and the emergence of a group of rules proper to discursive practice. These rules define not the dumb existence of a reality, nor the canonical use of a vocabulary, but the ordering of objects.
>
> (Foucault, 1972a: 48–9)

In this last sentence, Foucault stresses that we do not simply transcribe 'reality' through discourse, but we organise it through serious speech acts, or what he terms *statements* (l'énoncé).[8] And later in the same text, he says:

> The analysis of statements, then, is a historical analysis but one that avoids all interpretation; it does not question things said as to what they are hiding, what they were 'really' saying, in spite of themselves, the unspoken element that they contain . . .; but on the contrary, it questions them as to their mode of existence . . . what it means for them to have appeared when and where they did – they and no others.
>
> (Foucault, 1972a: 109)

This is of central importance to Foucault's analysis of what can be deemed 'true' in different eras and places, since writings about the empire are often characterised by their truth claims. It is in the analysis of statements that it is possible to trace women writers' ambivalence in their position in relation to power.

10

Secondly, Foucault's concern with the surface of discourse is also important: he is not concerned with the hidden meaning of the text, since for him this type of hermeneutic impulse is based on the notion of an illusory truth which awaits discovery. Hermeneutic analysis posits a level of 'reality' which is hidden from most people, but to which it has access through analysis. Foucault asserts that there is no *hidden* 'reality'; what is discovered beneath the primary interpretation is yet more interpretation. For him, 'there is no sub-text' (Foucault, 1972a: 119). Marxist critics, drawing on the work of Pierre Macherey or Louis Althusser, tend to attempt to unearth a meaning which is unsaid or unarticulated. For example, Peter Hulme, using a psychoanalytic Marxist framework, aims to 'make a text speak more than it knows' (Hulme, 1986: 11–12), and this leads him to describe Christopher Columbus's diary as 'a veritable palimpsest' (ibid.: 1986: 18). These statements imply a hermeneutic role for the colonial discourse analyst, deciphering layer after layer of meaning, and although Hulme's book is an extremely stylish analysis of colonial texts, both insightful and inspiring, it is this delving for hidden meanings which is superfluous. To me, these colonial texts seem to be all surface.[9]

Thirdly, in this context, it is important to draw on the work of a theorist who is aware of the problems of claiming scientificity and truth for her/his own statements. A number of Marxist theorists, most notably Louis Althusser, have proposed systems of knowledge whereby there is a distinction between ideology and scientific knowledge (Althusser, 1984), but Foucault does not attempt to privilege the status of his own work and knowledge. He says:

> The notion of ideology appears to me to be difficult to use for three reasons. The first is that, whether one wants it to be or not, it is always in virtual opposition to something like the truth. . . . The second inconvenience is that it refers, necessarily I believe, to something like a subject. Thirdly, ideology is in a secondary position in relation to something which must function as the infrastructure or economic or material determinant for it.
>
> (Foucault, in Morris and Patton (eds), 1979: 36)

Dreyfus and Rabinow note: 'The practitioner of interpretive analytics realises that he [*sic*] is produced by what he is

11

studying, consequently he can never stand outside it' (Dreyfus and Rabinow (eds), 1982: 125). Thus, the interpreter has no privileged place in relation to the material s/he works on. Foucault constantly draws attention to the power of discourse in the structuring of his ideas. In an interview he states that he has not revised his answers to written questions 'not through any belief in the virtues of spontaneity, but in order to leave a problematic character, voluntarily uncertain, to the assertions advanced. What I have said is not "what I think" but often what I wonder whether it couldn't be thought' (Foucault, in Morris and Patton, 1979: 58). Rather than set up a scientific knowledge against which ideology is viewed, Foucault locates his own work within the discursive framework he has described. In much the same way, I am very aware that my concerns within this book, and what I discover, are conditioned by the theoretical frameworks and larger discursive structures circulating in Britain in the 1990s.

FOUCAULT AND FEMINISM

Since feminism is not a unitary theoretical position, it is essential to specify which elements of feminist thought I am drawing on, and how feminist the use of the work of Michel Foucault can be. Feminist literary theory can be split into those theories which are usable but naïve and those which are interesting but unusable (roughly translated as Anglo-American and French feminism). As I show in a recent book (Mills *et al.*, 1989), this division is not at all as clear cut as its geographic boundaries would suggest. Nevertheless, it is often difficult to find a theory which will enable you to make interesting and insightful statements about a text, which you would not have been able to say without the theory. In general, feminist textual theory has restricted itself to the analysis of literary texts and has been concerned with analysis of the text in itself.[10] This book aims to analyse texts which are not generally considered 'literary', and to consider both their production and their reception. I show that women's travel writing is constructed within a range of discursive pressures and in its reception it has frequently been labelled 'autobiographical'. This labelling should be seen as an attempt to deny women the status of creators of cultural artefacts. However, the analysis is still

12

she considering
autobiog as denigrating

further complicated by the fact that, whilst labelled 'factual', doubts are frequently cast on the truthfulness of women's accounts. This is especially the case in women's travel writing, where their texts are subject to accusations of exaggeration and falsehood. Thus, although my work is analysing 'factual' texts, I will be asking very 'literary' questions of them. A mixture of certain elements of feminist theory and Foucault helps to analyse this complexity.

Both Foucault and Edward Said are good examples of theorists who are inspiring and yet disappointing for feminists. Neither Foucault nor Said mention women writers in any detail in their work. Foucault devotes a part of *History of Sexuality* to a discussion of the hystericisation of women, but this is only a section alongside which he deals with other 'marginalised' groups, such as children and homosexuals.[11] As Sandra Bartky notes, Foucault is 'blind to those disciplines that produce a modality of embodiment that is peculiarly feminine' (Bartky, 1988: 64). Said discusses a wide range of writers on the Orient but he only deals with one woman writer, Gertrude Bell, despite the prevalence of women writing within the colonial context. So how can feminists use their work as a theoretical base? This book is concerned with the way that feminists can use and transform these models.

Being a feminist makes one suspicious of adopting a male theoretical 'guru'. However, in search of explanations, feminists may fall under the sway of a theorist, male or female, who seems to be able to provide plausible explanations or readings. Recently, Foucault has gained a certain amount of popularity in feminist circles.[12] With Foucault the problem of having to take a theory wholesale is perhaps less marked than with other theorists, for a number of reasons. Firstly, because, as I mentioned earlier, he explicitly questions the truth status of his own discourse repeatedly and alludes to the ways in which his position is not consistent. Secondly, he says that he does not want people to 'buy' his theories wholesale. It should be stressed that using theory of any kind is an *appropriation*, since Foucault himself states, the reader: ' . . . is of course, free to make what he [sic] will of the book he has been kind enough to read. What right have I then to suggest that it should be used in one way rather than another?' (Foucault, 1973b: ix). Thirdly, as I mentioned earlier, there is a sense in which Foucault's work

13

is so diverse and contradictory that it would be impossible to use it as a coherent theory in the traditional sense of the word. However, despite these objections, in literary theory debates, one is often involved in taking up positions and these involve a set of theoretical assumptions which you either have to adopt or oppose. This can seem for feminists like a form of infatuation, as Meaghan Morris has put it, like 'being screwed' (Morris, in Morris and Patton (eds), 1979: 148), because, by adopting male theoretical work, feminists risk colluding in potentially anti-feminist positions. Morris states:

> Even if his own texts did not take their own precautions against application, I doubt whether Foucault would apply himself at all well if put directly to work for women. Foucault is a profoundly androcentric writer . . . one only needs to flirt with the possibility of censorship in the act of translating his texts to feel 'Homme' . . . resound like a mantra.
>
> (Morris, in Morris and Patton (eds), 1979: 152)

Feminists, in basing their work on male-authored theories, also risk adding to the body of knowledge which suggests that theory is in fact male.[13] So acute is this problem of using male theoretical work that some Anglo-American feminists like Elaine Showalter and Dale Spender have called for, in effect, a boycott of male theorists' work (Showalter, 1982 and Spender, 1982). For them, if one uses the work of male theorists, feminism appears as a parasitic discourse with no new hypotheses of its own, but simply as a feminist dimension to male theories. Showalter states that feminists should reject 'male critical theory' since it 'keeps us dependent upon it and retards our progress in solving our own theoretical problems' (Showalter, 1982: 183). This leads Toril Moi, one of Anglo-American feminism's main critics, to assert that if we ignore male theorists then we run the risk of turning feminist theory into an untheorised subject (Moi, 1985). She considers that it is not possible only to draw on the work of women theorists, or, for that matter, only men theorists. In that male and female critics construct the discursive formation within which we are working, the work of male theorists cannot be ignored (Moi, 1989). Instead, feminists must use males' theories and adapt them, reformulating them in the light of feminist work. Moi comments that this problem

14

of adopting/adapting male theoretical work does not cause such problems in France as it does in Britain:

> French intellectual life has had a considerable impact on French feminist thought, particularly since French feminists on the whole have been eager to appropriate dominant intellectual trends for feminist purposes . . . . Although not entirely absent, intellectual separatism (the desire to do without 'male' thought; or the search for an all-female space) has had less impact on feminist thought in France than in some other countries.
>
> (Moi, 1987: 1)

From a slightly different position, Chris Weedon notes that there are historical reasons for this dominance in theory by males:

> It is no coincidence that these theorists are all men; this is a consequence of the gender relations which have structured women's absence from the active production of most theory within a whole range of discourses over the last three hundred years.
>
> (Weedon, 1987: 13)

However, it is not necessary to ignore male theoretical work because of this domination. Indeed, it is more appropriate to consider feminist appropriation of male- and female-authored theories as constituting feminist theory, much as male appropriations are considered to be theories themselves.[14]

Irene Diamond and Lee Quinby consider that the convergence of Foucault's work and feminism can be productive:

> Both identify the body as the site of power . . . both point to the local and intimate operations of power rather than focussing exclusively on the supreme power of the state. Both bring to the fore the crucial role of discourse in its capacity to produce and sustain hegemonic power and emphasise the challenges contained within marginalised and/or unrecognised discourses, and both criticise the ways in which Western humanism has privileged the experience of the Western masculine elite as it proclaims universals about truth, freedom and human nature.
>
> (Diamond and Quinby (eds), 1988: x)

There are certain elements of Foucault's work, therefore, which

15

I will be concentrating on as I analyse women's travel writing: firstly, the notion of power and knowledge; secondly, the way that discourses structure textual production and reception; and thirdly, the notion of discipline and the confessional.

Foucault's work is particularly useful because of his insistence on the centrality of power, especially when instantiated in knowledge. He attempts to move away from conspiracy theories, for he says: 'If power was never anything but repressive, if it never did anything but say no, do you really believe that we should manage to obey it?' (Foucault, 1979: 36). Foucault believes we should give up the master/slave view of power because it leads to a unified view. This is important in attempting to theorise or describe patriarchy. If one only has a repressive model of patriarchy, then it is very difficult to explain how it is that so many women have managed, against the odds, to write and react against the supposed rules, thus transforming those rules. In this repressive model, Foucault notes that:

> power is conceived as a sort of grand, absolute Subject . . . who articulates what is forbidden. On the side on which power is suffered, there is an equal tendency to 'subjectivise' it, by determining the point at which the acceptance of the interdict occurs, the point at which one says 'yes' or 'no' to power.
>
> (Foucault, in Morris and Patton (eds), 1979: 54)

This notion of resistance is important here; many theories of patriarchy are so formulated that there is no way of explaining how resistance can come about. For Foucault, it is not simply a matter of changing consciousness on an individual basis, but resistance being a necessary part of power. He sees the knowledge that archaeological and genealogical work can produce as a way of creating a counter-knowledge, what Michel Pecheux calls a 'counter-identification', that is a form of identification which rejects the terms of subjectivity which have been proposed (Pecheux, 1982: 159). Simply identifying a position which one has been assigned and rejecting it may not be adequate in Pecheux's terms, but it has been of great use in work on representation in colonial discourse, such as that of Edward Said, Gayatri Spivak and Homi Bhabha. There is potential for this work to be used by feminists who are trying to resist views of women and women's writing which emanate from a patriarchal

16

system of thought. As Frigga Haug suggests, a more productive analysis is one which analyses both the way we have resisted power structures and the way that we have complied or actively worked with these structures. She states that we should

> refuse to understand ourselves simply as a bundle of re-actions to all-powerful structures, or to the social relations within which we have been formed . . . [we should] search instead for possible indications of how we have participated actively in the formation of our own past experience.
>
> (Haug (ed.), 1987: 35)

Foucault rejects the posing of the subject as the locus and origin of meaning, and he wishes to develop a system which does not refer to the subject as an originary position, but rather as a result of discursive forces. The supposed 'death of the subject' or 'death of the author' is in fact rather the turning away from the subject as the prime focus of analysis, and as the primary explanatory motor. It is this undermining of the certainty of terms which has been productive for feminists working with Foucault, as Erica Carter states in her introduction to *Female Sexualisation*:

> The most unsettling contention of 'discourse theory' from a feminist point of view was that the categories hitherto deployed by cultural analysts as 'givens' – class, gender, race, generation and so on – were constantly being produced anew within different and competing discourses, and that they were therefore more fluid and shifting than had previously been assumed.
>
> (Carter, in Haug (ed.), 1987: 17)

This unsettling element in discourse theory can also be its most productive moment.

Much feminist work on travel writing has used a largely untheorised model of patriarchy. At present, with a few exceptions, patriarchy is referred to almost without defining one's terms. It is self-evidently something which oppresses women and which must be opposed.[15] Chris Weedon suggests that we see patriarchy as a set of institutional structures and representational practices which 'rest . . . on the social meanings given to biological sexual difference' (Weedon, 1987: 2), and she states that 'to say that patriarchal relations are *structural* is

17

to suggest that they exist in institutions and social practices of our society and cannot be explained by the intentions, good or bad, of individual men or women' (ibid.: 3). Within a Foucauldian framework, it is possible to see patriarchy as a system without intentions as a whole, which is supported by, resisted, given into or passively gone along with by both males and females. Foucault notes:

> power is not constructed on the basis of 'wills' (individual or collective), no more than it is derived from interests . . . . This is not to say that power is independent, or that it could be deciphered outside of the economic process and the relations of production.
>
> (Foucault, in Morris and Patton (eds), 1979: 71)

And Weedon comments on this view of power that:

> This is not to deny that individual women and men are often the agents of oppression but to suggest that we need a theory which can explain how and why people oppress each other, a theory of subjectivity, of unconscious thoughts and emotions, which can account for the relationship between the individual and the social.
>
> (Weedon, 1987: 3)

Thus, in drawing on Foucault's work on power, it is possible to avoid the excesses of a conspiracy theory of *all* men against *all* women, which feminists such as Dale Spender implicitly propose (Spender, 1982), without nevertheless basing our theories in discourse alone, where there is nothing to react against and no way to resist. The women travellers whose writing I describe constructed their texts within a range of power nexuses: the power of patriarchy which acted upon them as middle-class women, through discourses of femininity: and the power of colonialism which acted upon them in relation to the people of the countries they describe in their books. It is the convergence and conflict of these two power systems which determines the style and content of women's travel writing.

In Foucault's work on the changes in the eighteenth and nineteenth centuries in the mechanisms of power he says: 'there was a new "economy" of power . . . procedures which allowed the effects of power to circulate in a manner at once continuous, uninterrupted, adapted and "individualised" throughout the entire social body' (Foucault, in Morris and Patton (eds), 1979: 37). It is this individualisation which is interesting here, particularly in the way in which it relates to women's lives and writing. As Paul Patton states:

> what distinguished this new form of political investment of the body was, firstly, the scale of control involved: this was minute, a matter of treating the body not as an undifferentiated unit, but of working on it in detail at the level of its individual movements and gestures.
>
> (Patton, in Morris and Patton (eds), 1979: 121)

This change manifested itself, at least in part, in the confessional, as Foucault notes: 'The Christian West invented this astonishing constraint, which it imposed on everyone, to say everything in order to efface everything, to formulate even the least faults in an uninterrupted, desperate, exhaustive murmuring, from which nothing must escape' (Foucault in Morris and Patton (eds), 1979: 84). By the confessional we can infer all manner of disciplinary practices, from diary and letter writing (interestingly gendered activities) to the religious confessional itself. The confessional can be analysed, as Frances Bartkowski has suggested, not as the expression of 'the voices of women, children, homosexuals, perverts, but the voice of power as it institutionalises, domesticates and suppresses those very discourses by which it shores itself up' (Bartkowski, 1988: 45). In describing confessional writing, we are thus describing the way power is resisted (and I would add also the complicity with power) and the way it is enacted. Women's travel writing can be seen as a response to disciplinary pressure, tending to exhibit a concern with displaying the 'self'.

THE STRUCTURE OF THE BOOK

The book is divided into three main sections. In the first, I examine the way that critics have analysed women's travel writing, both the conventional biographical approach and the more theoretical. I focus particularly on the problems which both of these approaches present. I then move on to a discussion of the way that gender has been discussed within the critical study of colonial discourse. Gender cannot simply be added to colonial discourse theories; the theories themselves need to be reconsidered in the light of feminist analyses. In the second section, I set out my theoretical framework, particularly Foucault's work on discursive constraints. This is an analysis of the range of constraints which work upon the production and reception of women's travel writing. In the third section, I take a number of case studies to examine the way in which these discourses work out in a range of different textual strategies. The texts themselves are markedly different one from another; however their differences can be set within a range of parameters defined by a group of conflicting discourses. The book aims to provide a workable model of analysis for texts such as women's travel writing, but I hope my analysis has implications for many other texts.

The three case studies stress certain key elements: firstly, the relation of women's writing to colonial discourse. I centre on the problematic relation of the texts to colonial discourse and also the way that different women's texts comply with or resist some of the discourses I describe in chapter 3. I also focus on the way that the discourses of femininity contest or comply with discursive representations of women. Secondly, I stress that these accounts cannot be read simply as autobiographies, but must be read as textual constructs emanating from a range of discourses in conflict.[16]

I focus on three texts: Alexandra David-Neel, *My Journey to Lhasa* (1927/1983); Mary Kingsley's *Travels in West Africa* (1897/1965); and Nina Mazuchelli, *The Indian Alps and How we Crossed them* (1876). My reasons for choosing these books are various. Firstly, the texts seem to exemplify a range of positions within the discourses of colonialism and femininity, and as such they go to show that women's writing, although difficult to generalise, does inhabit certain discursive parameters. David-Neel's text describes her journey in disguise to Lhasa, the capital of Tibet, which at that time was forbidden to foreigners. This exclusion was enforced by both the British and the Chinese, because of fears of Russian influence in the 'Great Game'. Tibet, like many of the other 'buffer-zones' around India, was considered of great strategic importance by the British. David-Neel's book comes in a long tradition of British texts which chart the dangerous journey of a white person to a forbidden city. Mary Kingsley writes about her visit to West Africa where the British colonial relation was very different, consisting primarily of trade and missionary influence. Because of this difference of colonial situation and because of traditions of writing about this region, her text concerns itself with very different representations. The specificity of colonial relations can be most clearly seen in Nina Mazuchelli's writing, since in her account of her travels to northern India and Bhutan she calls upon a range of discursive frameworks which are particular to the British presence and expansion in the Indian context. Each country described has a different range of discursive parameters, and each woman writer negotiates with these constraints, since her text is also acted upon by other discursive pressures. The second reason for choosing these texts is that I wanted to analyse both the well-known, widely available texts by 'indomitable lady travellers' like Mary Kingsley and Alexandra David-Neel, and also the more problematic (for feminists at least) works by writers such as Nina Mazuchelli, which have not been reissued.

All fall roughly within the period 1860–1930 and all describe travel to non-European countries which had some form of colonial relationship with Britain. I have chosen non-European, colonial countries, because colonial texts are produced and processed in a different way. Although women's travel writing is not given authoritative status (as I mention in chapter 4, the authors are often accused of lying), the texts add to the affirming and contesting of knowledges about the empire.

The authors travelled for very different reasons and in different countries, and wrote about their travels within a multiplicity of constraints – gender, class, purpose of their journey, textual conventions, audience and so on – which acted upon and formed their writing. These factors determine that the texts will be constructed differently, both from texts by other women and also those by men. And yet what the narrators write about the people amongst whom they travelled and their attitude to those people is surprisingly similar and seems to differ from the writings of male travel writers in the stress they lay on personal involvement and relationships with people of the other culture and in the less authoritarian stance they take *vis-à-vis* narrative voice. I demonstrate that these two factors result from women writers' problematic status, caught between the conflicting demands of the discourse of femininity and that of imperialism. The discourses of colonialism demand action and intrepid,

21

fearless behaviour from the narrator, and yet the discourses of femininity demand passivity from the narrator and a concern with relationships.

I am concerned as much with the elements which the texts share as with the elements which distinguish them one from the other. For example, it is interesting that many of the texts present the female narrator travelling without protection and without coming to harm; this seems to signal to the reader that the colonised country is so much under British control that *even* women can be represented travelling through it without the 'natives' daring to approach her. In many ways they present the colonial countries as *empty*, or populated by harmless, loving children. There is little conflict mentioned in the travel writing of women, again reinforcing the colonial presence. A further reinforcement is gained by the fact that none of the writers questions her presence in that country; it is presented as self-evident and the motive for travel is often portrayed as being simply for personal reasons. As I mentioned earlier, in fact, this representation of the colonised country as a safe place for women to travel may have developed from precisely the problem of women writers describing sexual matters; it would have been considered improper for a woman writer even to allude to sexual matters. This is a notable silence in the texts.

A further element which is shared by the texts is a difficulty in the choice of narrative figure: rather than (or sometimes as well as) the bold adventuring hero of male travel texts, there are other narrative roles, such as the nurse/doctor, the invalid, the philanthropist, the angel in the house and the caring mother or wife. Implicitly, some of these roles reinforce a vision of 'femininity', paradoxical though that may seem for texts which portray women within the public sphere. This 'femininity' is undermined, because of the narrator's relation with other characters, for example, the fact that the narrator is shown in a position of power and is never portrayed as being disobeyed. These narrative positions are ambivalent, both drawing on the dominant discursive formations and yet being excluded from full adoption of them because of their position within the discourse of the 'feminine'. Through elements such as humour, self-deprecation, statements of affiliation, and descriptions of relationships, which stress the interpersonal nature of travel writing, these texts constitute counter-hegemonic voices within colonial discourse. Considering travel writing in this way enables us to see oppositional forces at work in colonial texts. What are generally regarded as limitations on women's writing (the discourse of femininity restricts what can be written, women are unable to draw on colonial discourse in the same way as men) can in fact be seen to be discursively productive, in that these constraints enable a form of writing whose contours both disclose the nature of the dominant discourses and constitute a critique from its margins.

Part I

CRITICAL RESPONSES TO WOMEN'S TRAVEL WRITING

1

FEMINIST WORK ON WOMEN'S TRAVEL WRITING

From the fourteenth century onwards, western women have written accounts of their travels.[1] Much of this writing, although widely read at the time, has been neglected, and has not been reprinted.[2] The ones which have been reprinted are those which are most stereotypically 'women travel writers': the indomitable eccentric spinsters; the many other texts which do not fall into that mould have by and large been ignored by present-day critics and publishers alike. This 'rediscovery', primarily by Virago, of women travel writers is a part of a larger 'reclaiming' of the Victorian period for women's history. The aim of this rewriting process has been to dispel the various mythologies circulating in contemporary Britain about women's position in the Victorian period. For example, Martha Vicinus works against the notion that all Victorian women were confined to the home and the private sphere, chaperoned when outside, swaddled in clothes which restricted their movements and had little or no economic or political choice about their lives. (Vicinus (ed.), 1972, 1980). For many Victorian women, especially those from the middle class, this was indeed the case; however, the lives of working-class and aristocratic women were very different from that of the stereotypical 'angel in the house'. Even whilst it must be admitted that the lives of many middle-class women were restricted, it is surprising that it is primarily from the ranks of the middle class that women travel writers sprang. One begins to wonder whether these images of Victorian women and their restricted lives are more discursive than actual.[3]

27

HOW DO FEMINISTS READ WOMEN'S TRAVEL WRITING?

There has been a substantial amount of work on women's travel writing, much of it an attempt to examine more closely the public/private divide, and to question whether in fact women were, or have ever been, entirely confined to the private sphere. Analysis of travel writing from a feminist perspective must ask a number of questions. Firstly, we must decide how we are going to write about these women travel writers and for what purpose. We must ask whether we are simply going to reproduce parts of their texts to make them more accessible to a wider public, since, in many cases, the texts can only be found in reference libraries. Are we going to be critical of some of the positions exemplified in the texts, for example, colonialist or racist statements, and will we be judging these works against some feminist standard? Or are we writing about them as part of a larger project concerned with the construction of an alternative women's history?

Secondly, we have to decide whether these texts share more features with other female-authored texts than they share with male-authored texts. It is a common assumption amongst critics on women's travel writing that women's writing is self-evidently different to men's, and very little work examines the features shared with male-authored texts. If we do decide that the writing is different from men's, we will then have to decide how to explain that implied difference. Mary Jacobus suggests that women's writing will always work to deconstruct male writing (Jacobus (ed.), 1979), although more recent work by Sandra Gilbert and Susan Gubar has shown that women's writing is not such a unified object (Gilbert and Gubar, 1988).[4]

Because of our concern as feminists to trace a 'female tradition' of writing, we might find that our readings of women's travel writing emphasise the shared elements within the texts by women in order to foreground their difference to men's writing. This is an understandable move, and one which I am often tempted by in reading travel writing. Reading in this way makes the texts more manageable, and enables the reader to read the texts within a well-defined framework. However, there is always a sense in which it is necessary to *reduce* the texts to a range of parameters in order to organise the reading of the text; one of

28

these parameters might be gender. The reduction of the complexity of the text to one main parameter usually means that a large number of features in the text which do not fit into that schema have to be ignored. In this analysis, I attempt to incorporate some of the elements which have been hitherto omitted in an attempt to construct a unified field of 'women's travel writing'. The features which are shared with male writers will be analysed as well as those which constitute the difference of women's travel writing.

A third question which a feminist reader faces when analysing women's travel writing is that one of the ways in which early women's texts are often read is in terms of trying to read them as proto-feminist; that means reading them to trace the features and ideas which would seem to be similar to the ones exhibited by contemporary feminist texts and concerns. For example, in the case of travel writing the texts are read as if they were a simple presentation of positive role models.[5] It is tempting to read these women travellers' writings as examples of strong, exceptional women who somehow managed to escape the structures of patriarchy. This type of analysis works fairly well as a reading strategy for the texts which have strong narrators and where narrative incident is the focus of attention, for example, Alexandra David-Neel's *My Journey to Lhasa* (1927/1983) or Mary Kingsley's *Travels in West Africa* (1897/1965), since these images of women travelling alone in dangerous situations transgress the notion of the necessity for women to be chaperoned. But this approach cannot deal with other more 'feminine' texts such as Nina Mazuchelli's *The Indian Alps and How we Crossed them* (1876) or Emily Eden's *Up the Country* (1866).

A further point that feminists have to deal with is the question of the relation of these texts to the colonial system; many of the women critics treat these writers as if they travelled simply as individuals and were not part of colonialism as a whole. I have written articles which argued precisely this point, and, in order to do so, I had to highlight certain sections of the text at the expense of others (Mills, 1986). I also had to ignore the fact that this view of women as outside the colonial enterprise is the conventional critical position on the relationship between women and imperialism. Catherine Stevenson argues that Mary Kingsley and Florence Dixie were actively opposed to colonialist intervention (Stevenson, 1985). Like other critics she feels it necessary to evaluate these writers on the extent of their feminism (i.e., Dixie is more feminist than Kingsley) and also on the degree to which they were involved in colonialism (i.e., Dixie is less involved than Kingsley). However, again this risks falling into the trap of accepting the discursive stereotypes of women's superior moral position over men.

Finally, women critics of travel writing need to consider whether these texts are factual, whether they tell the 'truth' about the journeys which were undertaken. Many critics see a biographical approach as the only way to read these texts, and they devote themselves to proving or disproving allegations against the writers. Many of the contemporary male critics read the texts within this framework and accused the women's accounts of falsehood or exaggeration. Far more women's texts were accused of falsehood than men's, although it must be recognised that these types of claims were made about travel writing in general from its very beginning.[6] A possible feminist position would therefore be to deny these claims and assert that the texts are factual or truthful. This is a position which needs to be strenuously resisted. It is possible to accept that these women authors travelled to the countries they describe and that they wrote accounts of their journeys, in good faith, but it is necessary to accept that there are perhaps other elements which structure these texts other than simply authorial intention.

The position which will be developed in this book will aim to deal with these questions. Thus, although I am dealing solely with texts written by women, it is clear that I do not want to align myself with a position of biological determinism, that is, if you are born biologically female, then you will necessarily write in a particular way. This is why I avoid describing women travel writers as if they necessarily write in a similar way. Given the diversity of the texts this would be an extremely problematic position to hold. Instead, it is necessary to recognise that women's writing practices can vary because of the differences in discursive pressures, but that they will also share many factors with men's writing. The most striking difference often lies not so much in the writing itself (although differences may be found there) but rather in the way that women's writing is judged and processed. It is for this reason that I have divided the book into the analysis of the discourses which affect the production of a text and those which affect its reception. It is because of these problems outlined above that I would like to formulate a feminist Foucauldian model, which, I argue, does not entail the notion of a coherent text-immanent reading, and therefore allows me to describe the way that the texts are not simply different because female-authored, but tend towards differences in their production and reception. It is a much more complex analysis and perhaps more unwieldy, yet it nevertheless allows the reader to deal with the texts in their complexity rather than attempting to reduce them to a clear but partial analysis.

CRITICISM OF WOMEN TRAVEL WRITERS

Male and female critics alike seem to adopt particular strategies for analysing women travel writers' work. As I have already noted, women's travel writing is generally ignored by male critics, and I will discuss this problem in more detail in chapter 2 (pp.57–63). Occasionally, a critic such as Percy Adams will mention a woman travel writer in passing, often for novelty value, because they are generally characterised as odd, exceptional or eccentric (Adams, 1983). And Charles Batten says of the eighteenth century: 'even the occasional woman travelled' (Batten, 1978: 2), as if this were a remarkable feat for a sex which is renowned for its underachievement. Most of the women critics who have produced books about women's travel writing share certain assumptions about the texts which seem to be in some sense problematic, and I will consider these in turn.[7] Much of this work has not set itself within a particularly academic framework, many of the books being full of pleasing and striking images of women travellers, aiming rather to draw wider public attention to these extraordinary texts. As a subject, the study of women's travel writing is usually considered as falling within the field of social sciences, as part of women's history – a history which is often characterised as being that of exceptional women. Women travellers are treated as 'oddities' – Mary Russell characterises them in the following way:

> It is easy to dismiss (women travellers) as oddities – as indeed they are – to be relegated to the bedlam of flat-

31

earthers, free-fall divers or indeed writers. That they exist cannot be denied, but the strange uncomfortable world they occupy lies well outside our everyday experience and can be dismissed, we tell ourselves, as an irrelevancy.

(Russell, 1986: 13)

This quotation characterises a great number of the assumptions about women travellers and their writing. Firstly, there is the assumption that women travel writers are rare; this is rather surprising, since, as I noted earlier, there have been a great many women travellers, especially during the nineteenth century. Secondly, it is clear from many of these critical accounts that women travel writers should not be considered ordinary women, but exceptional, and perhaps not always viewed in a positive way. There are many statements about the behaviour of the narrator figure which depict her as odd and freakish, for example, Davies, when writing about Mary Kingsley, says: 'When she wanted to know how deep the river was, she would test the depth with her umbrella!' (Davies, 1985: 21). In these accounts, the women themselves are presented as figures of fun. These critics present a remarkably homogeneous view of women travel writers: they seem to regard the texts as simple transcriptions of their adventures, and they see the authors themselves, whose lives they read back from the textual accounts, as indomitable, eccentric and mostly rather crazy. The spinster or old maid tag is often attached to these writers, and something of the ridiculous always lingers with those two terms (Birkett, 1989). There is also a sense in which there is something rather improper in these women's behaviour, as connoted in the term 'adventuress' which is used by Alexandra Allen (Allen, 1980).

This point of view is perhaps given the clearest definition in Mary Russell's comment: 'It seems a contradiction and denial of their sex that women should risk the very thing which only they can nurture and sustain, namely life itself' (Russell, 1986: 14). This seems a curious statement from a critic who recounts the exploits of many women who are supposed to have 'denied their sex'; similar texts from male writers would perhaps be viewed as perfectly normal, or even ideal accounts of behaviour. However, this is one of the contradictions within patriarchal discourses that women must be described as frail and weak, at

32

the same time as there are representations of women as strong, resourceful and independent available within women's travel writing. Charles Batten recognises the problems which are faced by critics who attempt to consider travel writing as history. He says:

> these socio-historical studies face a methodological prob-
> lem that renders their findings ambiguous at best and
> misleading at worst. By ignoring the literary conventions
> that govern what an author says, they assume that these
> accounts display the immediate, personal experience of
> travelers, and that these travelers, in turn, reflect the tastes
> of the century in general.
>
> (Batten, 1978: 4)

It is interesting that most of the critics have chosen to concentrate on the travellers of the Victorian period, and very few
of them consider writers of earlier periods or those who are
writing at present. This trend may have been encouraged by the
reprinting of Victorian women's travel writing by Virago, whose
avowed aim has always been to 'rescue' women's texts. It is also
part of a feminist enterprise which attempts to disprove the
stereotyped view of Victorian women – an attempt to rewrite
women's history. Whilst this redefinition of women's role in
history and women's achievements is crucial to feminists, it is
also necessary to be aware of how much the model of history
used owes to the patriarchal model which excluded women in
the first place, that is, that history is composed of exceptional
individuals.

In their attempts to include as many women as possible
within their accounts of travel writing, as I mentioned in the
Introduction (p.6), critics sometimes go so far as to include
women who have been kidnapped. Lesley Blanch includes, as a
traveller, Isabella Burton who travelled *by proxy*; as Blanch says:

> Her life story is one of the greatest adventure stories . . .
> because she loved 'Burton of Arabia', one of the greatest
> adventurers of his age . . . . She was never to accompany
> him on those desperate ventures which made his life so
> astonishing. But such is the power of love that she lived
> them all by proxy.
>
> (Blanch, 1974: 16)

Russell includes, as a travel writer, a woman who answered an advertisement to live with a man on a desert island in New Guinea (Russell, 1986). Possibly the most extreme example is also in Russell's book, where a fifth-century Irish nun who was reported to have crossed the Irish sea on a leaf is described as a woman traveller (ibid.).

Many of these critics, in an attempt to construct a history of women travellers which depicts women in a positive way (i.e., one which portrays them as strong individuals whilst still retaining femininity), are very selective with the accounts they give of women travellers, for example, they leave out accounts in the original texts of cruelty or deceitfulness. Stress is laid on feminine qualities, such as the care that was felt for the 'natives' of the country: for example, Davies says of Hester Stanhope:

Hester grew to love the people of Lebanon and Syria . . . .
She shared her money with the local people and caused herself to become very poor by the time she died. But the people loved her and thought of her as a queen.

(Davies, 1985: 8)

In this way the travellers are often reintegrated within the private sphere of the private/public divide. They may travel outside the home but they display all of the conventional characteristics of women within the home. Many of the accounts simply omit those incidents which show imperialist leanings. Mary Kingsley's views of the African as a separate and inferior species is often glossed over in accounts which stress her love for Africans. Davies states: 'most of the time she lived as the local people did, sleeping in the village huts and eating the same food as Africans' (ibid.: 21). Although this is true of part of the text, a large proportion is taken up with descriptions of Kingsley's visiting *European* settlers and staying in their houses, and much of her description of staying in African dwellings is in a very negative vein. Thus, as I mentioned earlier, in order to make these texts fit into a predetermined schema, very partial readings are undertaken.[8]

These critics also lack an overall perspective of the role of women's travel texts and the discourse of Orientalism, since they insist on treating these women's texts as expressions of personal endeavour and individualism rather than as part of a larger enterprise. Those elements which contradict the theme

34

of personal struggle against society's constraining forces are simply left out of the accounts. Instead, stress is laid upon the anti-colonialist statements of the women travellers, whereas in the texts themselves there are often both types of statement, both upholding and criticising colonial rule (Stevenson, 1985).

Writers on women travellers are especially uncritical about the status of these texts. None of the critics analyses the politics of production of women's texts. There is no real analysis of how these women managed to travel in an age which has been characterised as repressive and where many middle-class women could only move outside the house with a chaperone. For example, Davies remarks on the fact that some women 'just wanted to visit an unknown part of the world or to enjoy the fun and adventure of travelling' (Davies, 1985: 4). Their travels are simply seen as a personal escape from boredom and repression: for example, Lesley Blanch says of Hester Stanhope: 'She was not so much seeking fulfilment as a woman, as seeking escape from her own nature' (Blanch, 1974: 15). And many of the accounts of Isabella Bishop-Bird's travels make reference to the fact that she travelled in order to get away from the restrictions on her life at home (Birkett, 1986). Very frequently in the criticism there is mention of the tomboyishness of the author, which developed into a wish to travel: Alexandra David-Neel's biographer states that she ran away from home at an early age and spent the night in the Alps alone (Chalon, 1985), and Davies says of Lady Hester Stanhope: 'Even when she was a child Lady Hester Stanhope showed that she had a spirit of adventure', since she stole a boat and rowed across a lake. 'She did not get very far, but it gave her a liking for travel' (Davies, 1985: 5). There is no critical analysis of this 'escape', except to describe these women as remarkable, odd, eccentric and exceptional. The travel texts are then simply read as an extension of this adolescent tomboyishness.

None of these women critics question how these women managed to have their work published, or why they were and are still read to such an extent. To explain the popularity of these texts, they simply call on notions of vicarious pleasure on the part of women readers not able to go on such expeditions themselves.

35

PROBLEMS IN THE ANALYSIS OF WOMEN'S TRAVEL WRITING

One of the major problems in the analysis of women's travel writing is that of assuming that the texts are autobiographical, and that they are straightforward transcriptions of the lives of the women travellers. When talking about 'the self' in writing of any kind there are immediate problems. Firstly, we are making an assumption that we all know what the self is: it is used as an easy shorthand for something amorphous and untextualisable. The self is presumed to be the writer's self which is translated into the persona or narrative voice of the text. It is assumed that the reader can discover the 'self' of the woman travel writer in the narrator position in the text. But if we accept that the writer's self in the first place is not a coherent entity, nor is it entirely under the control of the writer, then we cannot imagine that what we read in the text is a faithful representation of the writer. Secondly, we have to deal with the problem of assuming that this self can be faithfully transcribed into a text. The self is not easily grasped in any case, but the representation of it is even less so because it is mediated by discourse, i.e., the writing system and its rules for making sense within the existing meanings of the time. This is further complicated with texts from another period where you cannot be entirely sure that you are reading with anything like the same frames of reference as the writers or readers of the time. Our notions of self conflict quite markedly with other periods' textualisations. In texts, we are dealing with an illusory textualisation of an illusory construct, and this representation is itself not coherent or unified since textualisation, although it may attempt some form of unity, always exceeds this attempt. Since words have potentially multiple meanings, and multiple reference, various connotations, and therefore different possible interpretations, dependent on the text's context or the reader's frame of reference, I would argue that a coherent 'self', in textual terms, is impossible. The text itself is not a stable field of meaning, but something which readers work on and interpret. Therefore the range of meanings which the unstable self of the writer attempts to encode are never decoded in a predictable way by the unstable self of the reader.

This may seem like meaningless problematisation of a

36

common-sense term, but it is necessary to set out the problems of the term in order to show why I have adopted such a tortuous route to my analysis of women's travel writing instead of simply assuming that these texts can be read as autobiographies. In order to be able to discuss the reading of texts as auto-biographies what is needed is a theoretical framework which recognises that the self in the text and the self outside are both different and overdetermined in their various ways, and also which will enable us to describe the way that the self within the text is structured from a range of discursive factors or pressures which are not within the control of the writer. Foucault's work is interesting in this context since he is interested in the 'dispersion of the subject' (Foucault, 1972a: 55). Although it is difficult to discuss texts which are 'authored' without reference to the subject who wrote them, it is a useful move in the direction away from autobiographical readings. Foucault makes it clear that the 'I' of the text can in no way be taken to bear a direct relation to the persona of the author, and he prefers to call the author the 'author-function' and refer to this function as an 'it'. By reducing the author-function to an 'it' he is not suggesting that the individual is simply the site of 'a sort of communal opinion' (ibid.: 122) that is imposed as a reflection of society's beliefs. He is simply trying to loosen the link between the author as an individual and the author-function as a textual entity. He is not denying the existence of the author as a person for, as he says,

> there can be no signs without someone, or at least some-thing, to emit them. For a series of signs to exist, there must – in accordance with the system of causality – be an 'author' or a transmitting authority. But this 'author' is not identical with the subject of the statement; and the relation of production that he has with the formulation is not superposable to the relation that unites the enunciating subject and what he states.
>
> (Foucault, 1972a: 92)

He goes on to say that we should try to break down this common-sense notion that a subject simply writes to express her/himself: 'If a proposition, a sentence, a group of signs, can be called "statement", it is not. . . because, one day, someone happened to speak them or put them into some concrete form

37

of writing' (ibid.: 95). Thus, for Foucault, it is the fact that there is a position for the subject to take up as an author-function that is interesting, rather than the fact that it is possible to recognise certain utterances as statements.

Thus, rather than imagining that each text has a 'person', one 'voice', which directs the text in a unified way, in a Foucauldian analysis, one would rather trace the different voices discursively produced.[9] The author serves to neutralise the contradictions that are found in a series of texts. Foucault does not say that the author as a person is totally irrelevant in the process of constructing meaning, as most critics have understood him to be saying, but he does state that there are a variety of positions within each text which, once the author has been dispensed with, cannot be formed into a cohesive whole.

One of the major problems with autobiographical readings of these texts is that there is no way of explaining how this type of writing came about; travel writing does not accord with the other discourses which we have about women at the time, and yet there is no way that we can describe these texts without referring to them in terms of anomaly and in terms of the strangeness of the women writers. How could a woman write and give herself a strong narrative voice and describe events which for many seem implausible within the discourses circulating around women at that time?

The notion of experience and its representation in text is a complex one, especially in the area of women's writing. Firstly, since the advent of post-structuralist criticism, many critics are wary of even considering the term 'experience' because of its associations with liberalism and intentionality, and the problems which these have entailed for literary criticism.[10] However it should be remembered that Foucault does not wish to dispense with the author entirely, and Said, using Foucault's work, is even more willing to retain some notion of author-responsibility for what is written, if only to be able to castigate someone for the racism of their texts (Said, 1978a). However, to write on a subject such as travel writing without discussing experience, in however problematised a form, would not be an adequate account since experience, for male and female writers, is the subject-matter of travel journals. The problem in most accounts of travel writing so far is that they have considered the experience of the writer to be unproblematically displayed and

presented in the text, rather than that 'experience' is chan-
nelled into and negotiates with pre-existent schemas which are
discursive in nature.

I have only found one woman critic, Elizabeth Joyce, who
considers the textual constraints on women writers (Joyce,
1984); all of the others consider the texts to be straightforward
biographical criticism, and they analyse them using the methods
of autobiography. Joyce shows that the role of the 'hardy adventurer hero' was simply not open to women writers. This can be
seen when Caroline Oliver mentions that there was a problem
for Harriet Ward when she wrote about her travels through
Kaffirland (South Africa): 'The tension between an assertive
opinionated masculine persona and an apologetic, ladylike
female voice reveals the problem of self-definition' (Oliver,
1982: 23). This is not a problem, in fact, for self-definition, but
a problem of textual constraint. There is no reason for equating
assertiveness, or for that matter opinionated behaviour, with
masculine qualities or an apologetic voice with female qualities.
As I argue in chapter 3, there is a textual clash here between the
constraints of colonial discourse and other discourses such as
femininity and feminism. Thus, these texts are not expressions
of individual subjects in the context of an alien country, but
rather are the site of various discourses which play on the text. As
Gayatri Spivak says, it is necessary to 'wrench oneself away from
the mesmerising focus of the "subject-constitution" of the
female individualist' (Spivak, 1989: 177).

WOMEN'S INVOLVEMENT IN COLONIALISM

Because the critical work on women travel writers has centred
on the women authors as individual rebels against the constraints of Victorian society, much of it has simply discussed the
women themselves and not their relation to the countries they
are describing or the part women travellers played in colonialism. It is very common in analyses of women's travel writing to
treat the accounts as simply about individuals, and this is
encouraged because of the stress within the texts on markers of
femininity, such as concern with personal relations and appearance. However, the texts are, just as men's texts are, about the
colonial situation, although their relation to the dominant
discourses differs.

Women's travel texts are constructed in the process of inter-action of colonial textual constraints and constraints of gender. As I show in chapter 4, these determine the way texts are constructed, the views that writers produce and even the way they present 'themselves' and their experience. Thus, an analy-sis of women's travel writing should be aware of the diverse elements, both socio-political and textual, which contribute to the construction of each text.

reception differ to production   *rather simple*

THE DIFFERENCE OF WOMEN'S WRITING

In order to understand what critics have to say about women's travel writing, it is necessary to consider women's production of writing in general. What many of these critics assume is that women's travel writing is necessarily different to men's writing. However, much recent work on women's literary production has militated against that assumption to a certain extent. There are elements in the process of production of the text which are different if the writer is female, for example, her access to a literary education and funding may be different, but, most important, it is the elements in the process of reception which differ markedly for female authors, and it is this which is not taken into account by critics in the main. I would like firstly to consider the process of production to attempt to delineate the ways in which this is a different process for women and how this affects the production of women's travel writing.[11]

reception what is different

As the Marxist Feminist Literature Collective notes: 'Female literary production breaks the cultural taboo against women as public speakers, a taboo felt by almost all women who defined themselves as writers' (MFLC, 1978: 44) This feeling of breaking taboos does not only apply to 'literary' writing but to other writing by women as well. Cora Kaplan, a member of the collective, states in a later article:

> in western societies (and in other cultures as well) public speech is a male privilege and women's speech is restricted by custom, in mixed sex gatherings or, if permitted, still characterized by its private nature, an extensive of the trivial domestic discourse of women.
>
> (Kaplan, 1987: 70)

She goes on to say that, for male speakers, this distinction between public and private speech is not so clearly defined. Many women were discouraged from writing since it was considered not only to be of high status but because it was seen to be sexually improper for a woman to enter into the realm of this public, high language.[12] As Nancy Miller puts it, 'To write is to come out of the wings, and to appear, however briefly, centre stage' (Miller, 1980: 266). Many women for this reason refused to put their names to their literary writing and others simply decided against writing or used pseudonyms.[13] It is this realisation that writing cannot come from simply anyone, as Foucault notes (Foucault, 1972a: 51) that makes women's writing different, because the conditions of production are different for most women.[14]

The taboos regarding women's writing were very great since, by writing about travelling, the women authors were bringing upon themselves criticism for both the writing and for the travels which they represented; they were laying themselves open to attack on charges of exaggeration and of sexual impropriety. Whilst this account is very appealing in many ways, there are obvious problems. It should be noted that although there are taboos on women writing, which have been reinforced by women's relative lack of education and for negative judgements on individual women authors, women have nevertheless continued to write.

For many women this 'centre-stage' position is too much of a challenge, and, as Linda Anderson shows, rather than produce texts which would be judged to be 'literary', women chose genres which were not so highly valued (Anderson, 1987). She considers the fact that there were so many women who wrote and published diaries and says that, historically, this form:

has offered the woman the possibility of laying claim to writing while allaying the anxieties of actual publication. Poised ambivalently between private and public statement, it can also be seen as a process, rooted in the private dimension of living which does not take as its goal or form from its status as social and cultural artifact. . . the diary for many writers can be regarded as a symptom of restriction, giving a provisional voice to women who were denied confident access to public expression.

(Anderson, 1987: 60–1)

41

Such a statement is of particular significance in this context, since travel writing has similarly been considered a low-status genre, and it also often follows the structure of a diary or journal. Furthermore, this view of women's writing accords with Foucault's work on the confessional, where rather than these genres being regarded as simply low-status genres where women felt able to write, they can be seen as genres where women were encouraged to 'reveal' themselves, and where the disciplinary forces of society were most at work (Foucault, 1981a).

As well as women choosing, or being encouraged, to write in low-status genres, and perhaps thus writing in a different way to male writers, their work is judged in a very different way. Dale Spender has shown how judgements made about women's writing have often been, in fact, judgements not about the text but about the writer's life (Spender, 1982). Elaine Showalter and Ellen Moers have both reported the sexism inherent in much male criticism of women's writing: for example, Bernard Bergonzi says 'women novelists. . . like to keep their focus narrow' (cited in Showalter, 1977: 7), and Walter Allen says of reading Fanny Burney: 'it is rather like having a mouse's view of cats' (cited in Spender, 1982: 279). Showalter remarks:

> it has been difficult for critics to consider women novelists and women's literature theoretically because of their tendency to project and expand their own culture-bound stereotypes of femininity, and to see in women's writing an eternal opposition of biological and aesthetic creativity.
> (Showalter, 1977: 7)

Women in the eighteenth and nineteenth centuries were restricted as to the type of language they might use and the sort of 'experience' they might depict, and thus their work was judged to be limited when compared to the relative freedom of male novelists. As a reviewer in the *North British Review* says of Anne North's work: 'She writes as English gentlewomen ought to write. . . her pages are absolutely like green pastures' (cited in ibid.: 26). It is this normative approach to women's writing which causes problems for analysis. The blandness which was seen as appropriate to women writers, in a form of circular logic, was then used against them as a reason for their exclusion from consideration by literary critics.

42

THEORISED READINGS OF TRAVEL WRITING

It is precisely the problematic nature of travel writing, in terms of its relation to truth and reality, which prevents me from adopting the strategy of reading women's travel writing as if it were autobiographical. It is also for this reason that I have chosen to ground my analysis in theoretical work.

There are other types of reading which could perhaps compete with a Foucauldian one in this context: Kay Schaffer's book, *Women and the Bush: Forces of Desire in the Australian Cultural Tradition* (1989) is an attempt to work within a basically Kristevan framework, which leads her to consider the notion of the 'feminine' as an important aspect in the way that writers, both male and female, respond in their work to the colonial context.[15] Schaffer argues that, within the Australian cultural tradition, the representations of the bush have been projected as a mother figure, the feminine, which is both seductive and cruel and which is 'no place for a woman' (Schaffer, 1989: 52); the figure of the Australian male has been as one who attempts to master the landscape. There are obvious resonances with the colonial situation, where it is clear that metaphors of virginity and penetration are frequently used. However, because of her use of psychoanalysis, Schaffer states that this has an effect on women writers who attempt to write about, in this case, Australia, and also it has an effect on the way females are treated in that country. For her, in order to write at all, women must take up a masculine position:

> In a phallocentric culture the masculine is valued, the feminine exists in an inferior relation to the masculine. The ideal self to which the subject (whether male or female) in culture attaches desire is an impossible masculine subject. As soon as the child speaks it assumes a subjective place in language as either male or not-male.
>
> (Schaffer, 1989: 10)

Thus, either women inhabit the category not-men and therefore do not write, or they write as men, as she says:

> The bush woman can stand in place of her husband, lover or brother and take on masculine attributes of strength, fortitude, courage and the like in her battle with the

environment. She could be called and have the status of a pioneering hero, even though she is a woman.

(Schaffer, 1989: 14)

What Schaffer has shown is the difficulties attendant on women attempting to write within a colonial context, where the figure who generally writes about the other countries is male and adventurous, supremely masculine, and where the land to be conquered or in the process of being conquered is represented as feminine and passive. She shows how the representation of women within the Australian situation has been limited to two positions: what she terms the figures of 'God's police' and 'the whore'. This seems to have resonances with the British colonial situation in general, but British women seem only to have been represented as 'God's police', the stern moral memsahib.

For Schaffer, 'Women speak and locate themselves through and within the metaphors of femininity' (ibid.: 23). In many ways this is true, but these are not the only pressures weighing upon their texts. If they were, women's writing would be far less diverse than it is. She goes on to say: 'To speak with authority she must wear a male disguise' (ibid.: 103): however, this does not seem to hold with the travel writing that I examine where, to write with authority, women align themselves with colonial forces and thus potentially with a predominantly male and masculine force, but they are not in that move wearing a male disguise. Many of these women strenuously guarded themselves against assertions of this kind by writing very much as 'feminine' women. Their writing seems more of a contest between masculine and feminine discourses, and other textual determinants. Schaffer acknowledges this complexity when she states that although women's writing may differ slightly from male accounts, they still uphold the basic metaphorical descriptions of landscape. She says:

> They depict the land in ways that are equally problematic. The women writers reiterate masculine constructions in their representation of the feminine. One might say that the fiction by women writers supports, even as it seems to challenge, the codes of national identity.
>
> (Schaffer, 1989: 107)

It is precisely this double-voiced quality of women's writing which I hope to explore in the following chapters. However, I should state that it is impossible to limit the whole of textuality to the simple binary opposition of masculine/ feminine; the texts themselves and their reception do not support this. Lacanian psychoanalysis, because of its stress on binary oppositions, is doomed simply to see all material in terms of those oppositions.

A further problem with psychoanalytic readings for me is their lack of address to the specificity of power relations: for example, Schaffer states:

> A dominant impulse in the narratives of exploration and discovery is one towards ownership, mastery or possession of the land, which might consolidate and guarantee identity to the subject. At least mastery over a threatening landscape allows the illusion of a unified identity to be countenanced.
>
> (Schaffer, 1989: 80)

And she goes on to say in a similar vein: 'The assumption that the masculine (man, Empire, Civilization) has an unquestioned God-given right to subdue or cultivate the feminine (woman, Earth, Nature) and appropriate the feminine to masculine domination is a constant structuring principle of Western discourse' (ibid.: 82). This seems to exclude the colonial context entirely until it is only a question of a psyche's attempt at union with the Other of the landscape. And there is no sense either of the discontinuities in the process.

Within Lacanian and Kristevan psychoanalysis, language and the Symbolic Order are crucial for the constitution of the self. For Foucault, discourse is a much larger term, and we have no choice about whether we are to enter it or not (it is not something we enter at a particular stage in our psychological or social development). Even madness offers no escape since it is constructed within discourse (Foucault, 1981b). Foucault's 'discourse' is made up of many different discursive formations and in that respect it is much more heterogeneous than the Symbolic Order. Psychoanalysis risks not being aware of the changing power relations circulating through society at a particular period, and is thus unable to describe differences in subjectivity and textuality; nor is it able to produce an account of the way in which these might change. It is because Foucault's theoretical work is based upon the notion of change and

45

discontinuity that he is most useful in this context.

In the Introduction I outlined the reasons why Foucault's work is the frame for this book, and it is necessary to go into slightly more detail at this point, to highlight the ways in which Foucault's discourse theories enable us to avoid some of the problems I have been drawing attention to in this chapter. I showed that autobiographical readings of women's travel writing force the critic to discard a large amount of the material in a text in order to make it fit the model. The material which is excluded in these critical accounts is mainly, but not exclusively, concerned with the colonial presence and expansion. What I would like to do is to describe the texts in all their complexity in order to trace, not the authors, but the conditions of production and reception of their texts. We will never be able to state that we have discovered those conditions, but discourse theory enables the reader to account for many of the elements which exist in a wide range of texts without recourse to autobiographical reconstructive work. Having discovered some of the problems with referring texts back to their authors in this context, I would like now to turn to an analysis of colonial discourse which sets works of this period within a political context and theoretical framework, but which largely ignores the work by women writers.

2

GENDER AND THE STUDY OF COLONIAL DISCOURSE

In this chapter, I consider the relationship between gender issues and the study of colonial discourse. I analyse the work of several theorists and point to some of the theoretical and analytical problems arising from their work in order to show that it is difficult to use their work as it stands for an analysis of women's travel writing. I deal with four main areas of difficulty with the study of colonial discourse: firstly, the potentiality of personal statements as a form of 'escape' from Orientalism, since women's texts often tend towards the personal; secondly, the supposed homogeneity of Orientalism, because although colonial discourse is described in a unified way, women's texts cannot easily be accommodated within its descriptive framework; thirdly, the truth-value of colonial discourse, since women's writing has a very problematic relation with authoritative status, particularly within the colonial context; and finally, the lack of address to women's writing and gender issues as a whole. Each of these problems is important for the analysis of women's travel writing. It is not simply a case of adding on gender to make colonial discourse analysis better, but thoroughly reformulating the model of textuality which is employed in critical colonial discourse analysis.[1]

PERSONAL STATEMENTS

Peter Hulme sums up most of the work on this area when he describes colonial discourse as:

> an ensemble of linguistically-based practices unified by their common deployment in the management of colonial

47

relationships. . . . Underlying the idea of colonial discourse
. . . is the presumption that during the colonial period
large parts of the non-European world were *produced* for
Europe through a discourse that imbricated sets of questions and assumptions, methods of procedure and analysis,
and kinds of writing and imagery.

(Hulme, 1986: 2)

This reinforces many of the ideas which were first formulated
by Edward Said in his influential book *Orientalism* (1978a).
This book draws together the work of Foucault and Gramsci to
describe the surface regularities of a wide range of texts which
were written about the Orient during the colonial period.

Said's basic thesis is that western writers, especially since the
eighteenth century, have constructed the Orient as the Other,
and have, in doing so, attempted to contain and make powerless the inhabitants of colonised countries by fixing them in an
object position, and hence retaining the subject, powerful
position for westerners. This is what Johannes Fabian terms a
'denial of co-evalness', the denigration by textual means of
another nation (Fabian, 1983: ix). Said stresses the textual
means whereby this opposition is achieved:

Everyone who writes about the Orient must locate himself
[*sic*] vis-à-vis the Orient, translated into his text, this
location includes the kind of narrative voice he adopts, the
type of structure he builds, the kind of images, themes,
motifs that circulate in his text – all of which adds up to
deliberate ways of addressing the reader, containing the
Orient and finally representing it or speaking in its behalf.

(Said, 1978: 20)

This means that Orientalism is manifested in textual features
which can be traced in a wide variety of texts.

In describing texts as Orientalist, Said is not simply writing
about the jingoistic, openly racist discourse which is often
found in colonial writing of the nineteenth century, where
'natives' are reduced to a sub-human or childlike species,
incapable of organising themselves without British intervention; instead he concentrates on the 'objective' writings of
philology, history and ethnography, where the professed aim is
to understand phenomena in the East, to explain them to a

western audience, supposedly without undue bias. This type of writing (through various strategies, such as making general-isations about the other nation, making valorised statements, fixing these people in an unchanging past or present tense and making them very much a textual entity) limits them to an object position and does not confer full human status on them. Said considers Orientalist discourse to be 'disregarding, essen-tialising, denuding the humanity of another culture' (ibid.: 108). It is this dehumanising element in many texts which constructs the Orient and other nations as the Other for European nations.[2] Said emphasises that it is the omission of personal statements which contributes to the denying of a subject position to others:

> the record of Oriental residence and experience by a European must shed, or at least minimize, its purely auto-biographical and indulgent descriptions in favour of descriptions on which Orientalism in general and later Orientalists in particular can draw, build and base further scientific observations and description.
>
> (Said, 1978a: 157)

Charles Batten, discussing eighteenth-century travel writing, has also shown that male travel writers omitted personal elements from their texts in the eighteenth century because of textual and publishing pressures, as has Mary Louise Pratt in her description of the 'manners and customs' style of travel writing, where personal details are omitted (Batten, 1978; Pratt, 1985). Even when a writer such as Chateaubriand does make highly personal statements about the Orient, Said labels this as 'equating the Orient with private fantasy' (Said, 1979: 176).

Said suggests that when a western writer makes a general-isation about another nation, for example, 'The Syrian lives in well-defended towns', there is no appeal against the statement and there is no means of refuting it. However, although this statement presents itself as holding true for all Syrians, and therefore claims factual status, the difficulty of challenging it is also true of a great deal of subjective, personal anecdotes. This is a problem not with generalisations as such but with writing which is consolidated by a range of other texts and by authority. Said suggests that the Orientalist 'seeks to convert each aspect of Oriental or Occidental life into an unmediated sign of one or the other geographical half' (ibid.: 247). In this case, Said is assuming a simple binary opposition between East and West, and every element in the Orientalist text can be positioned on one side of that divide. But as Sadiq Al Azm notes:

> If, as Said insists, the unfamiliar, exotic and alien is always apprehended, domesticated, assimilated and represented in terms of the already familiar, then such distortions and misrepresentations become inevitable. . . . If the Orient studied by Orientalism is no more than an image in the mind and culture of the Occident. . . then it is also true that the Occident in doing so is behaving perfectly naturally and in accordance with the general rule.
>
> (Al Azm, 1981: 9)

Personal statements are presented as somehow less Orientalist than generalisations as they emphasise the common humanity of both the author and the people described. Yet, if the personal is to be lauded over the scientific generalisation, where does that leave us with a travel writer like V. S. Naipaul who, in such texts as *An Area of Darkness*, strings together highly subjective anecdotes, personal encounters, etc., stressing his lack of analysis and generalising very little. Said, on this point, remarks: 'Either one writes science like Lane or personal utterance like Chateaubriand' (Said, 1978a: 175). Therefore, Said suggests something in between these two positions: a 'lively sense of an Oriental's human or even social reality' (ibid.: 176). But this is exactly what Naipaul does in, for example, *Among the Believers* (1981). The people he describes are differentiated as individuals: one does develop a sense of their way of life, their views, etc., and yet Naipaul's view of these people is extremely negative, to the point of racism. It is ironic, therefore, that on linguistic grounds his work would not necessarily be classified as Orientalist or as part of a residue of colonialism. It is clearly possible to make racist assertions even if *only* writing in a personal way.

For Said, the only possibility of change is, for the reader, critique, and, for the writer, a firm emphasis in the text on 'human experience' (Said, 1978a: 328) or as he says in 'Orientalism reconsidered', 'mutual recognition' (Said, 1984: 19). However, although Said's basic contention is correct – that the texts do attempt to place, or have been read as placing, the

50

other nation into a position of inferiority – it must be admitted that the texts themselves are much more complex than that, particularly women's texts. Said is describing the dominant reading of these texts, rather than the elements in the texts which are in potential conflict. What I mean by dominant reading is those elements which are foregrounded as the self-evident meaning of the text and which form a cohesive reading, especially with reference to other discursive structures which are circulating in the society of the time. The reader can recognise that this is the reading position she is to adopt, but may resist it. As we have seen with the reading of women's travel writing, the dominant reading tends to be an autobiographical one, which foregrounds those elements in the text which concern themselves with personal relations, self-revelation and other feminine characteristics. This reading is ratified by the common-sense assumptions about femininity which circulated at the time, and which, in many elements of the discursive structure, still circulate. With male colonial texts the dominant reading is quite different, in that elements relating to the colonial situation are often foregrounded. It is these elements which Said concentrates on in his analysis – the dominant readings rather than the other elements of the text. A more complex view of the production and reception of texts is necessary, since the writing of western women in the colonial period rarely underwent conversion to official status, which Said suggests was a characteristic of personal statements in Orientalist texts. For that reason, their work remains at the level of the personal.

HOMOGENEITY OF COLONIAL DISCOURSE

In the analysis of colonial discourse the object of study is often portrayed as more homogeneous than is, in fact, the case. There are major differences, as Peter Hulme has noted, between the way that texts deal with those countries which were colonised and which were settled by the British and those where the countries maintained their own independent government and legal system and yet traded with the West. (Hulme, 1986). There is a great difference between the representations and discursive structures circulating about countries which were considered civilised and those which were not. Sometimes

51

countries, such as India, slipped in and out of such categories at various times during the colonial period. Hulme analyses Christopher Columbus's diaries in order to show the way that the narratorial position vacillates between the discourse of the savage and that of the civilised Orient: the barbarous and the riches of Cathay. Africans can be portrayed as noble savages or savage cannibals depending on the colonial situation. Said's views of Orientalist discourse are too monolithic and unified; that is, he describes Orientalism as if it were unchanging and consistent, both internally and across discourses. As Porter says:

> Unlike Foucault, who posits not a continuous discourse over time but epistemological breaks between different periods, Said asserts the unified character of Western discourse on the Orient over some two millenia, a unity derived from a common and continuing experience of fascination with and threat from the East, of its irreducible otherness.

> (D. Porter, 1982: 181)

For Porter, this runs the risk of confirming Orientalist knowledge in its powerful position rather than challenging it, since it seems to suggest that Orientalism has always and will always exist. It is precisely this problem which other critics using a Saidian model have been unable to resolve; for example, Rana Kabbani repeats a Saidian analysis of colonial texts and extends this to more recent writers such as Thesiger, Canetti and Calvino (Kabbani, 1986). In this way, Kabbani does not distinguish between those texts which were written within the colonial period and those which were not. Thus, it would seem as if there were no end to Orientalist representations.

Furthermore, Said's analysis relies fairly heavily on the correlating of formal features with particular political positions. For example, he analyses the way that the present tense is used in these texts. Said here is drawing on the work of Johannes Fabian, who suggests that 'the present tense is a signal identifying a discourse as an observer's language' (Fabian, 1983: ix); yet this does not appear to be true for all instances of the present tense. There is a fundamental problem in correlating linguistic elements with semantic or larger-scale elements in a direct one-to-one relationship, even though they can be indicators of tendencies in text, if backed up by other

52

features.[3] Clearly, this model of textuality analyses features from a text-immanent position, ignoring those elements of reception which also determine meaning. Particularly in the case of women's writing, it is evident that features cannot simply be taken to refer to one specific set of assumptions, nor can women's writing be fitted into this supposedly homo-geneous vision of Orientalism.

TRUTH-VALUE OF COLONIAL DISCOURSE

On the question of truth, Said says: 'a representation is *eo ipso* implicated, intertwined, embedded, interwoven with a great many other things besides the "truth" which is itself a repre-sentation' (Said, 1978a: 272). This idea of truth as a representa-tion is very much a Foucauldian one, and yet Said seems to be arguing against the truth-value of the statements of colonialist writers, for he wants to 'study other cultures and peoples from a libertarian or non-repressive and non-manipulative perspective' (ibid.: 7). For Said, Orientalist representations are distorted; he wants a knowledge of other people which is untainted by power. But as Dennis Porter says: 'Even when [Said] praises an occa-sional scholar for a rare objectivity, he does not show how within the given dominant hegemonic formation such an alternative discourse was able to emerge' (D. Porter, 1982: 181). Porter also shows that, if Said is correct in his proposition that there is little difference between the biased accounts he describes and other forms of knowledge, then 'Orientalism in one form or another is not only what we have but all we can ever have' (ibid.: 180). He suggests that Said fails to acknowledge the importance of other knowledges, especially those at the margins of the dominant discourse. Porter says:

> The failure to take into account [the] efforts and contribu-tions [of those who are on the edge of specific hegemonies] not only opens Said to the charge of promoting Occi-dentalism, it also contributes to the perpetuation of that Orientalist thought he set out to demystify in the first place. . . . Even when he praises an occasional scholar for a rare objectivity, he does not show how, within the given hegemonic formation such an alternative discourse was able to emerge.
>
> (D. Porter, 1982: 181)

53

This problem confronts Rana Kabbani also, since she devotes a chapter to Wilfred Scawen Blunt, whom she praises for his sympathetic representations of the inhabitants of the country in which he travelled (Kabbani, 1986). In many ways, in this type of analysis, the question of colonial discourse as discourse is simply not addressed, and the question is reduced to one of whether such a writer is to blame or not for the negative representations within the text.

Porter gives two examples of counter-hegemonic voices in works which should be strictly Orientalist in Said's terms: Marco Polo's *Travels* and T. E. Lawrence's *Seven Pillars of Wisdom.* He shows that in these two works there is no unified vision of the East, and that the very nature of writing about another culture entails a heterogeneous discourse, marked by gaps and inconsistencies. He suggests that travel writing itself is subject to such a wide range of constraints and motivations that it is almost inevitable that it will not present a unified vision of a country. Said's failure to take account of other elements in texts and his view of Orientalism as a unified discourse with clearly identifiable author-intentions and volition is obviously an effect of his professed liberalism. Porter, coming from a more openly Marxist background, sees this as disenabling, and wishes to stress the fragmentary nature of texts – their attempt to present a cohesive ideological statement necessarily producing fissures and rifts in the texts which allow the possibility of critique on their attempts at a unified position. It is these other voices in the texts which, Porter states, destabilise colonialist statements, and thus, it is not necessary to rely almost entirely on a simple critique to combat Orientalism, as Said does. However, it must be noted that without the notion of a dominant reading, Porter is unable to explain the power that these texts have had. If they contain within them destabilising elements, then how can these texts have had any effect at all? Therefore, although Porter's critique is useful, it is necessary to be aware of the reception of these texts and of the fact that they did serve a role in the process of affirming and reaffirming Britain in its colonial position.

Porter also shows, in contrast to Said, that the portrayal of western society and values in works of this kind does not necessarily present the west as superior. This is not to deny that both T. E. Lawrence and Marco Polo often wrote about the east in negative terms, and made generalisations about people in the east in standard Orientalist fashion, and Porter does not attempt by any means to justify these statements; but he points out that these texts are not unified and consistent, and that these are not the only statements contained within the texts. Instead he notes that: 'western ideological representation may be perceived by an appropriately positioned reader to be both asserted and put into question' (D. Porter, 1982: 188). Orientalism is not, then, the unified discourse that Said describes, but is rather made up of diverse elements which both contest and affirm the dominant discourses and other discourses of which it is composed. Peter Hulme takes up this point when he describes the variety of discourses of colonialism, as I mentioned earlier (Hulme, 1986).

Lata Mani and Ruth Frankenberg, similarly, see Said's main problem as one of attempting to generalise about very diverse material:

> no 'general' answer can be sought to the question of representation in part because there is no universality to the standpoints of authors. Rather, each of us is located very specifically and differentially within discourses of power/knowledge. We write from these positions.
> (Mani and Frankenberg, 1985: 191)

I would not agree that it is impossible to make general statements in this field, since elements of Said's analysis of colonial writing are undoubtedly correct – Orientalist texts, in the main, do attempt to construct the Orient as different and inferior. However, it is the texts' diversity which must also be considered, their differential negotiation with the rules of discourse and the factors, particularly gender and generic conventions, which determine these differences.

Without drawing too close an analogy, I would like to suggest that the criticism of colonial discourse has undergone similar stages to feminist criticism. Within a Kristevan framework, in the first phase of feminist criticism, liberal feminism, there is an analysis of sexism in male texts; in the second phase, radical feminism, there is an assertion of female difference and separatism; in the third phase, revolutionary feminism, there is a deconstruction of gender difference.[4] There are striking similarities between the assumptions of Said and the first phase of feminism. Phallocentric writing is criticised for describing socially constructed difference between males and females as immutable fact, just as Said criticises colonial discourse for a similar failing (Millett, 1977; Spender, 1986). In this approach, phallocentric texts are seen as consistent statements of sexism, and contradictions within the texts are not considered. Women's writing is seen to have been repressed and women's silence is stressed; within a negative view of power we are left silent, and our own resistance cannot be accounted for.[5] Just as you would not want to have a sexual politics analysis of literature as the only form of feminism, nor would you want to be left with only a Saidian approach. That does not mean that we do not recognise the usefulness of Said, since Orientalist texts are still being written largely within the same framework as Said discusses. Early feminist criticism depressed many women with its visions of monstrous male individual writers oppressing females as a whole, and patriarchy being an all powerful, consistent entity which was extremely difficult to tackle.[6] Feminists now recognise the necessity of dismantling this idea or we will be adding to the strength of patriarchy instead of challenging it. In a similar way, with Said, there is a danger of describing Orientalism in a way which makes it difficult to destabilise.

In the second of the phases that Julia Kristeva describes, feminists revel in the notion of women's difference, reclaiming and celebrating qualities which they consider inherently feminine, but also those qualities which have been foisted on women. Sadiq Al Azm considers a parallel move in some Arab writing, which celebrates the difference of world-view due to Islam (Al Azm, 1981). He describes this as 'Orientalism in reverse'. With some radical feminists, especially separatists, there is a move to abandon 'male' methodologies, such as rationality, strict theoretical frameworks, academic conventions, etc. and to write in a much freer way; women work on their own histories (herstories) and reclaim women writers who have been ignored. Male writers are not studied. A parallel move can be seen in some countries against what are considered western dogmas, such as Marxism or democracy, and there are efforts to 'Arabise' education, institutions and representational practices. The problem with both of these approaches is that difference is stressed in much the same way as before, and it runs the risk of being just as essentialist and ahistorical.[7]

56

Kristeva then moves on to a third utopian, deconstructive phase, where the very differences on which gender distinctions are based are deconstructed: 'the very dichotomy man/woman as an opposition between two rival entities may be understood as belonging to *metaphysics*' (Kristeva, in Moi, 1986). The problem with Kristeva's third stage is that unless power differences dissolve, it is simply utopian. The man/woman dichotomy is not simply metaphysical in practice. In his article, 'Orientalism reconsidered', Said seems to be working on this third level, but unfortunately his methodology still belongs to the earlier stages (Said, 1984). He suggests that the critique of Orientalism does not simply apply to representations of Arabs, but can be used as a way of deconstructing anti-Semitism too, and there are even wider possibilities implied. He suggests that we should 'create a new type of analysis of plural as opposed to single objects' (ibid.: 23). He goes on to say that we must 'regard analysis as in the fullest sense being *against* the grain, deconstructive, utopian' (ibid.: 26). This is what Dennis Porter is referring to when he says:

> the feasibility of a textual dialogue between Western and non-Western cultures needs to be considered, a dialogue that would cause subject/object relations to alternate, so that we might read ourselves as the others of our others and replace the notion of a place of truth with that of a knowledge which is always relative and provisional.
>
> (D. Porter, 1982: 181)

That is why it is not enough simply to *add* gender to a Saidian analysis, for example, to analyse women travel writers along with the other writers considered, although that must obviously be done. We need to reformulate his work within a more complex model of textuality which women's writing entails, which is also aware of gender as a determinant in the production and reception of both texts by men and by women.

LACK OF ADDRESS TO GENDER

As I mentioned earlier, Said portrays Orientalism as 'peculiarly (not to say invidiously) a male conception of the world'. He says: 'Orientalism itself . . . was an exclusively male province; like so many professional guilds during the modern period, it viewed itself and its subject matter with sexist blinders. This is especially evident in the writings of travellers and novelists' (Said, 1978a: 207). Colonialism is certainly portrayed as a male preserve where females have a very secondary supporting role. Most studies which consider women and imperialism consist of descriptions of 'native' and British women as the objects of male gaze or male protection within colonial texts.[8] Little serious work has been undertaken to analyse women as agents within the colonial context. Thus, despite Said's useful critique, he risks becoming entangled himself in this very male view of imperialism since he ignores the fact that many women were actively involved in colonialism: they wrote about the colonial situation and their works were very widely read.[9]

It is thus incongruous that someone who seems to be claiming universality for Orientalism (in so far as it appears to be impossible to write about the Orient without using Orientalist discourse) should equate that universality with maleness, and that he should write an account which is so sensitive to issues of race representation and yet should not have considered the implications of gender. Therefore, following on from Porter's criticism of Said, an analysis of women's writing about other cultures should examine whether they conform to the Orientalist pattern, or whether there are more, and potentially more numerous, counter-hegemonic and multiply determined voices overlooked by Said (D. Porter, 1982). This would necessitate a full-scale revision of the Orientalist framework rather than a simple addition of women to the ranks of Orientalists.

Representations of women have been central to the process of constructing a male national identity in the colonial period, but that paradoxically has been based on an excising of women's involvement in colonialism. The issue of representation is important simply because these discourses of women's role within colonialism establish the parameters for women's writing about the colonised countries. It is surprising, given the quantity of writing produced by women during the colonial period, that their work has been largely ignored. Although women feature largely in the colonial enterprise as potent objects of purity and symbols of home, their writing is not taken seriously in the same way that male Orientalist writing is. Patrick Williams shows that the representation of British women's sexuality is seen as an essential component in the construction of Britishness, and, particularly, male Britishness within the colonial context (P. Williams, 1989). Females play an important part in the colonial enterprise as signifiers, but not as producers of signification. As John McBratney notes, the 'figuring of women' is at the centre of colonial discourse, but not presumably the production of 'figurations' by women writers (McBratney, 1988). There are two main types of figuration of women: the British memsahib, in need of protection from potential sexual threat; and in direct contrast, the sexually available colonised woman.[10]

The way that the memsahib is represented is curious, since as Pat Barr has shown 'Writers have handed down to us a fictional image of the typical "memsahib" as a frivolous, snobbish and selfish creature who flitted from bridge to tennis parties "in the hills" while her poor husband slaved "on the plains" ' (Barr, 1976: 1). However, much of what Barr describes falls into the same discursive traps of representing the memsahib, for example, when she states: 'the women loyally and stoically accepted their share of the white people's burden and lightened the weight of it with their quiet humour' (ibid.: 1). It is necessary to work against these notions of the 'feminine' memsahib, since it excludes all other sorts of representations. Her book is however interesting in that it focuses precisely on women's involvement within the colonial situation, and its negative representation. This very negative depiction of women is compounded by the widely held opinion that the coming of the memsahibs irrevocably spoilt the British relationship with India. James Morris describes the memsahib in the following terms:

Newly emancipated herself, she took to India or Africa or the South Seas her own frilled and comfortable culture, patting the cushions as the muezzin called in the twilight, and receiving once a week. Fresh and fragile, pink and white, innocent by convention and inviolable by repute, among the dark skins of the subject peoples she must have seemed exquisitely distinct. To those subjects she remained, for the most part, benevolent but aloof . . . . The Englishwoman wove a white web around her menfolk; and though there were unrepentant reprobates to steal down to the bazaars, or lie in another sweet bosom on the scented

59

shore, still she did drive a wedge between ruler and ruled, breaking the physical contact, and hurrying the Briton home along Hastings Road for his bridge.

(Morris, 1979c: 136)

Here, the white woman is represented firmly in the private sphere as she would be in the Britain of that time, and she is represented as the obstacle to good relations with Indians, that is sexual relations. For Morris, the colonial administrator 'believed physical intercourse to be much the best way of preserving the Empire' (ibid.: 135) and 'concubinage was one of life's solaces' (ibid.: 134) (perhaps a slightly masculinist view of the situation).

Anna Davin demonstrates the way in which this representation of woman within the colonial period was partly determined by eugenicist arguments about racial purity and fears of falling birth rates: 'If the British population did not increase fast enough to fill the empty spaces of the empire, others would' (Davin 1989: 10). She argues that it was therefore necessary to depict women's role as being centred around the family and the rearing of children to assuage this fear. Morris also notes that the memsahib figure, despite this trivialising and negative depiction, became one of the empire's key symbols in times when the empire was tested by resistance, for example, with the Indian Mutiny of 1857: 'It was a favourite horror story. The British saw it in terms of cowering white ladies in fetid cellars; goggle-eyed Indians, half blood-mad, half lustful, creeping unawares upon sweet English children in lace pantaloons' (Morris, 1979c: 136). This type of representation served two purposes: that of portraying the Indian as a dangerous and lascivious beast, who therefore needed the paternal rule of the British, whilst at the same time reinforcing British women within their roles as chaste and British males as their protectors.[11]

Set against this depiction of the memsahib as sexually chaste, much is made in the accounts of colonial writing of the eroticism of the description of 'native' women. Kabbani shows the way in which the Orient is constructed through depictions of sensual eastern women in harems and in baths, sexually available space. She also shows the way in which this representational practice was in stark contrast, and perhaps even made sense in terms of its opposition, to the way that Victorian British middle-class women were depicted: naked eastern, but curiously Caucasian, women, in baths and seraglios, against tightly corseted, well-covered British women in their drawing rooms (Kabbani, 1986). Alloula also shows the way that the representation of sexually available 'native' women, particularly in a harem setting, was widespread throughout seemingly sexually repressive Victorian Britain (Alloula, 1981).

This sexualised depiction also transfers to the depiction of the country to be colonised as female, and therefore weaker. Many of the colonial encounters Hulme describes were also sexual encounters, and the vocabulary of sexuality is frequently used to encode this: for example, colonial forces are often portrayed as 'penetrating the interior' and the country is seen to be offering 'herself' to the male invading forces (Hulme, 1986). Central to all of these representational practices is the notion of sexuality, and the representation of the colonial situation as sexualised is a key element in the problems which British women encounter in representing themselves and the colonial situation in their own texts.

As I have noted, women's travel writing, and in fact women's writing about the colonial situation as a whole, has been largely ignored, or has been negatively viewed. Indeed, Paul Fussell, in his book *Abroad: British Literary Travelling Between the Wars*, specifically refuses to grant inclusion to the only woman traveller he discusses, Freya Stark, because he says: 'to write a distinguished travel book you have to be equally interested in 1) the travel and 2) the writing' (Fussell, 1980: 197), and, for him, it is clear that Freya Stark has not shown sufficient interest in either of these (like all other women travellers, presumably). In so doing, he manages to suggest not only that these women writers do not qualify as writers, but also that they do not qualify as travellers either.

Neither Said nor other analysts include women's writing within their accounts of colonialist writing.[12] There is a tradition of reading women's writing as trivial or as marginal to the mainstream, and this is certainly the attitude to women's travel writing, which is portrayed as the records of the travels of eccentric and rather strange spinsters.

However, in this specific context, this writing seems to have been ignored for a further reason: because it does not exhibit

61

the same clear-cut qualities that men's writing does. It is more difficult to analyse women's colonial writing, since it is only possible to talk about tendencies towards alignment with discourses of colonialism or tendencies towards a writing dominated by the discourses of femininity, since the women themselves differed greatly in their positioning in relation to both discourses; however, it is clear that their writing is not straightforwardly Orientalist in the way that Said has described it. There are statements within the texts which are clearly colonialist, but there are also statements which undermine them. The way that their writing was received also means that it is not possible for them to be regarded as straightforwardly Orientalist.

Women's colonial writing seems to have been omitted from accounts of colonial discourse, partly because women were not seen as part of the colonial enterprise and also because their writing seems to be Orientalist in a different way from male-authored texts. It is interesting that a recent book entitled _Women and Colonization_ surprisingly does not deal with the relationship of women to colonialism as writers or active participants, but rather deals with the position of women of the colonised country. This practice reinforces the notion that women took no part in colonialism as agents but were rather the passive victims of colonial powers (Etienne and Leacock, 1980).

Worley suggests another reason, when describing women's travel writing about America:

> The relative paucity of published narratives written by women is certainly one reason for this neglect. A less tangible reason for this neglect may well be the very categories used to classify the literary and travel writers. Raymond Jurgen Apahn, for example. . . finds that the authors [of travel accounts] were either professional authors of fiction, men of means who wrote semi-scientific books, individuals commissioned by European governments to describe conditions for potential emigrants or 'persons urging settlement of a particular place usually because of vested interest'.
>
> (Worley, 1986: 40)

She goes on to say: 'These categories may seem to arise logically from the body of literature, but once these categories are in place, their parameters make it easy to overlook women authors' (ibid.: 49).[13]

Thus, whilst acknowledging the importance of Said's work, and that of many post-Saidian critics, their work needs to be seen to be lacking an account of gender. The work of women travel writers cannot be fitted neatly within the Orientalist framework, and seems to constitute an alternative and undermining voice because of the conflicting discourses at work in their texts. They cannot be said to speak from outside colonial discourse, but their relation to the dominant discourse is problematic because of its conflict with the discourses of 'femininity', which were operating on them in equal, and sometimes stronger, measure. Because of these discursive pressures, their work exhibits contradictory elements which may act as a critique of some of the components of other colonial writings.

Part II

CONSTRAINTS ON PRODUCTION AND RECEPTION

3

FOUCAULT AND CONSTRAINTS ON THE PRODUCTION OF TEXT

As I noted in the Introduction, there are constraints on both the production and reception of texts which lead to them being read and judged in certain ways. Although these elements work on the text as a whole, and it is therefore difficult to separate the constraints on production from those of reception (for example, the negative reception that women's writing receives may discourage women from writing, or may encourage them to write in particular conforming ways), for the purposes of this book it has been necessary to separate these constraints, and in this chapter I will consider the constraints on production.[1] Ngugi wa Thiong'o states that:

> Over the years I have come to realise more and more that work, any work, even literary creative work, is not the result of any individual genius but the result of a collective effort. There are so many inputs in the actual formation of an image, an idea, a line of argument and even sometimes the formal arrangement. The very words we use are a product of a collective history.
>
> (Ngugi, 1986: x–xi)

This notion of collective history is, in the case of women's travel writing, the history of imperialism, but it is also the history of many other struggles; I aim to show here how strongly that history impinges on the production of texts and constrains what is written. When one reads contemporary accounts of women's travel, one becomes aware of the fact that nineteenth-century women were writing within a different set of discursive constraints. For example, Dervla Murphy, Bettina Selby and Robyn Davidson – contemporary travel writers – share many of the features which I describe in nineteenth- and early twentieth-century women's travel writing, but the discourses of femininity and colonialism have changed beyond recognition and there are other discourses, such as feminism, which inform the texts more.[2] The project of this chapter is to trace the way the discursive situation determined women's travel texts in the colonial period. What differentiates this account from pure determinism is that there are possibilities for resistance to this process of constraints, and I concentrate on tracking down the resistances as much as the constraints as such.

By analysing the rules of discourse, Foucault has given us a vocabulary to describe how it is that there are surface regularities across a wide range of texts, and by showing that these are representational practices rather than 'scientific' accounts, he enables resistance to such practices. In 'The order of discourse', Foucault analyses the limits on the proliferation of discourses, in other words, what constraints there are on what can be said. He describes these limitations as attempts to 'gain mastery' over the 'formidable materiality' of discourse: 'as history constantly teaches us, discourse is not simply that which translates struggles or systems of domination, but is the thing for which and by which there is struggle' (Foucault, 1981b: 52–3). Discourse becomes not simply a grouping of written texts within a particular discursive formation, but, at one and the same time, the site of struggles for meaning and also a means of constituting humans as individuals. That is, discourses are not anonymous sets of writing which have little effect on people's lives, but they actively constitute us as subjects; individuals have some part to play in this process, both challenging and rewriting some of the positions within discourse.

Writing is constrained by a variety of factors; that is, texts are produced in situations where there are numerous textual, economic, social, political, historical and personal forces at work which impinge on the writing process. Texts are therefore heterogeneous entities, and the aim of this chapter is to demonstrate the way in which texts are constructed from these various discursive elements, at the same time being aware of the way in which discursive structures circulating in society lead to them being read in certain ways. This chapter is an exploration of the constraining factors in the writing process within the discursive formation of colonial discourses.[3]

The constraints which I describe should be understood in a Foucauldian sense not to refer only to factors which limit discourse, but also to those which enable discourse to take place. The chapter as a whole seeks to demonstrate that women's travel writing cannot be analysed as if the texts originated from one determining factor, such as the author, 'reality', imperialism or femininity, but rather that the texts are produced in the interaction and clashing of a variety of constraining factors. Texts are heterogeneous, made up of various elements in response to different constraints on the writing process.

These systems of discursive rules are seen by Foucault in *The Archæology of Knowledge* to be autonomous; that is, the rules are produced by texts/utterances, and by the rule-governed nature of discourse. However, in 'The order of discourse', and his work after this period, he begins to become more interested in the nature of the textual and extra-textual constraints on writing, especially those imposed by power relations (Foucault, 1972a, 1981b). By the term constraint, Foucault wishes to describe the rather surprising fact that, given that, in theory, writers can say anything, texts are, in fact, so repetitive and restricted in the range of their structure, tropes, language choice, tense, statements, events, narrative figure and so on. This is the case for many types of text, but it is particularly evident in colonial discourse, where, for political and economic reasons, a single view of the situation is presented.[4] In 'The order of discourse' he speaks of the 'rarefaction of discourse' and uses the term 'rarefaction' to refer to the fact that so little is written, or that what is written is so repetitious (Foucault, 1981b). Foucault states, in *The Archæology of Knowledge*, that 'On the basis of the grammar and of the wealth of vocabulary available at a given time, there are, in total, relatively few things that are said' (Foucault, 1972a: 118). He continues this analysis in 'The order of discourse', and suggests that what we should be concentrating on is not the proliferation of discourse, but the constraints on the writing process. In this article, he considers the constraints on who writes and on what is written.

With a Foucauldian view of text production, all texts can be seen to be heterogeneous, and the product of multiple constraints. So, for example, the text is not seen to originate in a subject. Travel writing cannot be read as a simple account of a journey, a country and a narrator, but must be seen in the light of discourses circulating at the time.

I would now like to consider some of the constraints in more detail with examples from colonial discourse to show that, as Said says:

> Because Orientalism is a cultural and political fact . . . it does not exist in some archival vacuum; quite the contrary, I think it can be shown that what is thought, said or even done about the Orient follows (perhaps occurs within) certain distinct and intellectually knowable lines.
>
> (Said, 1978a: 13)

That is, there are constraints on what can be said or written within the colonial context. However, it is necessary to integrate some analysis of gender and Carolyn Steedman's work on constraints is useful here. In her book, *Landscape for a Good Woman* (1986), she considers the difficulties that beset her as a writer when trying to depict her mother's life; she considers the way that depicting a working-class woman's life is constrained by the type of representations which have preceded her work and which construct the working class as an almost exclusively male domain.[5] Similar problems beset women's travel accounts in the way in which they try to insert themselves into a set of discursive constraints which are largely masculinist.

I therefore concentrate here on the way in which women writers have difficulty adopting the same voice as male travel writers. I do not see their work as deficient because of this, but as different and therefore not fitting in with Orientalist models. As Worley notes:

> Since men were assumed to possess such characteristics as activity, energy, independence, and intellectual prowess to be used in public life and the wide world, their travel and any writing based on these travels were fully in harmony with society's expectations. The situation was quite different from women for whom travel meant leaving the postulated 'female' sphere, a sphere limited to the interior realm and domestic life. Women travellers would thus most likely have felt conflict between their need to fulfill cultural expectations which viewed them as the weak, passive 'other', and their deliberate entrance, perhaps even escape, into a world of danger and difficulty, a world of travel to

faraway places. Women's travel narratives reflect these tensions, tensions missing in men's narratives.

(Worley, 1986: 40)

Although there are clearly tensions in women's travel writing, the texts need not be read as a reflection of a 'different subjectivity'. These texts are clearly produced within a different discursive context to men's writing, and this context must have some effect on the subjectivities thereby produced, but the link between the discursive context and the creation of subject positions is much less clear than Worley suggests. She goes on to state:

> A woman attempting to write an account of her travels would sense that her activities were diametrically opposed to those of the nineteenth century ideal . . . the selfless 'angel of the house' . . . for not only had she ventured out of the domestic circle into the wide world, but the very act of writing – especially a travel narrative with its strongly autobiographical element – might reveal an unwomanly preoccupation with the self.

(Worley, 1986: 40)

However, it is not so much the preoccupation with the self which causes these tensions, since it is clear that, drawing on Foucault's notion of the confessional, women have since the eighteenth century been encouraged to reveal 'the self' in writing through diaries, letters, etc. (Foucault, 1981b). Worley states that she notes a certain 'anxiety' about these narratives, 'in their compulsion to justify to the reader both the auto-biographical elements of their book and the journey itself, an anxiety not shared by . . . male travellers' (Worley, 1986: 41). These dissonances in the text can be more profitably analysed using discourse theory as an indication of clashes of discourses.

I now describe some of the discourses which women travel writers engage with when they produce texts. I deal firstly with the conventions of travel writing as a whole; secondly, I con-sider those discourses which construct the colonised nation as different and as objects of western knowledge (these are the more conventionally recognisable elements of colonial dis-course). As I suggested in chapter 2, this is a strong element in many texts, but it is not the only one. There are many discourses here: the discourse of ethnography, the discourse of racial superiority, savagery, the noble savage and so on. These discourses have been the most widely studied, firstly by Edward Said but more recently by Mary Louise Pratt, Homi Bhabha and Peter Hulme (Said, 1978a; Bhabha, 1983; Hulme, 1986; Pratt, 1985). None of these discourses is easily available to the woman travel writer since she has a further pressure to negotiate: that is the discourses of the feminine, although this did not necessarily prevent her from adopting the discourses of imperialism. In fact, in some cases, the discourses of femininity reaffirmed colonialist statements, whilst at other times undermining them. There are a variety of textual strategies which are at various periods termed feminine – the most important one is the confessional, as Foucault terms it. This strategy is the textualising of the 'inner self' (Foucault, 1981b). The feminine discourses stress concern with the presentation of a well-behaved self: there are frequent remarks in travel texts about the importance of the feminine discourse of clothes, wearing correct clothes, gloves, skirts of a decent length, not riding side-saddle and so on, but also of correct behaviour, of obeying the norms of British society. This could be read as a bow in the direction of the feminine in order to mitigate the force of some of the elements included within the colonial discourses. But there is also a a clash between discourses of femininity and discourses of feminism, the latter attempting to challenge the 'naturalness' of restrictive clothing for women.[6] The discourses of feminism inform many of the texts, since this was a period of feminist debate and action on a wide range of issues.

Travel writing, like all writing, is produced in the conflict of several discourses, which are both textual conventions and also texts which are circulating within society. For women travel writers, there is a conflict between several of the discourses, but there are moments when the discourses do reinforce one another, for example, in the case of philanthropy, which falls within both the discourses of femininity and those of empire, and there are elements like the 'angel in the house' figure which is constructed at least in part by imperial discourses, and which is drawn on in some of the women's travel narratives to construct a narrator figure. The conventions of travel writing obviously are constituted partly by the discourses of empire, but what I argue here is that there is a range of textual features

72

which also constitute the 'travel writing genre'. Thus, textual conventions are also part of the determinants of women's travel writing.

In discussing these constraints it should be borne in mind, as I noted earlier, that there is the possibility of resistance. Foucault, although slightly vague on examples of this more positive notion of power insists that the idea of resistance is contained, written into the notion of power. He says: 'Where there is power there is resistance' (Foucault, 1981b: 95), and, conversely, where there is no resistance there is no power. As well as seeing that resistance is entailed in power, he sees resistance to power as being multiple, just as the manifestations of power are multiple. Thus, textual power is not to be seen as a reflection of some other form of power, whether economic or political, but rather as a manifestation of power itself. Texts *are* relations of power.

CONVENTIONS OF TRAVEL WRITING

It is important to note that textual constraints on travel writing are constructed by certain regularities of discourse; that is, by the books which have already been written about other nations. Said notes that textual constraints are of great importance in colonial discourse: 'In the system of knowledge about the Orient, the Orient is less a place than a topos, a set of references, a congerie of characteristics, that seems to have its origin in a quotation' (Said, 1978a: 177). Many writers actively draw attention to the textual nature of travel writing, for example, Rose Macaulay, in her travel 'novel' *The Towers of Trebizond*, says: 'The trouble with countries is that, once people begin travelling in them . . . they are apt to get over-written' (Macaulay: 1956: 72). Macaulay's narrator frequently mentions other travel writers she has read who serve as a framework for her descriptions, and similarly, Redmond O'Hanlon says, in 'Amazon adventure', that a necessary part of his preparation for a four-month journey to Venezuela and Brazil was to 're-read my nineteenth century heroes', which consisted of the major travel writers on the region (O'Hanlon, 1986: 17). In this way, most travel writers portray members of the other nation through a conceptual and textual grid constituted by travel books. This close intertextual relation with other travel accounts

73

can be seen in the fact that travel writing has always appropriated other writing, sometimes explicitly but often by plagiarising. For example, Carrington notes that large parts of Mandeville's *Travels* (1322) were appropriated virtually verbatim from Friar Odoric of Pordonone's account, and Adams traces the numerous elements of previous authors which surface in travel texts (Carrington (ed.), 1949; Adams, 1962, 1983).

Within travel writing, there is even a tradition of textbooks which attempt to determine how other books are written. Charles Batten describes Count Leopold Berchtold's *Essay to Direct and Extend the Inquiries of Patriotic Travellers* (1789) which attempts to show travellers how to categorise information into tabular form in a remarkably complex system of categorisation. Batten remarks: 'The favourable reception enjoyed by Berchtold's *Essay* indicates that his suggestions, outrageously complex as they may seem, were taken seriously by his contemporaries' (Batten, 1978: 88). There were also textbooks which were addressed specifically to women travellers as I show later in this chapter (pp.100–3).

Travel writing is characterised by similarities of textual features, such as the narrative figure, narrative incidents and the description of objects, and these act as constraints on writing. Most critics only discuss the device of 'narrator' in 'fictional' writing, particularly in the novel; it is difficult to say whether this is due to the fact that they only analyse 'fictional' works, or whether they actually believe that there is no 'narrator' as such in 'non-fictional' works. However, it is generally possible to see the narrator as a device through which the narrative becomes comprehensible; the narrator is a construct which gives coherence to a variety of voices, or discourses. As Hayden White says:

> the capacity to envision a set of events as belonging to the same order of meaning requires a metaphysical principle by which to translate difference into similarity. In other words, it requires a 'subject' common to all the *referents* of the various sentences that register events as having occurred.
>
> (White, 1980b: 1)

Mary Louise Pratt shows that there are essentially two types of travel writing, each with their own narrative figure: what she terms the 'manners and customs' figure, and the 'sentimental' figure, the main difference being that the former is largely impersonal, where the narrator is absent, and the latter foregrounds the narrator (Pratt, 1985). Even within travel texts, the narrative figure is not a unitary source of information; that is, all of the statements within travel writing do not issue from the same narrative figure. In the manners and customs figure, certain statements emanate from an impersonal source which is not identical with the narrator who travels from place to place. Pratt says these statements come from 'an unknown site behind the speaking "I" – behind the periphery of what is seen, from a seat of power that should probably be identified with the state' (ibid.: 126). Although I would agree that these generalising statements issue from a place other than the 'I' of the narrator, they do not necessarily come from the state, although it is very difficult to trace their source. They certainly seem to emanate from the framework of knowledge about the other nation which travel writers have normalised. Pratt concentrates her analysis of the manners and customs figure in Herbert Barrow's eighteenth-century text on South Africa, where little account of human interaction is given. Instead, people only occur in the texts as representative figures, or as *traces*. Numerous travellers write about the traces of earlier civilisations whilst not attempting to describe their interactions with the present occupants of the country. Landscapes are described as if they were empty of people: as Pratt says 'signs of human presence, when they occur, are . . . expressed as marks upon [the face of the country]' (ibid.: 123). It is a convention that western travellers write about ruins in their accounts, but Pratt suggests, as Said has also, that the reason for this is to 'reduce current . . . societies to vestiges of a glorious past' (ibid.: 130). Instead of human interaction, there are many descriptions of the landscape. She says: 'In the main, what is narrated proves to be a descriptive sequence of sights/sites, with the traveller presented chiefly as a kind of collective moving eye which registers these sights' (ibid.: 123). She notes how the narrative is surprisingly agentless, and that the reader is forced to infer the progress that the narrator makes, rather than that progress being described.

The second type of narrator which Pratt describes is the sentimental traveller, where the narrator and the individual

indigenous inhabitants are portrayed as taking part in a dramatic narrative. Whereas the authority of the manners and customs
type text comes from the informational, scientific nature of its
content, the more 'experiential' text gains authority from the
fact that it is concerned with people as individuals. Here,
individuals from the country are presented in dialogue with the
narrator, often in the framework of the courtly encounter. Pratt
notes:

> If the land-scanning, self-effacing producer of information
> is associated with the state, then this sentimental, experi-
> ential voice must be associated with that critical sector of
> the bourgeois world, the private sphere, home of the
> solitary, introspecting Individual.
>
> (Pratt, 1985: 133)

It is hardly surprising, given this concentration on the private
sphere, that many of the women travellers chose this narrative
figure for their texts. However, Pratt notes that these texts,
although they seem more personal than the manners and
customs texts, are just as much a part of European colonial
expansion as others; their avowed intent of making the country
known to Europeans is submerged in their personal tales of
adventure, but their function is still that of expansion and
domination.

There are also common plot and narrative structures for
travel writing. The adventure narrative, it has been argued, by
such critics as Martin Green, is 'the energising of myth of
empire' (Green, 1980: xi). He says: 'To celebrate adventure was
to celebrate empire' (ibid.: 37). In many ways the history of the
imperial situation is often described in terms of adventure – for
example, James Morris states: 'In Africa the British seemed to
be storming belligerently everywhere, seizing territories or
abasing chieftains for reasons that were basically economic or
strategic, but were often sublimated on the spot into the sheer
love of a scrap' (Morris, 1979c: 118). Green has described the
way in which this myth is profoundly gendered in that it is more
easily available for male writers:

> Adventure seems to mean a series of events, partly but not
> wholly accidental, in settings remote from the domestic
> and probably from the civilised . . . which constitute a

76

challenge to the central character. In meeting this challenge, he performs a series of exploits which make him a hero, eminent in virtues such as courage, fortitude, cunning, strength, leadership and persistence.

(Green, 1980: 23)

Rebecca Stott also confirms this when she notes: 'Imperialist discourse [is] . . . a man-made discourse, expressing male fantasies, fears, anxieties. It is a discourse that emphasizes the importance of male camaraderie and which implicitly warns of the debilitating effects of women' (Stott, 1989: 70).

This should not lead us to imagine that women could not write within this framework, but as Elizabeth Joyce (1984) has shown the choice of narratorial voice is more problematic for women writers (Joyce, 1984). To argue that this is a male narrative voice, we have only to look at some of the critics who write on adventure: for example, Paul Zweig in *The Adventurer* states that 'adventurers always flee women and reinvent themselves as men, in order to find wholly male pleasures' (cited in Green, 1980: 346). The fact that adventure narratives usually include descriptions of cannibals, which for Green 'is the archetype of everything monstrous and appalling in primitive cultures' (ibid.: 80), or of other incidents of a bloody nature, effectively puts off limits a large number of narrative incidents for women travel writers, since the conventions for descriptions by women writers would decree these elements improper. The adventure hero is the perfect colonial subject, or at least the perfect colonial *male* subject. The narrator must keep 'face' and a 'stiff upper lip'. Such a narrator figure, whilst available to women writers to some degree, is also undermined by other elements within their texts.

Hulme states:

It might be said that the 'pure' adventure story, which has to take place outside metropolitan Europe, and preferably in as remote an area as possible, reached its apogee as the tentacles of European colonialism were at their greatest reach in the late nineteenth century.

(Hulme, 1986: 183)

Thus adventure narratives were at their height when women travel writers were also writing in great numbers. Since this was

77

one of the conventions of travel writing they adopted the plot form, but very often there was a degree of uneasiness about such adoption. As Joanna Russ has shown, there are only a small range of hero positions available to women within narrative (Russ, 1984; see also Pearson and Pope, 1981), and the adventuring hero role clashes with other discursive constructions of how women behave. The type of hero who is master of a situation and who maintains a 'stiff upper lip' is so immediately masculine that women writers have difficulty adopting this role with ease. That is not to say that the role is not adopted by women, but that when it is it is often modified by disclaimers and by humorous interventions, as I show in chapter 6, or by stress on the difficulties of travel, as I show in chapter 7.

There are conventions about the type of event which can be included in a travel journal, and these are very specific in women's travel writing. As Dervla Murphy comments in her introduction to Ella Maillart's book *Forbidden Journey*, originally published in 1937:

> This is what travel – and travel writing – is all about . . . . If there were fleas or lice, they bit her; if a pony or camel collapsed, she walked; if there was no food, she went hungry; if the sun was too hot, she sweated; if blizzards blew, she froze.
>
> (Maillart, 1983: xvi)

Maillart's text is seen to be of value since it contains descriptions of events which require physical endurance, and therefore it conforms to the norms of this type of travel text.

There are numerous incidents which are frequently included in travel narratives, and thus they seem to form part of the genre expectations. One of these, which Pratt (1985) points to, is to imagine the scene before the narrator peopled by the British. In this way, the landscape is emptied of 'native' inhabitants and British 'order' is imposed.

One of the most important incidents of this kind is the panorama. Pratt suggests that 'the fantasy of dominance . . . [is] commonly built into this stance' (Pratt, 1985: 124). Thus, in the physical act of describing the landscape the narrator is also mastering it. This recalls Foucault's work on the panopticon.[7] In travel writing the narrator gazes at the 'natives' – and is irritated if they have the temerity to gaze back, as is the case with both Mildred Cable's and Isabella Bishop-Bird's narrators – and at the same time, s/he amasses information about them (Cable and French, 1927; Bishop-Bird, 1880/1984). Pratt suggests that the panorama is always a device for seeing the country as a future colonised country, and thus the narrator who includes a panoramic scene arrogates to herself the power of the colonial position.

In travel writing there are conventions for what type of information can be included. These conventions are not static, as Batten has shown, for he notes that, in the eighteenth century, travellers generally described architecture, but then there came a radical change to descriptions of soil and crops (Batten, 1978: 95). He also says:

> Whereas mountains, plains and rivers had formerly served to instruct the reader concerning their utility as boundaries, sources of food, defences, and their influences on national manners and customs, these natural features [in the eighteenth century] become the primary topics of description serving for the most part simply as a source of amusement for the traveller and his readers.
>
> (Batten, 1978: 99)

Mary Louise Pratt sees it as the task of the writer within colonial discourse

> to incorporate a particular reality into a series of interlocking information orders – aesthetic, geographic, mineralogical, botanical, agricultural, economic, ecological, ethnographic, and so on. To the extent that it strives to efface itself, the invisible eye/I strives to make these informational orders natural, to find them there uncommanded, rather than assert them as the products/ producers of European knowledges or disciplines.
>
> (Pratt, 1985: 125)

These informational constraints produce what is described, for example, Batten describes the way in which, in Horrebow's *Natural History of Iceland* (1758), chapter 72 is entitled 'Concerning snakes', and the chapter consists of the sentence: 'there are no snakes to be met with in the entire island' (Batten, 1978: 36). In this way it is the informational order which has determined the structure of the text. Writers are constrained, since

79

these narrator figures share the 'will to knowledge'. The narrator is shown to be in control, and also to be in a position of knowledge, superior to that of the inhabitants of the country. The narrator maintains an air of sang-froid, in marked contrast to the emotionalism of the other characters, who often only serve the purpose of buttressing the status of the narrator: for example, in *A Voyage to the Pacific Ocean* (1784) Francis Drake recounts how he was worshipped as a god by the inhabitants of San Francisco Bay, and how he was begged to be their king.[8] To a lesser degree the same is true for many of the more recent travellers: for example, Mildred Cable notes the compliments that her driver pays to her, and she has him say about her: 'you are good people' (Cable and French, 1927: 272). She also remarks: 'the visitor can never become intimate . . . until he shows himself able to share [the country's] . . . outlook on life and for this he must be familiar with the language, sayings, customs and traditions of the people' (ibid.: 35). The implication of this statement is that Cable *is* in fact conversant with the language and customs and, therefore, she is in a position of intimacy with the inhabitants of the country which gives her the authority to describe them. Rather than attacking these statements for their 'egoism', it should be noted that they emanate from a larger discursive formation, whereby the narrator of travel texts must adopt a position of mastery where her/his face is not threatened. This poses significant discursive problems for women. Description is also constrained by the fact that the narrator often wishes to distinguish himself/herself from other travellers by stating openly that the account offered is about the 'real' town or country, whereas other travellers' accounts only show a westernised 'non-real' version. Foucault radically questions the notion that writing can simply describe the world. Travel writing has constructed conventions for describing landscape, places and people and objects in that landscape. Mrs Piozzi, a travel writer in the eighteenth century, shows herself to be aware of these problems when she says: 'descriptions are *so* fallacious, one half despairs of communicating one's ideas as they are: for either well-chosen words do not present themselves, or being well-chosen they detain the reader, and fix his mind on *them* instead of the things described'.[9]

As I noted in chapter 2, non-fictional writing, i.e., the assertion of truths, has been largely a male domain because education was restricted primarily to males until the late nineteenth century.[10] However, this statement needs some qualification since it is primarily that type of 'factual' writing which requires 'authorising', for example, history and scientific writing, which has rarely been written by women. The type of 'factual' texts which can be written by women is often that which needs little authority. Examples of the latter are autobiography and travel writing, although, with both of these, the 'facts' which are included have to accord with a set of discursive conventions of what females can and cannot do.

A further constraint on women travel writers is that there are certain subjects which women are not supposed to know or write about – sex is the most obvious one. Within this stereotype, women are supposed to travel in order to paint butterflies and flowers, as Marianne North and Margaret Fountaine did. As Joanna Trollope says: 'Plants – as long as they were not too grossly tropical – were a safe subject, just sufficiently aesthetic without any danger of being intellectual, and properly sexless' (Trollope, 1983: 156). Women travel writers are not supposed to become experts on fish (as Mary Kingsley did), discover unknown mountain ranges (as Fanny Bullock Workman did) or provide statistical information about a country (as Isabella Bishop-Bird did).[11]

That these constraints work actively on women's writing can be clearly seen in Dorothy Middleton's account of a woman traveller:

> Mrs Alec-Tweedie, a handsome, courageous, young widow – one of the first professional travel-book writers – could have given many more delightful pictures of herself and her friends rattling through Finland in carts if she had not been so anxious to explain the political and social position of women in the Scandinavian countries.
>
> (Middleton, 1982: 5)

For Middleton, despite Mrs Alec-Tweedie's 'professional' status, women writers are supposed to write within a 'confessional' framework, revealing personal information, and not writing on serious topics. When women travellers do attempt to give 'scientific' accounts, their work is seen to be aberrant, for example, Middleton notes of women travellers:

> It is almost as if they feared it was wrong to travel for

pleasure and that to bring back notebooks of statistics and pages of drawings was necessary to justify the frivolity of bicycling across Java or living among the Hairy Ainu of Japan.

(Middleton, 1982: 5)

If the reader expects that the texts should only deal with pleasure or with trivial domestic information, then statistical information will not meet those expectations.

A further example of the way that conventions structure the way that a text is produced is Jane Duncan's account:

I was in the saddle for seven and a half hours continuously that day without feeling tired . . . . I gave this account of crossing the Chang La to a literary friend to read, and his criticism was that I did not harp sufficiently on the agonies of the journey; but as I did not suffer any agonies, I do not quite see how the harping is to be done . . . . I have no gift of fine writing to cast a glamour over it and make it seem the tremendous achievement it was not.

(cited in Middleton, 1982: 16)

There are also subjects which women are supposed to avoid, and are advised to exclude from their texts by publishers. None of the travellers I have read refers to the other country in the same terms as some of the male writers, as a female sexualised body. Nor do they mention 'indelicate' subjects in the main; surprisingly, few of them refer to any fear of sexual harassment, one of the discursive constraints which is the strongest in the context of women and travel, especially in accounts of women travelling alone. If they do mention subjects which seem 'unfeminine' in some way, many of them use a distancing strategy in their texts, such as mediating the information: for example, Fanny Parks reports on Thug atrocities in India through incorporating letters from a friend containing the accounts (Parks, 1850). This conflicts with many of the genre requirements of adventure since thrilling and often blood-thirsty episodes should be included, and since, as I noted earlier, adventure is one of the necessary requirements for an account of empire, women's writing is problematically con-structed. Russell demonstrates that women were supposed to write on certain topics, but that in doing so their texts were

82

judged inferior – a conventional literary double-bind:

> They became observers, not of places but of people and we
> owe them an eternal debt, for their records of sights and
> happenings complemented the scientific data remitted by
> male explorers. Used to the minutiae of the household,
> they observed the trees within the wood, but because of
> this their observations were often dismissed as trivial.
>
> (Russell, 1986: 213)

She goes on to detail the way in which this affected women's
writing: 'Aware of this negative attitude and wanting to disarm
their critics in advance, many women travellers adopted a self-
effacing pose, unnecessarily belittling their aims and denigrating their achievements' (ibid.: 213).

Women writers are clearly not given the same discursive
possibilities to assert as male writers and many are singularly
modest in their assertions. For example, Mildred Cable and
Francesca French, in *The Gobi Desert*, state that they 'went out
not knowing whither' (Cable and French, 1942: ix), but J.
Stuart Holdern remarks that 'It would not be true to say that
"they went out not knowing whither", for they had studied the
available maps and pondered the known problems of the
course they must traverse' (Holdern, in ibid.: ix). The reasons
why they make this statement is that women's texts are not
supposed to be 'scientific' and authoritative, but rather,
supposed to be amateurish. This problematic positioning of
these texts often leads to the writing being prefaced with a
disclaimer which denies any scientific, academic, literary or
other merit; this occurs very frequently with women's travel
writing in the nineteenth century. A further result of this
problem with adopting a 'scientific' voice is that some women
travel writers concentrate their descriptions on those elements
which fit their texts in with the feminine discourses, and
therefore avoid reference to the colonial context or to scientific
subjects.

  The constraints on travel writing are also evident in the
structuring of description, that is the different sites/sights
which could be described when writing a travel account. This
stems from the origin of travel writing in accounts of pilgrimage.
During the era of the Grand Tour the itinerary of travellers was
fairly fixed; there were only certain towns and cities in Europe

83

that were considered worth visiting and describing. Texts decreed which sights should be seen and how these sights should be viewed. Many travellers took guide books or other travel books which listed the most important, worthwhile sights, and rated them for the traveller. Before the traveller had even arrived, the site was thus already categorised. Philip Dodd notes that in different periods there are different sets of discursive constraints on what constituted a 'site': 'The Edwardian traveller tended to search out uncultivated terrain, and to draw from the landscape values against which the place he had left, and to which he wrote, was to be judged' (Dodd (ed.), 1982a: 127). It is possible to see the arbitrariness of this notion of 'place' most clearly when we notice that its definition has changed; for, with the Romantics, mountains and wastelands suddenly became transformed into 'places' which were considered beautiful and which one should visit, whereas before they were considered to be simply dangerous obstacles between cities, and areas to be avoided.[12]

Travellers normally only write (and are published) under the following circumstances: firstly, if they travel to well-established places (in this case, the writer has to produce something which is novel, witty or erudite to compensate for the fact that they are writing about the well-known); secondly, if they write about travel to non-places (the Gobi Desert, Tibet, that is, places which have not been written about before); or thirdly, if they describe travelling by a difficult means of transport.[13] The very fact of being female is considered to be one of the elements which make travel difficult enough to write about.

The travel writing genre has experienced a number of changes in its conventions over time, as I mentioned earlier. For example, Charles Batten shows the way in which there was in the eighteenth century – as Hayden White and Michel Foucault have discussed – a radical break-up of writing from an essentially undifferentiated 'news/novels' discourse, to use Davis's term, to a situation where books are either 'factual' or 'fictional' (Batten, 1978; Davis, 1983). By the nineteenth century, Batten notes that travel writing either tends towards the 'factual' guide book or the 'literary' text. In the late eighteenth century he notes that this split can be seen in the pressures on certain writers to change their texts. For example, Marianna Starke revised her travel book on Italy several times, until by

84

1832 it had become a guide book; Beckford's *Italy* (1834) had originally been published as *Dreams, Waking Thoughts and Incidents* in 1783, and on each subsequent new edition had been revised so that the autobiographical sections were omitted. Writers such as Boswell and Arthur Young both decided to order their writing into two distinct sections, one for their journal and one for general observations, and it was only the latter which was published. By the nineteenth century this was almost a convention for most travel writing, and demonstrates the way in which external discursive factors structure the format of the text.

In Foucault's terms 'what happened' and 'what was seen to happen' and 'what was written' are entirely dependent on the rules of discursive formations, which allow certain things to be described; hence, there is no question of a 'simple transcription'. There is a common assumption made about travel writing that travellers carry a notebook with them in which they note down all of the things which they see and which happen to them whilst travelling and then, when they return to Britain, they have this published. It is also assumed that travellers send letters to their friends and relatives whilst they travel, which they have published when they return. However, these forms should be recognised as conventions. Many of the letters which form travel books were scrupulously written with a view to publication, and some writers composed their writings in the form of letters only when they returned. For example, Robert Byron's travel book, *Road to Oxiana* (1937), is always considered very 'immediate' and 'spontaneous' and yet, as Paul Fussell (1980) remarks, he took several years to arrange the material from his notebooks to achieve that effect. Travel texts, like all other texts, are written within the conventions established by discourse and cannot therefore be seen as 'transcription'.

In addition, Paul Fussell notes of Robert Byron's *Road to Oxiana*: 'So conscientiously is it disguised as a book of hurried entries into a diary that a reader may easily and pardonably read it too quickly, mistaking it for an amusing record of an amusing trip and no more' (1980: 320). Among the other elements which critics, such as Adams, consider central to the structure of the travel book is the interpolation, or digression (Adams, 1962, 1983). Although, as he points out, this has been seen as irrelevant material in the novel, digressions can be

85

interpreted as foreshadowing, as echoing the main plot and characters, and, therefore, as not extraneous. He suggests that these digressions are essential in the travel text because they authenticate the journey: 'What may be called digressions in some forms of literature are for travel accounts structurally inherent' (Adams, 1983: 209). Similarly, Fussell considers that the 'anomaly' is central to the structure of the travel book:

> Like any genre, the travel book carries about it the marks of its origins, and if the wonders of Antiquity, the Middle Ages, and the Renaissance have in the full bourgeois age, attenuated to mere anomalies, these anomalies are still a necessary element in travel writing.
>
> (Fussell, 1980: 166)

He states that, in fact, travel writing is an 'implicit quest for anomaly', as if the travel writer were searching for something strange to describe (ibid.: 167). And yet, he feels that this is only because in describing the anomaly the writer is affirming the societal norms of England, a view surprisingly close to that of Edward Said.

One of the striking features in all of the descriptions of other countries is that objects are presented only in terms of their *difference* to objects in Britain. And this difference is portrayed as 'strange'; as Said mentions: 'The Orient was almost a European invention, and had been since antiquity, a place of romance, exotic beings, haunting memories and landscapes, remarkable experiences' (Said, 1978a: 1), and he states that 'The Orient becomes a living tableau of queerness' (ibid.: 103). Very little space is accorded to similarities with the British landscape or British people. The importance of difference is foregrounded by Ella Maillart when she says, of her companion: 'Peter mocked me for beginning all my opinions [about China] with the remark: "We must at all costs try to understand", when everything was incomprehensible' (Maillart, 1983: 41). The conventions of travel writing thus present a framework of largely masculine narratorial positions and descriptive patterns with which women writers negotiate when they construct their travel accounts.

DISCOURSES OF IMPERIALISM

Peter Hulme, as I noted in chapter 2, states that there are several discourses within colonial discourse, two of which concentrate on the discourse of the civilised other and the discourse of savagery (Hulme, 1986: 21). In an analysis of Christopher Columbus's diaries, Hulme traces the moment when the discourse of savagery, for purely pragmatic reasons, begins to dominate the discourse of the civilised Orient. For him:

> the radical dualism of the European response to the native Caribbean – fierce cannibal and noble savage – has such obvious continuities with the classical Mediterranean paradigm that it is tempting to see the whole intricate web of colonial discourse as weaving itself in its own separate space entirely unaffected by any observation of or interchange with native Caribbean cultures.
>
> (Hulme, 1986: 47)

Hulme shows how, within one geographical area, the division civilised/savage was made by Europeans between Arawak and Carib, and the Carib were associated with cannibalism, since they resisted colonial rule. This distinction can also be seen in Fanny Parks's work, when she contrasts the 'savages' she visits on the way to a more 'civilised' India (Parks, 1850). However, it is interesting in her account that the two discourses are never entirely separate, since the supposed 'civilised' India is still portrayed as degenerate, and inferior to western civilisation.[14]

The main thrust of Hulme's argument is that there are many discourses circulating within colonial texts and it is not simply a question of Said's monolithic Othering or Orientalism. There are more discourses at work than Hulme describes in the whole of the colonial situation. Each colonial relation develops narrative and descriptive techniques particular to its setting and history, which draw on a range of discursive practices. It is my aim in this section to describe the range of discourses brought into play in colonial texts, and also to describe the range of resistances which writers could draw upon.

Foucault says of eighteenth-century travel writers that they had 'schema' for collecting their data (Foucault, 1980a: 74). Whilst posing themselves as objective, they were, in fact, describing people and events from a particular position which had been constructed mainly by colonial discourses and hence from the demands of colonial power. Most travel writing presents a clear notion of the difference between the British as a race, of whom the narrator is a representative, and the nation which inhabits the country which is being described. As Said has shown, this 'Othering' process is essential for Europe to regard European behaviour as the norm and hence to assert itself as a superior race. Lévi-Strauss notes that western Europe in the Renaissance experienced:

> that crucial moment . . . when, thanks to the great voyages of discovery, a human community which had believed itself to be complete and in its final form suddenly learned . . . that it was not alone, that it was part of a greater whole, and that, in order to achieve self-knowledge, it must first of all contemplate its unrecognizable image in this mirror.
>
> (Lévi-Strauss, 1973: 30)

Said implies that 'Othering' is an inbuilt psychological mechanism which is simply part of human nature. Every nation attempts to construct other nations with which it is in conflict as the Other, but for Lévi-Strauss, the concept of the Other is something which comes to the fore especially at certain historical moments, particularly in colonial expansion.[15] In periods of imperialism, 'Othering' is one of the ways in which the conquering nation organises thoughts and actions towards the colonised nation, but each colonial context develops a specific range of colonialist discourses dependent on the type and length of colonial relation.

Mary Louise Pratt asserts that 'Othering' is achieved through language choices:

> The people to be othered are homogenised into a collective 'they', which is distilled even further into an iconic 'he' (the standardised adult male specimen). This abstracted 'he'/'they' is the subject of verbs in a timeless present tense, which characterises anything 'he' is or does, not as a particular historical event but as an instance of a pregiven custom or trait.
>
> (Pratt, 1985: 120)

She goes on to show that these traits which are seen as belonging to the whole nation, are 'likely to focus on the Other's amenability to domination and potential as a labor pool' (ibid.: 120). Thus, far from being 'objective' descriptions of the way the nation is, these descriptions are largely determined by the socio-historical context within which they are written, i.e., colonialism, and the needs which Britain as a colonial nation has for these people. Pratt discusses the conventional ways of describing people from other nations, and details the similarities between texts as diverse as those of John Mandeville and Christopher Columbus. And as I noted earlier, Johannes Fabian has shown the way in which the Other is consigned to another time sphere which is not the present, as he says: 'Time . . . is a carrier of significance, a form through which we define the content of relations between the Self and the Other' (Fabian 1983: ix). Fabian states that travel writers and anthropologists consign the other nation to a time which is distant from their own, through the use of words with temporal aspects such as 'primitive', 'backward' or 'developing'. Lucie Duff-Gordon, in *Letters from Egypt* (1865/1983), uses temporal adjectives like 'feudal' or 'medieval' to describe Egyptian society, and she describes scenes as being similar to the Old Testament and the Arabian Nights. In this way, she relegates contemporary Egypt to a European past. She and Isabella Bishop-Bird describe other people as 'savages' (Duff-Gordon, 1983: 377, and Bishop-Bird, 1984: 76) which, for Fabian, is also a temporal term. And in more recent writing, Jan Morris describes people in India as 'Bosch figures', that is, at once medieval and grotesque (Morris, 1984: 60). Another strategy is to consign the other nation to a time-scale which is unchanging: thus, for example, Jan Morris describes India in a similar way: 'I wish I could be original about the experience. I wish I could say something new. But Calcutta is always Calcutta' (ibid.: 61). A further way of distancing a nation temporally is through describing the inhabitants of a country as children; in this way, the people are considered distant from the time of adult Europeans. This 'denial of co-evalness' can be seen at work in travel accounts such as that of Mr Adamson, *A Short Account of that Part of Africa Inhabited by the Negroes* (1768): 'The simplicity of the natives, their dress and manners, revived in my mind the idea of our first parents; and I seemed to contemplate the world in its primitive state' (cited in Carrington (ed.), 1949: 243).

A further way of 'Othering' a people is not to describe them as full individuals, but as composed of separate parts of the body.[16] For example, William Dampier in *Captain Dampier's Voyage Round the Terrestial Globe* (1697) describes the people of 'New Holland' in the following terms:

> The inhabitants of this country are the miserablest people in the world . . . . They are tall, straight-bodied, and thin with long small limbs. They have great heads, round foreheads, and great brows. Their eye-lids are always half closed, to keep the flies out of their eyes . . . they have great bottle noses, pretty full lips, and wide mouths . . . . They are long-visaged, and of a very unpleasing aspect, having no graceful feature in their faces.
>
> (cited in Carrington (ed.), 1949: 354)

These people are not individuals but a list of features. In the same way, Lucie Duff-Gordon describes the bodies of Egyptians; each element composing their bodies is described in turn, in terms of their supposed difference from the British. Her descriptions relegate the bodies of these people to the status of objects: for example, she states that she wishes to send her husband pictures of the naked women, as their 'breasts are so good', and she remarks on the 'superb black arms' of her servant Mabrook (Duff-Gordon, 1983: 364). Janet Schaw, in *Journal of a Lady of Quality* (1774–6), describes Africans in a similar way: 'Their features are in general high and very regular, they have charming eyes, fine teeth, and the greatest quantity of hair I ever saw, which they dress with taste, and wear a great deal of powder' (cited in Carrington (ed.), 1949: 255).

There are several other constraints on writing about other nations: one of these is portraying the other nation in terms of abhorrent smells and filthiness.[17] Mary Douglas demonstrates that this assigning of dirtiness to the other nation is a common way of separating the colonised nation from the coloniser (Douglas, 1966: 2). For example, Isabella Bishop-Bird describes a place as 'the lowest abyss of filthiness', and Mildred Cable says of an inn-room that it was 'unspeakably filthy' (Bishop-Bird, 1984: 106; Cable and French, 1927: 84).

Mary Russell states: 'it is one of life's small ironies that women – their own position in society not unlike that of a colonised country – were themselves able to take a ride on the great wave of colonisation that burst outwards into the unclaimed world' (Russell, 1986: 38). Apart from her assumptions about the colonies being 'unclaimed', it is important to note that Russell, at least, includes women as part of colonial expansion, even though she only accords women a subsidiary role, following in the footsteps of the great male explorers. Colonialist statements can be found throughout women's travel writing, for example, Mildred Cable describes Buddhist prayer wheels as 'the offerings of a blinded people to its undiscerned god', a statement which positions the other nation negatively in relation to a British, and in this case Christian, norm (Cable and French, 1927: 30). It is clear that women writers assume the powerful textual position afforded by colonialism in much the same way that men do. Later in the text, in order to demonstrate the worthiness of the missionary enterprise, she describes a monastery:

> From the faces of most of the child lamas all boyishness had fled, leaving only lack-lustre eyes and a dull apathy, while on the features of the greater number of older men, nameless convulsive passions had left their hideous traces, showing unmistakeably the disintegrating nature of the Power at work. In a country where personal cleanliness is practically impossible during nearly three quarters of the year, owing to climactic causes; where women are the common property of a plurality of possessors; where one sixth of the population is segregated in a so-called celibacy given over to idleness, and such family life as exists is destitute of the very rudiments of decency or sanitation, nothing short of the deliverance of the individual – body, soul, and spirit – from the grasp of this stultifying Power can effect anything radical.
>
> (Cable and French, 1927: 70)

Cable delivers this classic Orientalist statement about the other nation; in all respects these people are presented as inferior to westerners – they have neither decency, cleanliness nor moral scruples. The statements about the nation are exactly the same as other statements by Orientalists writing from a more economic colonialist position, and yet this comes in a text which exhibits great concern and respect for these people.

Whilst many of the women were able to adopt this colonial voice at least in part of their texts, there were many others who

openly rejected the discourses of colonialism. Several critics
have noted that some women writers tend to criticise the way
that imperial rule is conducted within the country in which
they are travelling. Critique of cruelty or mismanagement
by the government or administrators occurs fairly frequently in
most of the texts, except for the ones like Emily Eden's *Up the
Country* (1866/1983) where there is a strong alignment with
that colonial power. This is usually explained by the fact that
women are unable to speak wholeheartedly from a position
within colonial discourse, or it is explained by the fact that
because of their marginalised position within western society as
a whole, they somehow understood and sided with the colonised
country.[18] This latter position is one which Catherine Stevenson
has adopted in her examination of the work of Florence Dixie
and Mary Kingsley when she asserts that they found 'an outlet
for their anger in a distant land' (Stevenson, 1985: 7), and 'the
later women travellers ventured into the controversial male
arena of foreign policy and struggled to find an acceptably
feminine voice for their angry and trenchant criticism of British
imperial policy towards Africans' (ibid.: 9). Stevenson argues
that 'they eagerly and passionately embraced the cause of the
African I would argue because the situation of the colonized
native provided a mirror image of their own plight as women in
an imperialistic society' (ibid.: 8). It is true that the way women
and Africans were discussed is similar: simple, childlike, deceitful, passive, not capable of intellectual thought, and more
closely allied to nature. What Stevenson's analysis ignores is
precisely the difference in power relations between the western
women travellers and the people amongst whom they travelled.
This analysis also lacks a way of explaining why it was that
although some women travel writers expressed some affiliation
with the other nation, many did not, and also that those who
did express affiliation, at other points of their texts expressed a
belief that the colonised nations were in fact inferior to western
nations. For example, Mary Kingsley, for all her supposed
affiliation with the cannibal Fans, still thought that they were
inferior and like children, a standard colonial statement
(Kingsley, 1897/1965). Stevenson also suggests that in order to
gain this 'freedom' in their texts, these women writers took
over male personae: 'This voice indirectly attests to the lure of
Africa for female travellers like Kingsley: there free from gender-

based restrictions, the woman can become what her imagination dictates – in Kingsley's case, that means becoming a man' (Stevenson, 1985: 15). This statement unwittingly suggests that the only type of free woman that there can be is one who imitates a man, thus concurring with the view that the male is the norm.

Stevenson sees the expression of resistance to the colonial presence which she detects in their texts as a displacement of their feminism: 'Thus when Kingsley and Dixie returned from Africa to champion the cause of Africans, they were, in fact, unconsciously reacting to their personal experiences as women and displacing their anger into positive, social action for the good of others' (ibid.: 9). But we might ask why must this be seen as displaced from action; if they had been able to channel their anger as feminists, then, the implication is that they would not have bothered to champion the cause of Africans. Stevenson draws attention to the contradictions in Kingsley's texts, for example, when Kingsley writes that she 'went down to Africa to die' and yet elsewhere she states that she felt 'like a boy with a new half-crown' (ibid.: 14). These contradictory statements can only be understood, for Stevenson, as evidence of Kingsley's 'bifurcated personality', divided between allegiance with her father and freedom and her mother and confinement.

Clearly, Kingsley's writing cannot be read as straightforwardly feminist, or as autobiographical since, in a letter, Kingsley says about her personal feelings: 'I keep them out of print just as I keep them out of almost all of my conduct . . . for they are savage things that would make people . . . shrink from me' (cited in Stevenson, 1985: 15). Such a statement is a clear warning against arguing that Kingsley the person can be found in her texts since she herself draws attention to the fact that she has consciously excised her 'feelings' from the text. It also shows us how clearly Kingsley felt the pressures on her to conform textually.

Thus a more productive analysis is one which attempts to see the clashes of discourses in texts, for example, as Worley mentions, women travel writers often concentrate on details of domestic arrangements, but 'These women however all concern themselves at length in their books with . . . politics and the public sphere. At this point the discrepancies and contradictions engendered by the clash between the internalised

concepts of the feminine ideal and their own activities emerge'
(Worley, 1986: 45). This type of analysis does not lead us to
make judgements about the author, but leads us rather to try to
discover the discursive frameworks which informed the texts, to
see the texts as a series of traces rather than as providing
unmediated access to the authors.

Thus, Othering and resistance to Othering are strong parts
of many texts about the colonial situation, but it is not the only
discourse. It is clear that within each text Othering plays a role,
for example, portraying the inhabitants of the country as
savage; yet this is not all that the texts contain. Women draw on
these conventions in much the same way as men, and yet the
discourses of femininity undercut many of the statements that
they make.

DISCOURSES OF FEMININITY

Femininity is a set of socially constructed discursive frameworks. As Susan Brownmiller and Frigga Haug have shown, the
parameters of these discourses change over time, because of
women's resistance and other factors (Brownmiller, 1986; Haug
(ed.), 1987).[19] But there are certain elements within these
discourses which have stayed much the same since the nineteenth century. These discursive structures lay out for women a
range of behaviour patterns concerning sexuality, morality,
their relations with others which are there to be contested (they
are, after all, only discourses), but they are also there to be
complied with, in as much as that is possible. As Haug notes, it
is difficult to trace the discourses of femininity which have
determined the production and reception of texts in a period
which is not one's own, but nevertheless it is possible to
produce an archaeology of the period, however partial that may
be, and however determined by present discursive frameworks
it may be.

The discourses of femininity, in the late nineteenth and early
twentieth centuries, set out for middle-class women a range of
roles, largely situated within the private sphere.[20] 'Feminine'
women concerned themselves with their families and maintaining relationships, but also tended to the spiritual and moral
well-being of the family group. These discourses had a clear
effect on the way that women's travel writing was constructed,

for example, as Shirley Foster notes, when a publisher asked Sydney, Lady Morgan to write on Italy, they asked her to write on 'morals and manners', whilst her husband was to write on the laws and government institutions (Foster, 1988: 3). Thus, women are reinforced into a position of writing on personal relations, the private sphere, even whilst they are venturing into the public sphere, through describing travelling.

In order to discuss this notion of the depiction of relationships and personal involvement of women's travel writing in its historical context (rather than positing, for example, that women are inherently more interested in personal relations than men), it is worth considering middle-class women's position in Britain in the late nineteenth and early twentieth centuries, since women travellers were mainly from this class. This explains in some measure why many women travellers wrote about other nations in a way which was different from the standard Orientalist description. Within the discourses of femininity, women of the middle class were presented as very restricted in their movements: it was considered necessary for middle-class women to be chaperoned, both to protect them from what was considered rampant male sexuality and because of the importance of the notion of female purity for the construction of male identity.[21] For middle-class women, work outside the home was considered demeaning, and they were treated as frail beings, frequently suffering from a range of debilitating illnesses, unable to fend for themselves and in need of help and protection from males.[22] Middle-class women were defined by the status of their husbands or fathers, and social advancement was possible primarily through marriage; however, on marriage, women became civil minors and were not allowed to own property until 1857.[23] Women were not represented in the political structures, in the church or in the legal system, and therefore the general position of women at this time was one of relative powerlessness and invisibility in the public sphere. The discourses of 'femininity' which circulated throughout society at this time aimed to make this feminine position seem 'natural' for middle-class women, and they were an exceptionally strong force in socialising women into these limited roles.

Surprisingly, however, despite this a remarkable number of women did manage to travel, many of them travelling alone, and many of them wrote about their experiences either in the form of private letters to family and friends or in published work. Any women who published travel accounts at this time were potentially revolutionary in showing that, in direct contradiction to the discourses of femininity, women could in fact travel alone without coming to harm. However, this revolutionary possibility was undermined, as I mentioned earlier, because they were labelled 'eccentric', which was a way of warning off other women in case they were tempted to generalise from such behaviour to their own lives. Given their general lack of effective intervention in their own culture, women were denied the possibility of drawing on the predominantly male discourse of Orientalism with the ease that male travellers had, since they were more strongly positioned by the conflicting discourses of 'femininity'. That is not to say that they escaped the constraints of colonial discourses, but rather that the constraints upon them were different in kind.

The discourses of femininity designated certain areas of experience as 'feminine' and often attempted to elide this with 'female'. In western culture in the nineteenth and twentieth centuries, certain character traits such as sympathy and interest in emotions and relationships were designated as feminine and classified as 'natural' for women.[24] Denied the outlet of waged work, middle-class women were encouraged to care for others and consider the maintenance of relationships as their domain. It is not surprising therefore that women, because of socialisation, should consider relationships and interest in other people important, since these traits defined them as 'feminine' women. This is also interesting when one considers that the type of writing which women were encouraged to do was mainly concerned with this emotional sphere (autobiography, letters, the novel).[25]

Rather than seeing the concern that women travel writers express in their texts as a simple gesture of solidarity with people of other nations, it should be seen in its discursive history as belonging to a discourse of philanthropy which circulated through the nineteenth century and involved middle- and upper-class women. Many commentators on women's travel writing have remarked on the way in which the women tend to describe their relationships with the members of the other nations extending sympathy towards them in a way which does not occur in male travel writing to the same extent. The representations seem to be more concerned with presenting an equality in their relationships. However, we must be wary of making assumptions about the equality of these relationships, and their representations, since these women travelled very much within the colonial context. Their presence and their sympathy must be seen in the context of the philanthropic movement which developed mainly between the 1830s and the 1860s in Britain. For some critics, philanthropy developed because 'in the middle classes, where women were burdened with neither an excess of privileges nor privations, there was a vague sensation of discontent and emptiness' (Thomson, 1956: 14). Thomson suggests that because middle- and upper class women were largely forbidden from taking up full-time, paid employment, they could nevertheless gain a sense of worthwhile work, affirm themselves in their feminine and religious role and gain a sense of power through dispensing help to others lower down in the social scale. Many women from the middle and upper class also devoted their time to raising money for charities, particularly for missionary work in the colonised countries. In this way many of them had an interest in imperial expansion, seeing it as the duty of the Christian nations to colonise the 'heathen' nations, in order to convert them. In imperial terms, much of the empire was considered to be quite literally the 'white man's burden', that is, it was thought to be a religious and moral duty to bring civilisation to these regions of the world which seemed so 'primitive'. The discourse of philanthropy justified to those engaged in the empire and those at home financing it their presence in other countries. It also informed women's writing since, when adopted in their texts, it enabled the narrator to be in a powerful position, without contravening the discursive positions established for women.

Many of the women travel writers also concentrated on descriptions of relationships with members of the other nation, foregrounding their individuality rather than membership in another nation. This can be seen clearly even in writers in the twentieth century such as Dora Birtles's description of a journey by yacht, in *North-West by North* (1935/1985), where rather than an adventure narrative being adopted, as might have been expected from the subject-matter, a concern with the way that relationships function takes precedence.[26] The elements which can be labelled as 'feminine' – a concern with relationships, domestic description, a concern with Christianity and morality – are often included in the texts. These descriptions of relationships and positive depictions of individuals counterbalance the unfeminine actions they describe which were determined by colonial discourse. Furthermore, women writers, as well as being concerned with interaction with others, were, because of their socialisation as sexualised objects of a male gaze, generally more aware of the way the narrator appears to others, of themselves as objects.[27] Women travellers often remark on the way the narrator must seem to the inhabitants of the country, as Selina Martin notes: 'whenever we appear, we are followed by men, women and children, as if a show of wild animals had appeared among them' (cited in Foster, 1988: 12). There are few male travellers who describe concern for the way in which they appear to others (except perhaps with regard to the maintenance of face), and they certainly would not portray their narrators in such a potentially negative light.

I would like to introduce the term 'going native' here in an effort to reclaim it as a phrase to describe much of women's travel writing in the colonial period. Although the use of the term is fraught with difficulties, even within inverted commas, I feel it can nevertheless reflect the interesting and problematic status of western women colonial writers of this period. I am not therefore claiming that these women writers are exempt from racism, or involvement in imperialism, nor am I claiming an unproblematic empathetic status for their writings, rather I am stating that their texts display an alignment with other nations. Indeed the problematic nature of this term embodies the contradictory status of these texts.[28] 'Going native' is a phrase which describes the way in which certain European travellers and residents abroad adopted the dress and customs of the people of the colonised country, and potentially aligned themselves with that culture. The phrase is interesting because, conventionally, it has strong negative connotations – integrating and identifying oneself with a colonised community is seen to be 'letting the side down'. I recently came across a reclaiming of the phrase, when it was used in a positive sense in a book by Anita Desai, *Fire on the Mountain* (1977), where an Indian hill station reverts to Indian occupation on Independence. In Desai's work 'going native' is used to mean 'returning to its rightful indigenous owners'. I would like to reclaim the term in a slightly different way here to describe the way women travellers' accounts of their journeys seem to be positioned not only in alignment with an imperial discourse, but also affiliated to the 'natives', however problematic that alignment might be. These women writers are undoubtedly part of the colonial project, and yet colonialism is more notable by its absence in many of the accounts; the addressing of large-scale issues, such as the role of the journey in relation to colonial expansion or description of potential colonial sites, is notably absent. Instead, their accounts demand a recognition of the importance of interaction with members of other nations, not as representatives of the race, as in male-authored accounts, but as individuals. This alternative, more personalised form of writing by women, this 'going native' by women, constitutes both a challenge to male Orientalism and a different form of knowledge about other countries.

Many of these discourses of femininity are interlocking, and it is very difficult to compartmentalise them strictly. Some of the women travel writers display some of the features of femininity and not others. In the process of textual production there are various discursive pressures on women writers which encourage them to write in particular ways. That is not to say that all women write in the same way, but rather that there are pressures which they either resist, negotiate or simply give in to. These pressures are both ones which act upon women writers in general and also ones which are specific to women's travel writing.

In order to trace the discourses which acted upon women's texts, it is necessary both to use the text as a repository of traces, and also, drawing on Peter Hulme's notion of the congeneric text, to analyse those texts which were published at roughly the same time which 'can cast light by virtue of their deeper similarities, independently of any putative influence' (Hulme, 1986: 93). These congeneric texts which act as indicators of the discourses of femininity are the didactic texts which advised women of the time: cookery books, conduct manuals, etiquette books, which set out to elide the difference between feminine and female and locate the female firmly in the private sphere.[29] A book which might be considered congeneric is Lilias Camp-

99

bell Davidson's *Hints to Lady Travellers at Home and Abroad* (1889), and this may help us to locate the ways in which femininity is constructed and leads to the inclusion of certain textual features. There is no comparable book for male travellers.[30] Paradoxically, the book consists mainly of advice on how to maintain propriety whilst violating the codes of society by travelling outside the woman's place – the home. Davidson advises women how to travel without compromising one's respectability; as such, it forms part of a larger discourse which sees women as there to be advised.[31] Much of Davidson's book is concerned with warning women travellers about possible dangers:

> As a broad general principle, a woman's place in the moment of danger is to keep still and be ready for action. It is so much an instinct with the stronger sex to protect and look after the weaker, that in all cases of the sort, if there is a man at the head of affairs, he had better be left to manage matters without the hampering interference of feminine physical weakness . . . . If there is no man, the woman will have to act for herself, but even then she will find it the best plan to keep still till the decisive moment arrives.
>
> (Davidson, 1889: 12)

These remarks have two effects: firstly, that of equating travel with danger (the first heading in her book is 'accidents': 'It seems somewhat ominous to begin a book of hints on travel with so disastrous a subject' (ibid.: 11)); and secondly, that of portraying women as frail and dependent on men for protection.

As well as the dangers of travel, much of the text is concerned with advice about the things which should be taken on journeys. Most of the items are preparations for accidents: 'It is wise never to travel unprovided with a small flask of brandy and water, a tiny case of court plaster, with scissors, and either strong smelling salts or sal volatile' (ibid.: 13), and she also suggests taking a bath and 'a tiny case of needles, etc, a map and road book, some lighter literature' (ibid.: 39), 'air cushions, suitably covered with chintz or satin, for putting under the feet' and 'for nervous invalids, the addition of another cushion to sit upon is a still further prevention of headache and that shattering of the nerves which makes the mere thought of a journey by rail or carriage a nightmare to the imagination' (ibid.: 35). However, whilst stressing the dangers of travel, she also at the same time states 'Never anticipate accidents . . . . I mean, don't feel convinced, every journey that you set out upon, that peril lurks in ambush in your path . . . . Don't see collision in every jolt of the train and scent shipwreck in each lurch of the steamer' (ibid.: 14).

As well as the physical accidents, she deals with the problems of swindling and sexual harassment which can beset a woman travelling alone: 'Cabbies will often make the most pre-posterous charges with perfect audacity . . . when their victim is a lady travelling alone, and the younger and more easily deluded she looks, the better for their purposes' (ibid.: 30). She draws attention to the problems of sexual harassment, yet locates the problem firmly in female behaviour, for example: 'It is seldom or never that [women] find themselves subjected to either rudeness or annoyance . . . . Nevertheless it is as well to bear in mind certain simple rules – to ride by day only . . . to avoid lonely and unfrequented roads at untimely hours' (ibid.: 41), and she goes on to say:

> Much has been said about the danger to women, especially young women, travelling alone, of annoyance from im-pertinence or obtrusive attentions from travellers of the other sex. I can only say, that in any such case which has ever come within my personal knowledge or observation, the woman has had only herself to blame. I am quite sure that no man, however audacious, will, at all events if he be sober, venture to treat with undue familiarity or rudeness, a woman however young, who distinctly shows him by her dignity of manner and conduct that any such liberty will be an insult. As a rule women travelling alone receive far more consideration and kindness from men of all classes than under any other circumstances whatever, and the greater independence of women, which permits even young girls in these days, to travel about entirely alone, unattended even by a maid, has very rarely inconvenient consequences.
> (Davidson, 1889: 63)

This advice is interesting, since it locates the discourses which were circulating about women's culpability for sexual harassment, and also links travel with the threat of this type of behaviour. In women's travel writing, I have found no references to fear of or experience of sexual threat, even though within Davidson's text the subject merits a lengthy discussion. It seems a most significant silence, almost too important to be addressed by writers.

In the parts of the book which are not concerned with potential dangers, Davidson lists the types of clothes that should be worn: suede gloves in summer, woollen muffatees in winter, etc. Her main concern is with 'how to look respectable' (ibid.: 46). For mountaineering wear, she advises:

> Let the skirts be as short as possible – to clear the ankles. I must however draw the line at the modern feminine costume for mountaineering and deer-stalking where the skirt is a mere polite apology – an inch or two below the knee, and the result hardly consistent with the high idea of womanhood.
>
> (Davidson, 1889: 152)

Clothing is thus a key element in reducing the possibility of sexual threat.

One of the more interesting discursive turns of Davidson's text is when there is an attempt to transform the public space of travel into a private space, for example, she states, when travelling by train:

> To the lady who has a long journey . . . let me recommend that she remove her outdoor garments . . . as if she were in her own drawing room. It will be found a most comfortable plan to take with one a pair of house-slippers.
>
> (Davidson, 1889: 176)

The carrying of immense amounts of luggage also turns the public sphere into the private, and she even suggests taking 'fine yellowish brown paper' to line drawers, since 'there is something not particularly tempting in the idea of placing one's possessions in a place where one does not know what preceded them' (ibid.:214). She complains about waiting rooms, but remarks 'Of course one does not expect to find a waiting room fitted up like a South Kensington boudoir' (ibid.: 217), and yet, in some sense, it is precisely this transformation of the public space into the private that she is attempting to bring about.

In Davidson's text as a whole, travel is constructed as physically dangerous and a site for sexual threat; the woman traveller is constructed as a physically weak figure, concerned with her appearance and respectability and fearful of accidents, and this image accords very well with the discourses of femininity circulating elsewhere in conduct literature. These discourses of femininity have certain effects on women travel writers. Firstly, women travellers are aware when they write that they are entering discourse in a different way to men: whereas men could describe their travel as individuals and as representatives of the colonial power, women could only travel and write as gendered individuals with clearly delineated roles. The effect in the travel texts themselves is that women travel writers constantly allude to femininity, by producing statements which accord with the discursive rules, by negotiating those rules or sometimes by openly rejecting them. Whichever narratorial role is adopted, these discursive rules nevertheless play an important part in the construction of the text. Secondly, the discourses of femininity lead to an emphasis on the hazardous nature of travel for women; again, either this 'common knowledge' is agreed with or rejected. For example, Alexandra David-Neel details the hazards she endures, and poses herself as different to other women in that she can overcome them, yet Nina Mazuchelli describes the difficulties of travel in order to show that she is truly 'feminine' (David-Neel, 1927/1983; Mazuchelli, 1876). The two positions are very different and yet they are both determined by these discourses of femininity.

A further element in women's writing which is determined by the discourses of femininity is the fact that many of these women's accounts were written in the form of letters or diaries or a mixture of the two. It is interesting in this context to read Stevenson's account of the writing process for women travellers:

> Women often cast their narratives as a series of letters home to a predominantly female audience interested in both the minutiae of everyday domestic life and the writer's psychological reactions to a new environment . . . . The loose accretive epistolary form serves as an ideal vehicle for leisurely descriptions of diverse subjects.
>
> (Stevenson, 1982: 9)

In this way the form of travel journals is made 'natural' –

103

women write in the form of letters and diaries because they are the only forms which are loose enough to contain their un-structured narratives. Stevenson goes on to suggest that this is a feature of women's autobiography in general and, one must assume, their lives since, she says, men write:

> formal distilled autobiographies in which the primary concern is an objective evaluation of the significance of the whole life or journey. Women, in contrast, produce more private, fragmented, episodic autobiographies . . . which impose no overarching design on their lives or travels . . . . Women tend to record, to surrender to experience; men to judge, to schematize experience.
>
> (Stevenson, 1982: 10)

This is a discursive tendency in autobiography, however, as Maggie Humm (1989) has shown, rather than one inherent to males and females.

In women's travel writing there is a strong influence of the 'confessional' model of texts, so that although women are depicted performing strong and adventurous acts, they are far more self-revelatory than men's. There are significant discursive pressures on women writing travel accounts to position them within the confessional mode. However, it is not possible to consider these texts as referring in some unproblematic way to the lives of the women writers. There is no sense in which it can be assumed that reading a travel journal gives the reader information about the life of the writer. What should be analysed are the 'various positions of subjectivity' within this confessional field which women writers can occupy and con-struct for themselves.

One of the interesting elements which is rarely considered in accounts of women's travel writing is the way that feminism informed the texts. The period 1870–1930 was one where great transformations were taking place in terms of women, both politically, in terms of the vote and changes in legal status, and socially, in terms of permissible dress and behaviour. Women began to be involved in trade union activity and in campaigning on single issues such as alcoholism and the abolition of slavery. This was the period of the New Woman, although it should be noted as Hobsbawm remarks: 'statistically the women who opted for the defence of their sex through piety enormously outnumbered those who opted for liberation' (Hobsbawm, 1987: 210).[32]

Many of the narrators state clearly where they position themselves in relation to feminism, either explicitly, like Fanny Bullock Workman whose text contains statements of concern with votes for women (the cover of her book shows her planting a placard stating 'Votes for Women' on a mountain top), or implicitly, like Isabella Bishop-Bird and Mary Kingsley, who state that they are feminine women in their concern for the correctness of dress, and are not tempted by the clothing reform advocated by feminists of the time (Workman, 1895; Bishop-Bird, 1880/1984; Kingsley, 1897/1965). Descriptions of dress in these texts is a central concern because of debates about clothing reform, and the possibility of women wearing trousers or bloomers, as Gattey notes: 'trousers were the symbol of the male and of male domination and the proposal that women should adopt them . . . was seen as a threat to the whole structure of society' (Gattey, 1967: 13).

Even in the travel texts which present anti-feminist statements, the representations of women which are embodied work towards presenting a thoroughly subversive view of women. The texts seem to be transgressive in many ways, but they can only be so because they conform to discursive pressures at so many points. In many of these texts there is a presentation of female characters violating the norms of Victorian society: the characters subvert the notion that the woman's place is in the home and that women are too frail to go outside the home and to physically exert themselves. The texts are also transgressive of the notion that male sexuality is so dangerous that respectable middle-class women need chaperones, even if only because they omit to mention fear of attack. These texts negotiate these constraints by showing women fearlessly wandering abroad without representing them being attacked. This seems to be possible because of the influence of the adventure genre which the travel book is in large part built upon, and yet these adventure elements can only be portrayed, as I showed earlier (p.82), when sufficiently modified by other elements. One important element which allows the adventure narrative to be employed is the feminine discourse which denigrates the text itself; at many points of the narrative, the scientific status or quest nature of the text is called into question, and instead it is asserted that the journey is as Mary Kingsley called it simply 'a lark' (Kingsley, 1897/1965), or as Naomi Mitchison calls it 'mucking around' (Mitchison: 1981)

Some of the texts also transgress the notion of imperial rule, making fun of some of the heroic adventure figures which can be found in male travel texts. Thus, the clash of feminine and colonial discourses constructs texts which are at one and the same time presenting a self which transgresses and which conforms both to patriarchal and imperial discourses. In short, women travellers could not wholeheartedly speak with the voice of colonial discourse, at least not consistently, firstly, because of their role in western society and the way this was structured by the discourses of femininity, secondly, because some of them had rejected this role by travelling unchaperoned, and thirdly, because they had few discursive places within western colonial institutions.[33] Thus, western women writers' accounts often display a tension between the negotiation of two groups of discourses, neither of which completely overrides the other. They were certainly not considered to be 'speaking for' the imperial project in their work. The discourses of 'femininity' determine that women writers are more likely to describe their interactions with people rather than solely relating these accounts of the country to larger colonial issues or strategies. I am not suggesting that women's writing should therefore be considered better than men's writing, or that it escapes imperialist ideology, but rather that elements of women's travel writing are more heterogeneous and that these elements may act as a critique of the colonialist enterprise since there is a stress on personal involvement and investment on the part of the narrator. This stress on people from other countries as individuals is in marked contrast to much Orientalist work, where the divide between 'us' and 'them' is carefully policed. It is this lack of demarcation in women's writing which constitutes the point at which colonial discourse is most unstable, and which women's writing helps to expose.

By attempting to locate the discourses of femininity and colonialism, it is possible to view these texts by British women in the colonial period as the site for many discursive conflicts: the writers were at one and the same time part of the colonial enterprise, and yet marginalised within it. Their role as women writers and as travellers was circumscribed by conflicting dis-

106

cursive pressures – those of colonial discourses, and those of femininity. As anomalous travellers in the public sphere, their writing can be seen as the traces of discursive struggles over the 'proper' place of women.

4

CONSTRAINTS ON THE RECEPTION OF WOMEN'S TRAVEL WRITING

As I have mentioned in previous chapters, most of the critics discussing travel writing have not considered the way that the texts are received by both readers and critics. And yet the way that these travel texts are received has a crucial effect on the way they are read, what they mean and also, ultimately, on the way they are written. The texts are analysed as if in a vacuum. Few critics seem to be concerned with the fact that, in contrast to men's travel writing, most of these women's texts are accused of exaggeration or lying. Although, as I noted earlier, travel writing as a whole has a problematic history in its relation to 'truth', women's writing is systematically judged to be exaggerated.

There seems to be a range of constraints on the reception of women's writing in general. For example, several feminist critics have noticed the disparity in the reviews of male and female writers. Toril Moi reports on the reviews of the Danish poet Cecil Bødtker, whose first name is non sex-specific (Moi, 1985), When her poetry was first published, a reviewer, assuming that Bødtker was male, wrote a very positive review. The following year, the same reviewer wrote about Bødtker's second collection of poetry, by this time having realised that she was a woman. Surprisingly enough, the review was very different – the poetry was described as 'pleasant' and the review was far less enthusiastic. Moi's conclusion is that:

the critic's attitude unconsciously reveals the fact that . . . male reviewers just cannot attach the same degree of authority to a voice they know to be female. Even when they do give a good review to a woman they automatically select adjectives and phrases that tend to make the woman's poetry charming and sweet (as women should be), as opposed to serious and significant (as men are supposed to be).

(Moi, 1985: 35)

Several other critics, most notably Alicia Ostriker, note that critics praise writing which tends to fit in with their stereotypical views of women's writing, and criticise other women's writing for not fitting these preconceived ideas. For example, she notes that certain types of poetry, such as Marianne Moore's, is praised for being 'modest', hardly an adjective which one would use as a term of praise for poetry written by a man (Ostriker, 1987). Christine Battersby has also examined the way in which there is a covert system of value judgements on what it is acceptable for women to write, and this determines how women's writing is judged (Battersby, 1989). In a similar way, women's travel writing is criticised and accused of falsehood because very often the representations in the text do not fit in with a stereotypical conception of what women can do.

Women's writing is frequently read as if it were auto-biographical, as a 'confessional' as I noted in chapter 1. This strategy has two effects: firstly, the downgrading of the value of the texts (if the text is simply an overflow of emotions, then it is not an artistic production); and secondly, the text is read as only relating to the individual concerned and not related to the colonial context. For example, when Jean Larnac writes about women's writing he says: 'In the centre of every feminine novel, one discovers the author . . . . Incapable of abstracting a fragment of themselves to constitute a whole, they have to put all of themselves into their work' (cited in N. Miller, 1980: 253–4). Joanna Russ discusses this devaluing of women's writing when she shows that critics often accuse women writers of being unable to write, for example, stating: '*She didn't write it; he did*' (Russ, 1984: 21), suggesting that women, because incapable of writing, have their male relatives or friends write for them. A more subtle version of this is, as she states, to say '*It wrote itself*' (ibid.: 21). This statement suggests that women writers are incapable of 'creative' writing, but instead can only write as an outpouring of emotion, without authorial control. For example, Ellen Moers suggests that Mary Shelley was 'not so much an author . . . as . . . a transparent medium through which passed the ideas of those around her' (cited in Russ, ibid.: 144).

This critical reception of women's literary writing can also be seen to hold true for women's travel writing which is considered simply to be a transcription of everything which happened to the narrator during the travels. One of the main current critical assumptions made about women's travel writing by feminists and others is that it is non-literary. As I noted in chapter 1, it is assumed that the texts are simply reproductions of journals or letters to families, whereas, in many of the cases, the women wrote the texts in the form of journals because that was the convention of the times. Many of them had not kept journals during the journey and therefore the journals are fictional inventions after the fact. For example, Alexandra David-Neel, who wrote an account of her travels to Tibet in 1920, states that she was not able to keep a journal for fear of being discovered, but her book nevertheless is written as a journal.

However, as well as the texts being devalued because they are seen to be merely autobiographical, they are also accused of being falsifications of events; again, Alexandra David-Neel is accused of having exaggerated and lied about her trip to Lhasa because it did not fit in with the discourses about women's position circulating at the time. Her account consists of a narrative of her walking from northern India across the mountains to Lhasa, a forbidden city, existing on a diet of Tibetan tea and barley, and at one stage having to carry her injured male companion to safety. As I show in the chapter on David-Neel, these strong representations of women do not fit in with the stereotypical codes for representations of women of the time. I have already mentioned that several of the women writers had to exclude elements from their texts because the publishers did not believe that the events had taken place, or did not consider certain types of information appropriate for a woman's book.

Not all travel writing is judged to be factual; some travel accounts have been categorised as 'literary travel writing' or as 'literature', and therefore the way these texts are read is different. In recent years one of the selling points of travel writing has been to pose texts as 'literary' and to dissociate them from the tradition of dull, information-laden accounts. Most recent advertisements for travel books contain references to the 'fine writing' of the author. For example, the first *Granta* travel writing anthology is termed 'the finest prose anthology for years' by the *New Statesman*.[1] Other writing is similarly described as 'literary': for example, Jonathan Raban's *Coasting* is described by *The Times* as 'quite beautifully written', and by the *Guardian* as 'A joy to read'; the *Mail on Sunday* comments that 'Raban's writing is a delight', and the publisher Collins-Harvill describe it as 'A brilliantly observed tragicomedy'. *Journey into Cyprus* by Colin Thubron, is described by Lawrence Durrell as 'full of poetic insight', and such literary terms as 'romantic' and 'classic' are used to describe modern texts.[2] Patrick Leigh Fermor's book, *Between the Woods and the Water*, is described as 'picaresque' by the publishers and Philip Toynbee states of another of Fermor's travel books, *A Time of Gifts*, that it is

> more than just a Super-travel book . . . it is a reminder that the English language is still a superb instrument in the hands of a writer who has a virtuoso skill with words, a robust aesthetic passion, an indomitable curiosity about people and places; and a rapturous historical imagination.

Another review by Jan Morris states that the book is a 'masterpiece'.[3] Thus, the framework for describing travel writing can be clearly seen to be 'literary'. However, within these advertisements there are very few for women's travel writing, except within the Virago catalogue. There, Lucie Duff-Gordon's *Letters from Egypt* is described, not in terms of the quality of the style, but rather as 'a valuable historical document', and Emily Eden's *Up the Country* is described as 'an invaluable historical record'.[4]

This difference in reception can also be noted in awards for travel writing. Thomas Cook have, since 1980, awarded an annual Travel and Guide Book Award. Sir John Cuckney, the chairman states: 'Travel has provided the stimulus for some of the world's finest literature, from Homer and Herodotus to Dickens and Durrell. We therefore thought it appropriate to encourage the art of writing about travel by offering an award.'[5] Since 1980, there have been six male winners of the award and one female (Robyn Davidson for her book *Tracks* (1982)). In several of the accounts of the male winners, the style and manner of presentation is drawn attention to. However, no such attention is paid to the 'literary' qualities of Davidson's book. It is simply presented as an excellent book since it confounds the stereotypes of the content of women's travel writing: that is, what it is thought possible for a woman to do.

Women's travel writing is almost invariably described by critics in terms of exceptional individuals: each travel writer is written about in terms of her strong personality which is manifested in the text. Most critical accounts of women's travel writing concentrate on describing the difficulties which the individual writer had to overcome to travel; they are not concerned with that individual text's relation with the rest of the colonial enterprise, and thus the truth-status of the text often depends upon the strength of the narrator figure – which in turn poses problems of credibility because strong women narrator figures conflict with the cultural norms for women.

Jane Gallop gives details of a factor which plays a part in travel writing being judged false, and that is that women, in conventional wisdom, are judged to be deceitful. She says that several 'myths' are in play when women's writing is judged:

> our culture . . . has [a] myth about woman's relation to language – the myth of Woman as essentially a liar. According to this tradition, Woman spoke, neither to enlighten with philosophy or science, nor to give her word as the guarantee for some joint enterprise: she spoke to deceive.

> (Gallop, 1980: 274)

The idea that women are not to be believed can be seen in another context, that of court-room discourse, analysed by William O'Barr and Bowman Atkins. They examine court-room practice manuals, which advise lawyers that women witnesses should be treated in a different way to male witnesses. For example: 'Women, like children, are prone to exaggeration; they generally have poor memories as to previous fabrications and exaggerations' (cited in O'Barr and Atkins, 1980: 95). In their analysis of the style of language adopted by witnesses in court-rooms, O'Barr and Atkins find a strong correlation between authoritative styles of speech and the testimony being believed. They discover that, rather than there being a 'woman's language',[6] there is a group of features which characterises 'powerless language'[7] which both men and women use. They note that more women than men use this 'powerless' speech style, 'at least in part [due] to the greater tendency of women to occupy relatively powerless social positions' (ibid.: 104). Because of the use of this speech style, women witnesses are consequently not believed. However, they note that 'It could well be that to speak like the powerless is not only typical of women because of the all-too-frequent powerless social position of many . . . women, but is also part of the cultural meaning of speaking "like a woman" ' (ibid.: 110). This last clause is of central importance here, since it suggests that *whatever* the speech style adopted by women, their statements are judged to be 'powerless language' and therefore not believed. In women's travel writing, when women write 'like a woman', that is when they adopt elements of the discourses of femininity in their work, they may run the risk of the whole of the text being judged as exaggerated. Furthermore, if they write texts which do not draw on these discourses to the same extent, for example, if they draw on the discourses of imperialism and adopt an adventure hero narrator figure, they may also be judged to be exaggerating, since their text will clash with other discourses about women.

Lying has been a consistent charge levelled against travel writing, and one could say that it is an element in the light of which each travel writer must construct her/his text. Travel writers, especially after the eighteenth century, write very much within an atmosphere of an assumption of exaggeration and possibly falsification; they thus have to adopt strategies to counter this, such as including maps, photographs and even testimonials (in some cases, publishing disclaimers), by adopting a documentary, 'objective' style and including certain types of information. Adams shows how one of the major determinants of the way texts are constructed after the eighteenth century is the fear of being accused of falsehood (Adams, 1962). So many texts were labelled as false accounts that all texts within the genre became subject to suspicion. However, before this stage of the development of the genre, 'truth' was not considered to be one of the major criteria brought into play when evaluating a work. For example, many of the pre-eighteenth-century texts are striking in that they are characterised by the inclusion of elements of the 'fantastic'. Francis Drake in *The World Encompassed* (1578) describes 'strange

113

monsters' in Tierra del Fuego, and describes Patagonians as 'giants' (cited in Carrington (ed.), 1949: 331–4); the size of the Patagonian giants was one of the main debates sparked off by Drake's accounts. Not only are people described in these alien terms, but the landscape in other countries is similarly 'fantastic', for example, Walter Raleigh's descriptions of the New World in *The First Voyage Made to the Coasts of America* (1584):

> Grapes tumbled out of the rich forests into the very waves of the sea; there was an unbelievable profusion of birds and animals, fish and fruit; the corn grew three times in five months, and the trees were more splendid than any to be seen in the most celebrated forests of the Old World.
>
> (cited in Carrington (ed.), 1949: 278)

Sir Francis Drake describes huge mountains in the Pacific which he considers as one of the wonders of the world. Because of this history of 'travellers' tales', there is a constant tension within travel texts between the authority vested in them since they are written by representatives of the colonial powers, and this fictional, fantastic quality which is also evident from early travel writing.

Paradoxically, at the same time as certain texts are accused of falsifying, there is a contrary trend which assumes that these texts are, in some way, telling the 'truth' about the nations described, simply because they are written by westerners. Not only is the question of the 'truth' of travel writing problematic from the point of view of the way it is interpreted by the reading public, but it is also problematic in the assertion of truth about other countries. Said says: '[An Orientalist] text purporting to contain knowledge about something actual . . . is not easily dismissed. Expertise is attributed to it. The authority of academics, institutions and governments can accrue to it, surrounding it with still greater prestige than its practical successes warrant' (Said, 1978a: 94). Western writers on the east have obtained their authority to state the 'truth' from two main sources. Firstly, their status as white westerners (especially in contrast to the 'native' who is frequently constructed as an inveterate liar in texts). Secondly, many male travel writers were attached to government missions, embassies, trading or exploratory missions funded by the government; thus, even

114

when they travelled alone, they were very much representatives of the colonial power. Indeed, Foucault goes so far as to say that not only did they have authority from this source, but their accounts were directly drawn upon by the colonial powers: 'Those seventeenth century travellers and nineteenth century geographers were actually intelligence gatherers collecting and mapping information which was directly exploitable by colonial powers, strategists, traders and industrialists' (Foucault, 1980a: 75). It should be noted, however, that western women who published accounts of their travels in great numbers at the end of the nineteenth and beginning of the twentieth centuries rarely travelled with official status. Partly because of this lack of governmental backing, their work is seen to have a curiously ambivalent position in relation to truth.

Many critics accuse women travel writers of exaggerating their accounts. Alexandra Allen's explanation for this is that 'Lady travellers were strange animals and it took some time before they were officially recognised as reputable and trust-worthy travellers' (A. Allen, 1980: 11). However, a more plausible explanation for this problem of 'falsehood' can be summarised as follows: firstly, travel writing is a genre in which one of the expectations of the reader is that the text will be far-fetched; secondly, there is a European cultural stereotype which casts women as duplicitous; and thirdly, women char-acters in literary and other texts are often portrayed as passive objects, dependent on men characters. Thus, the female char-acters which are represented in women's travel writing appear discursively anomalous.[8] These stereotypes and representations inform the work of women critics on travel writing. For example, Middleton says of Annie Taylor who travelled to Tibet in the 1890s: 'She put her name to a book which gave a dramatic and by no means accurate account of her adventures' (Middleton, 1982: 124). And she goes on to note that when Taylor settled in Tibet, she accused the Customs Commissioner of drowning his illegitimate children in her well, which, Middleton comments, was 'surely a flight of fancy' (ibid.: 127). Kate Marsden, who travelled to Siberia in the 1870s to visit leper colonies, had to publish a book entitled *My Mission to Siberia: a Vindication* in 1921 because so many people had accused her of lying. Even Middleton accuses her of 'ludicrous' situations (Middleton, 1982: 182). Mary Kingsley was accused by her publishers of fabricating, in her account *Travels in West Africa* (1897/1965) because she stated that she had piloted a boat drawing 18 feet of water up Forcades creek. She became very angry at this accusation, since she stated that she had piloted the boat up this river not once, but *three* times. Kingsley cut many elements from her text because of fear of not being believed. Indeed, Isabella Bishop-Bird was forced to exclude certain material from her account *The Golden Chersonese* because the publishers considered it to be unfeminine. Because of stereotyped notions of what women can do, when there are representations of women behaving as strong, independent people, it is assumed that the account must be false.

Percy Adams considers that whether a text is considered true or not is dependent on the amount of personal comment it contains:

> Since the beginning of time, travel books have varied widely in the amount of subjectivity they include. That is, the less they have, the more they seem like a guidebook; the more they have, the more they approach the novel and seem to be lying.
>
> (Adams, 1962: 97)

Thus, women's travel writing, which because of discursive pressures, may seem to contain more of the personal, may by that inclusion seem also more prone to accusations of lying. Adams also states that there is a correlation to be made between truthfulness and dullness in travel writing, and hence those accounts which he considers 'fascinating' he also considers 'partly untruthful' (ibid.: 101).

What seems to be brought to bear on these texts is a 'common-sense' view of what constitutes credible accounts of women's behaviour. For example, critics often accept notions of 'reality' which exclude events which it is difficult to prove empirically. Especially when dealing with the 'reality' of other countries, it is often the case that critics judge to be lies those events which contradict or do not fit in with a Eurocentric picture of 'reality'. George Woodcock, writing about early travellers to Tibet, such as Bogle, Manning and Turner, and comparing their accounts with that of Alexandra David-Neel, states quite clearly what 'reality' and its 'transcription' in a travel book does *not* consist of. In the more modern travel books on Tibet, he says:

there will be wonder, as there always is in the unfamiliar; there will be adventure, as there always is when men go to new places or travel in disguise or on forbidden roads; there will be the personalities of the travellers, differentiating themselves in their reactions to what they see and those they meet. But the journey will not lead to a land of wizards or . . . to the kind of haven free from earthly troubles that James Hilton projected when, in *Lost Horizon* he gave voice to another modern conception of Tibet as far from reality as that projected by the occultists. [This refers to David-Neel.] Perhaps I should end this comparison between the modern romantic view of Tibet and the soberer view of earlier travellers with the comment that . . . I find the pictures evoked by Bogle and Turner and Manning nearer to the real Tibetans, even as they are today, than the fantasies of those who have tried to abstract from the symbolism of Tantric cults a world of chimerical marvels.

(Woodcock, 1971: 22)

This account of 'occult' and 'sober' descriptions of the 'reality' of Tibet is interesting for two reasons. Firstly, Woodcock places David-Neel in the same category as the novelist James Hilton, implying that both their works are distanced from 'reality' to a similar degree, i.e., Hilton's work is considered to be distanced as it is 'fictional', and David-Neel's work is distanced because an 'occult' work cannot be 'factual'. Secondly, it would seem that Woodcock, like many critics on travel writing, assumes that there is a more 'real' Tibet which can be discovered and described, and which David-Neel and Hilton are patently not describing. He prefers the descriptions of Tibet which are closer to a European 'reality', in his terms, which make the description more truly 'real' than the descriptions given of the mystical elements of Tibet, which cannot fit quite so easily into a European framework, with its obsession with empirical evidence and scientific objectivity. Philip Gove also puts forward the view that if a writer describes unusual events the text is more likely to be thought of as a 'fiction'. In describing Mme Godin's travel account, he notes that any reader who was told that the writing was 'fictional' would 'accuse the author of the novel of lacking *vraisemblance*' (Gove, 1941). Thus, it is clear that what can be believed in travel writing is not limited to the

117

'rational' and that which can be 'empirically' verified, but rather to that which appears probable, much in the same way as this is a constraint on the writers of the novel. For example, Percy Adams describes certain writers who did not travel and yet whose works were read and believed for many years. He suggests: 'Mme d'Aulnoy, probably without ever going to Spain, as she claimed, was able to write realistically about it because of her reading' (Adams, 1962: 76).

As I noted earlier, Paul Fussell considers anomaly central to the structure of the travel text, but this is also perhaps one of the central problems for the travel text: on the one hand, the writer is supposed to describe anomalies, because of the conventions of the text, and yet if s/he does so, there is a risk of being doubted. As Adams notes: 'So strong was the tradition [of lying] that . . . medieval travellers, afraid readers would think them liars, often denied they were and in denying simply confirmed the general opinion' (Adams, 1962: 85).

Women's travel writing is often described as if it were trivial because it contains descriptions of relationships and domestic details, as well as the more conventional descriptions of colonial relations. As Jane Gallop notes, it is quite common for women's writing like their speech to be regarded as trivial: ' "The silent sex" was never considered to be actually non-speaking. Talking constantly, women emitted chatter, gossip and foolishness. Gushing forth torrents of empty words, babbling contradictorily, all sense cancelled out, leaving merely white noise' (Gallop, 1980: 274). It is not surprising therefore that, with such a characterisation of women's speech, the texts that women produce are not viewed as accurate accounts. However, as I have already noted, women writers are caught in a double-bind situation: if they tend towards the discourses of femininity in their work they are regarded as trivial, and if they draw on the more adventure hero type narratives their work is questioned.

It is clearly not simply the process of production which is at issue here, because the reception of the text determines to a certain extent what that text means. Which books are published sets up a tradition of which books will be written and published in the future; the way that they are classified as autobiography, fiction, etc. also has a determining role in what type of interpretation is given to them and the way that the narrative

118

voice or self is viewed. The way that the texts are marketed also has an effect, for example, the travel writings which have recently been reissued by Virago are marketed and read in quite a different way to the way that they were read at the time of their issue. They are now bought, in the main by feminists, eager to read texts which contain alternative visions of women in the Victorian period. Despite the atmosphere of falsehood which surrounds women's travel writing for critics, readers of the texts have always been aware of their transgressive possibilities. Given their 'factual' status, women's travel accounts of the nineteenth and early twentieth centuries are potentially extremely subversive, since they portray women characters as strong, active individuals in stark contrast to their representations in the novels, plays and poetry of the time. That these travel narratives are read as 'factual' also makes their potential impact on women readers stronger. As Nancy Miller states: 'To justify an unorthodox life by writing about it . . . is to *reinscribe* the original violation, to reviolate masculine turf' (N. Miller, 1980: 263). By this statement, I take her to mean that representing a 'life' which is considered to subvert the norms draws into question the 'naturalness' of those 'norms', and each time the text is read the norms are destabilised.

However, whilst there is a sense in which the texts can be read as subversive, this potential is undermined, as I have already mentioned, since the women who wrote them were considered 'eccentric'; that is, they were labelled as abnormal, and the 'experience' related in their work could not be generalised to refer to other women. There is also a sense in which the terms used to describe these women – 'eccentric', 'adventuress' and 'globe-trotteress' – already mark the work of these women as slightly ridiculous and strange. This 'eccentric', marginal status casts the 'truthfulness' of the text into doubt. Also, women's travel writing is constantly gauged against the social 'text' of what women are capable of, which is constructed from the representations that a society makes of itself. Linda Anderson notes:

> It is necessary to take into account the fact that the woman who attempts to write herself is engaged by the nature of the activity itself in re-writing the stories that already exist about her since by seeking to publicise herself, she is

violating an important cultural construction of her femininity as passive or hidden.

(Anderson, 1987: 59)

Thus, before a woman begins to write, she must take into
account the 'stories' which have been constructed around
women in her society. The texts are being judged according to
the standard of *vraisemblance* which a society constructs of its
representations. Peggy Kamuf notes that the term contains
within it two aspects: 'As a "vision of the world" *vraisemblance*
provides a standard for logical judgements – probability. As a
"system of values" *vraisemblance* catalogues a social group's
ethical judgements, its ideology' (Kamuf, 1980: 292). These two
aspects, what 'life' is like and what 'life' *should* be like, are
inextricably tangled. Thus, judging women's travel writing as
false, or accusing the writer of exaggeration, is perfectly logical
within the realms of *vraisemblance*, since the representation of
women within these texts accords neither with society's view of
what women are like, nor what society believes they *should* be
like. This prescriptive meaning of *vraisemblance* is discussed by
Peggy Kamuf in her work on the debate over the authorship of
The Portuguese Letters. She shows that giving these letters a male
'literary' origin provides: 'a shield between [the critic] and
whatever is shocking or scandalous in this text written (possibly)
in a woman's hand' (ibid.: 29). In a similar way, denying that
travel writings by women are 'true', or by challenging these
representations of women, is a way of denying that women
could behave in the way they are portrayed in these texts: as
strong, self-motivated individuals.

The way that women's travel writing was received also made
some impact on their writing. Worley reports that there were
many negative reports of women travellers, for example, Henry
Tuckerman wrote 'There are few situations in modern life more
suggestive of the ludicrous than that of a woman "of a certain
age" professedly visiting a country for the purpose of critically
examining and reporting it and its people' (Tuckerman, 1864,
cited in Worley, 1986: 43). Tuckerman describes the details in
women's texts that he loathes: the details of dresses, dancing,
meals, trees, furniture, etc. Worley states:

In the light of the possibility of such vicious attacks, it is not
surprising that these women would repeatedly reaffirm the

120

accuracy of their accounts or would tend to limit . . . the content of their narratives . . . to those aspects . . . of life felt to be most in keeping with what was accepted as woman's role in society.

(Worley, 1986: 44)

One of the major problems for women travellers was whether their texts would be believed or not. This had certain effects on the way the texts were produced. This is not to say that the texts are necessarily different because they were written by women, but that conventions have a determining role in the way a text is produced and judged. Women writers knew that their accounts would be considered odd and eccentric, and would be accused of falsehood, therefore they adopted several strategies. One of these was to play down the adventurous parts of their texts. Mary Kingsley notes how she omitted several sections of her book, *Travels in West Africa* (1897/1965), for fear of not being believed, for example, the sections where she helped villagers to kill a man-eating crocodile, and an incident where she kept back a hippopotamus with her umbrella. She reserved these incidents for another book which was not destined for the general public. Catherine Stevenson shows how Fanny Barker admitted to falsifying her account of her journey with her husband to Basutoland in 1870s because she felt that if she had told the 'truth' about the hardships she endured, other women would be discouraged from attempting to follow her (Stevenson, 1982). Some critics suggest ways in which women writers should attempt to authenticate their travel accounts: Hopkirk suggests that Alexandra David-Neel (whose account he casts doubt upon) should have taken a photograph of the lamas she describes. Other suggestions he makes are the inclusion of maps and sketches. However, Hopkirk does believe one account by David-Neel, for he describes it in the following terms: 'This seemingly paranormal phenomenon which enables *sadhus* . . . to survive half-naked in sub-zero temperatures has, it should be said, more than once been attested to by independent and sceptical European witnesses' (Hopkirk, 1983: 224). Thus, the fact that there are other texts about similar events, written by 'independent' authors rather than by 'occultists', leads Hopkirk to assume that it is 'true'.

Women's travel writing has a problematic relation to 'truth'

121

claims, adventure narrative and the reporting of certain types of event which are seen to be 'unfeminine'. Because of these constraints women are led to write their texts within a range of conflicting parameters and this may lead to their texts being produced and read differently to men's travel writing. These judgements on their work have profound effects on the women writers. Some publishers ask women to cut or modify their texts, but also the writers themselves internalise at least some of these norms. Writing within these discursive frameworks, it is clear that women writers set out to authenticate their texts and guard themselves against accusations of falsehood.

Part III

CASE STUDIES

5

ALEXANDRA DAVID-NEEL:
MY JOURNEY TO LHASA
(1927)

[handwritten: 1st published Voyage d'une Parisienne à Lhasa]

In this analysis I focus on Alexandra David-Neel's writing, in particular on the critical reception of her work and the status her text has in terms of 'truth'. David-Neel, born in France, is the only non-British writer whom I will consider; however, she wrote *My Journey to Lhasa* in English.[1] She has an enormous reputation in France as an expert on Tibetan life and customs, and, in particular, on Tibetan Buddhism and Tantric practices.[2] *My Journey to Lhasa*, when it was first published, sparked off a major debate, because the events recounted in the text seemed to describe events which were in western terms 'improbable' in two ways: firstly, because few people could believe that a woman had managed to travel to the capital of Tibet, Lhasa, on foot disguised as a Tibetan peasant, subsisting in freezing conditions on a diet of Tibetan barley meal tea. It was forbidden for foreigners to travel to Tibet, and both the traveller and the Tibetans who sheltered her ran the risk of imprisonment if discovered by the authorities. And secondly, in this book she related the occurrence of several events which, in western terms, were 'fantastic', for example, the appearance of a ghostly lama figure and mysterious events explained by reference to supernatural agency. Her text is a good example of how women have had to structure their texts in the light of potential accusations of exaggeration and falsehood, and how they have had to deal with accusations of lying after publication.

My Journey to Lhasa is in many ways a classic 'eccentric' Victorian woman's travel text: the narrator is a strong, determined figure who battles against extremes of hardship, rarely losing face or making reference to 'feminine' concerns. The text concerns the attempt of the narrator to walk to Lhasa, at

[handwritten margin note: Tibetan peasant]

125

that time a forbidden city for Europeans. She describes her attempts to disguise herself as a Tibetan peasant, dying her hair and skin, and she is accompanied by her adopted son, a Sikkimese named Yongden, who poses as a lama. Most of the text is taken up with the threat of discovery, but there is also a great deal of information about Buddhist and Bön religious customs in Tibet, some of it concerned with mystical practices.[3]

In this section, I consider the type of reception that David-Neel's text had when published. The main critical attention to Alexandra David-Neel's travel writing has come from Jeanne Denys, who wrote a book entitled *Alexandra David-Neel au Tibet*, whose sub-title is: *Une supercherie dévoilée*, that is, 'trickery uncovered' (Denys, 1972). Denys reports that she originally went to work for David-Neel to help her organise her library, but later began to doubt that David-Neel had, in fact, been on her journey to Tibet at all. What concerns me here is not to prove that David-Neel did or did not go to Tibet, nor to show that Denys's account is itself 'true' or 'false', but to analyse the methods Denys uses to attempt to show that David-Neel falsified her account of her journey as an example of the way that these standards of judgement are used on women's travel writing as a whole.[4] These methods are interesting from a Foucauldian perspective, since they serve to define quite clearly what is meant by a 'true' woman's account within western society.

Firstly, Denys sets David-Neel's text in a general atmosphere of suspicion (generated by other experts): 'This prodigious exploit [David-Neel's account of her journey] undertaken by a woman excited a great deal of admiration, but also, here and there, a certain scepticism' (Denys, 1972: 11). Denys consistently uses impersonal forms to distance herself from such accusations ('On s'étonna'), and in this way locates the questioning of 'truth-value' to a more authoritative position, which is unnamed and which the reader can only assume refers to critics, or to a more generalised common sense. Thus, Denys's own later claims are substantiated by being set within this general unspecific context of suspicion.

Secondly, Denys calls upon other texts which, for her, have greater validity, and she compares these to David-Neel's account. It is not perhaps coincidental that the travel texts she chooses to compare to David-Neel's are all written by men. When introducing their work she describes in great detail the authority they have to tell the truth. For example, when attempting to dismiss David-Neel's account of her interview with the Dalai Lama, Denys considers a similar interview which was described by Commander d'Ollone, and she draws attention to the fact that 'Commander d'Ollone was given charge in 1906 by the French government of an important exploratory mission to Tibet' (Denys, 1972: 36). Here, Denys stresses the fact that d'Ollone is a member of the armed forces, that it is the French government which has sent him to Tibet and that his mission to Tibet is 'important'. Other writers whose accounts of meetings with the Dalai Lama she cites are described as 'Le Professor G. Tucci' and 'Sir C. Bell'. A writer such as David-Neel without this government sponsorship (without even an official document) is seen to be in a less authoritative position, and is referred to throughout the text as 'notre romancière'. Denys quotes in full d'Ollone's account of his meeting with the Dalai Lama as an example of what a 'truthful' account should be like. This account gives a detailed description of the Dalai Lama's dress and features, and the various stages of their interview. D'Ollone also mentions the difficulties that he had in making himself understood through an interpreter. None of this is mentioned in David-Neel's text: she simply records the questions she asked the Dalai Lama and his replies. A further 'fact' which proves, for Denys, that David-Neel's account is a falsification is that Charles Bell published the letter which he received from the Dalai Lama bearing a seal, whereas: 'since A. David-Neel has never published the note which was sent to her in 1911, bearing the seal, we should be persuaded that she never interviewed His Holiness the 13th Dalai Lama' (Denys, 1972: 40). The only time in Denys's book where she admits that David-Neel might have been to Tibet is on a journey where she was arrested after five months in the Marches of Tibet. Here at least there are authoritative eye-witnesses, and textual evidence since David-Neel was deported from Tibet. Denys goes on to state exactly what a travel account should consist of. She describes what David-Neel should have written in her account of her meeting with the Dalai Lama:

The mission of a reporter is to inform his readers above all, he must submit to the observation of facts, he must contextualise the atmosphere of the meeting, centre the focus of attention on the interviewer and not on himself; he must look in order to describe. However, A. David-Neel has seen nothing, nor has she described anything.

(Denys, 1972: 36)

Textual conventions of what should happen within an interview (and what does not happen in this report of an interview) lead Denys to assume that David-Neel is lying. She says: 'Our reporter . . . could have told us . . . plenty of other things' (ibid.: 36). This is indeed the case, and, if David-Neel had structured the report of the interview in a more conventional way, her account would perhaps have been believed. Yet, given that Denys notes that one of the central problems with the account is a textual one, it is surprising that she does not see this as undermining her whole hypothesis. Had David-Neel written the account in a more conventional way, would it then have been 'true'?

According to Denys, 'authoritative' texts and people are the sole means of deciding whether the 'truth' is contained within an account. There is no attempt on the part of Denys to suggest explicitly in what way these texts have greater validity than David-Neel's, or why the statements of people in authority should be believed rather than the statements of people without authority, except that the former texts have greater pretensions to scientificity and adhere to the conventions of travel writing in general. So strong are textual conventions in relation to the assertion of 'truth', that a travel account has only to differ slightly from other travel accounts to be no longer 'in the true'.

In relation to these other travel texts, Denys asserts that David-Neel's account is lacking in certain types of information; this lack, she suggests, has some effect on the 'truth-value' of the text as a whole. For example, she says about David-Neel's text:

> Much was made of the absence of all trace of chronological sequence in this travel account, as was the lack of detail about the itinerary which was followed, geographical notes, etc. and the contradictions between this text and the writings of explorers.

(Denys, 1972: 11)

She continues the list of elements which are missing from the text which render it suspect:

128

About the conditions of existence of the Tibetans, their customs, their resources, their jobs and their pastimes, about their language, their particular physical and moral characteristics, and the traditions belonging to each region, the author tells us nothing.

(Denys, 1972: 12)

With reference to the text itself, this lack is in fact debatable since large sections of David-Neel's account are devoted to descriptions of the people of Tibet. However, it is interesting that Denys is clearly convinced that this lack of certain types of description, which would normally be found in a travel journal, disqualifies David-Neel's account from being considered 'true'. Thus, if the text does not conform to the conventions, it has to be considered a non-text. She states that David-Neel does not include maps as other explorers have, and she asks: 'Should we accord more credence to an itinerary or to a topographic model established by an explorer using modern techniques of cartography?' (ibid.: 134). She also mentions the fact that David-Neel does not include a bibliography of texts in her book; a bibliography would have set her work within a system of authority and scientificity.[5]

Denys analyses David-Neel's text in the minutest details, even down to descriptive passages, which she feels lack the detail necessary in such accounts: 'One finds that about the regions between Jyekundo and Salwen, A. David-Neel tells us practically nothing; and the little which she tells us does not lead us to believe that she ever set foot there' (Denys 1972: 111). Again, in order to prove that David-Neel's text is false, she compares it with accounts by two explorers which are more detailed, or at least which give the conventional type of description which one would expect in a travel journal. The conventions of 'factual' travel writing demand an 'objective' method of description; Denys points out that one of the problems of David-Neel's landscape descriptions is that they are 'literary' ('des couplets purement littéraires' (ibid.: 158)); therefore, in Denys's terms, these descriptions could refer to almost any landscape.

Denys notes that other writers produced documentary evidence of the fact that they had travelled to the regions mentioned. For example, several of them produced detailed maps. David-Neel produced sketch maps (see figure 1), but she

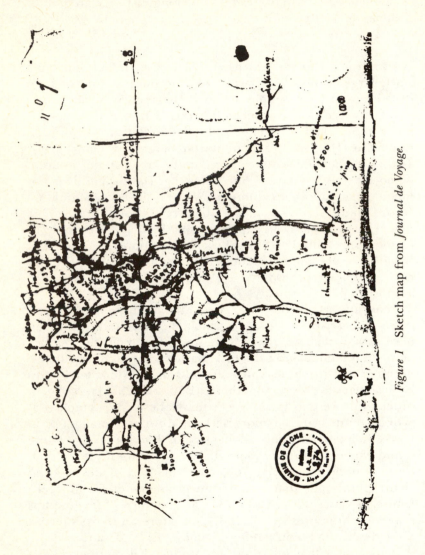

Figure 1   Sketch map from Journal de Voyage.

did not produce detailed full-scale geographical maps, since, within the text, she states that this would have been inconsistent with her disguise as humble beggar. Denys compares the accounts of David-Neel's arrival at Tashilhunpo monastery with that of D.W. Freshfield and W. Montgomery MacGovern. David-Neel's account stresses her personal actions – the fact that she was invited to dinner, the meal that she had at Patour monastery, the problems of crossing the river Tchi Tchou, the weather conditions which forced them to pitch their tents quickly. In the space of this passage of nine lines, David-Neel manages to describe in detail her actions and the causes of those actions. Freshfield and MacGovern use quite a different style: that of impersonal geographers, giving general information about the history of the region and the physical setting of the monastery. The two accounts are radically different, but for Denys the fact that David-Neel's is a more personalised account is evidence that the text is 'false', which is interesting when we consider that the two texts are determined largely by different discourses of scientificity and femininity.

A further reason that Denys gives for doubting the account is that the journey which David-Neel maintains she made could not possibly have been made in the time stated, especially since the writer was middle-aged. Great stress is laid by Denys on the fact that David-Neel was female and that she must therefore have been frail and unable to undergo such a strenuous journey, especially in view of the fact that she was over 40 at the time and 'without experience of climbing' (Denys, 1972: 115), a statement which she does not attempt to justify. She adds: 'It was surprising that a frail woman, without help apart from her young adopted son, was able to achieve such a feat with the rudimentary equipment which she took with her' (ibid.: 11). It is possible to recognise that Denys is drawing on a discourse of femininity here which defines women's capabilities. She goes on to a more specific citation from someone who is named R.P.Ch.:

> Mme David-Neel was overweight and nothing less than ungainly, to get her mounted on a horse was hard work; there is no way you could think of her as an active person capable of undertaking a trip of 12–15000 kilometres on foot with a heavy Tibetan load on her back.
>
> (cited in Denys, 1972: 69)

131

really? – overweight (?)

Denys draws on this feminine discourse of women's physical inferiority to prove that the journey could not possibly have been made.[6]

Denys also accuses David-Neel of being unscientific, since she describes in great detail events which in western terms would be considered 'fantastic'. David-Neel states throughout the book that she feels that she is looked after by a friendly spirit. Denys says:

> In the work [*My Journey to Lhasa*], we enter, with our *romancière* into the domain of the supernatural, of the extraordinary. She believes in communication between the world of men and that of the gods, in exceptional beings in whom the latter communicate their will or announce the future; she tells us of miracles, of mirages, of apparitions, of her premonitions and hallucinations as much auditory as visual, of her bewitching 'officials, soldiers and thieves', of her knowledge of 'Thumo' which allows one to bear extreme cold.
>
> (Denys, 1972: 119)

good pt

The very fact of reporting such 'irrational' events is enough to call the entire account into question, for she says: 'the predominance given to the irrational element leaves no place for scientific information of the most elementary kind' (ibid.: 120). Denys also states that David-Neel could assert whatever she liked simply because Tibet was such a 'blank page' in the public's knowledge that anything could be written upon it. She says: 'the general public . . . were almost totally ignorant of whatever happened in Tibet, and it was therefore impossible for them to appreciate exactly how much the facts as reported by this woman traveller approximated to reality or not' (ibid.: 11).

Even the photographs which David-Neel provides are attacked by Denys. She compares the photos which were taken by Sir Charles Bell of the mother of the Trachilama to those taken by David-Neel, and she states that the two figures do not resemble each other; therefore the photograph that David-Neel claims is the mother of the Trachilama must be false. Furthermore, she examines a photograph which has become central in the criticism of the text, that of David-Neel and her adopted son, Yongden, in front of the Potala, one of the most important

132

buildings in Lhasa. She states that the photograph has been faked. The first reason she gives is that Yongden is wearing glasses, and this would have caused consternation in Lhasa, since glasses were not used; the second reason is that there is a small Tibetan girl in the picture with them, and no Tibetan family would have trusted their daughter to two 'beggars'. Thirdly, Denys states that no Tibetan would have taken a photograph in front of the Potala, as it would have been sacrilegious. David-Neel stated that she had this photograph taken by Tibetan photographers at Lhasa, as she herself had been unable to take a camera with her; Denys responds that there were no Tibetans who took photographs in Lhasa at this time. She quotes, again, a male expert, R.P. Gore (who, in turn, quotes another male expert): 'A well-known Orientalist remarked that the photograph of the Potala in the volume entitled *Voyage d'Une Parisienne à Lhasa* is manifestly fake, because the group sitting in the foreground does not have a natural position' (cited in Denys, 1972: 65). In the light of these comments, it is interesting to note that the fact that she did not take photographs of certain events was also attacked; Hopkirk complains in describing her account of a lama's flying: 'Why, one may ask, did she not attempt to speak to, or at least photograph this apparition?' (Hopkirk, 1982: 225). At the end of her book, Denys puts forward the remarkable suggestion that David-Neel was, in fact, a government agent who was working secretly during this period on the French and Belgian mining interests in China, and that her journeys were simply a front. This would explain the governmental acclaim that she received.

I have dwelt on this extraordinary text by Jeanne Denys at some length because it shows clearly the techniques by which women's texts are invalidated or questioned. Denys does not attempt to see ways in which the text is determined by factors other than the personality of the author. Texts, however, within a Foucauldian framework are more complex and, as I show later in this chapter (pp.136ff.), this particular text has its origin in several different discourses. This diverse origin explains in part why the text's 'truth-value' has been questioned, but it would seem that gender is the major factor in many of the particular accusations.[7]

A further factor which leads to the text's status being questioned is its textual background and the construction of

Tibet as a 'mystical' land. In the case of *My Journey to Lhasa*, 'Tibet' has been produced textually by British writers since the seventeenth century. Because of its geographical position, surrounded by high mountains, which are impassable in certain seasons, it was a country about which very little was known in the west. It was characterised as a place which very few western travellers managed to reach and the Tibetans were portrayed as extremely distrustful of foreigners. Tibetan society was therefore constructed (as most 'primitive' societies are by the west) as unchanging and as spiritual. Tibet was portrayed as a fabled country, and the titles of the texts which were written about this country add to this image of mystery and secrecy.[8] So mysterious was Lhasa seen to be, romanticised as the 'forbidden' city, that Frétard describes it as 'the unreal city of the lamas' (Frétard, 1985: 58). In the blank space that was 'Tibet', European writers could write more or less as they chose (within the conventions of other such texts). This view of 'Tibet' culminates in Rudyard Kipling's *Kim* where the lama Teshoo comes to embody the spiritual nation, and in James Hilton's *Lost Horizon*, where 'Tibet' becomes 'Shangrila', a community set apart from the rest of the world, devoting itself to spirituality (Kipling, 1901/ 1987; Hilton, 1947). Mysticism has always been an important part of the view of Tibet, and many travellers' tales related the 'fantastic' things which happen because of the Tibetans' concentration on spiritual matters and supposed magic powers. Alexandra David-Neel records several events, such as lamas who seem to fly as they are running, and who can endure freezing conditions. Within our 'regime of truth' these events are unbelievable, and in the introduction to David-Neel's book, *My Journey to Lhasa*, we are urged by Peter Hopkirk (himself a travel writer on Tibet) to scepticism about certain sections of the book. He notes that there were allegations about the veracity of David-Neel's account and dismisses them as 'absurd' and 'vindictive'; yet he goes on to say that although he believes her account of *thumo* 'one of her claims does stretch credulity to the limit, or mine at least' (Hopkirk, 1983: xv). This was the account of *lung-gom*, the art of flying, which writers such as David-Neel claim is within the powers of certain lamas. Hopkirk likens the account to 'someone reporting a flying saucer', and therefore the writer must 'expect to face ridicule' (ibid.: 225). However, he suggests that perhaps, within its historical context, the events would have seemed believable:

> Half a century ago, when this was written, the reading
> public was more receptive to such possibilities than they
> would be now. This after all was the era of the Indian rope
> trick, and everyone knew someone who knew someone who
> had seen *that*. In secret and mysterious Tibet almost any-
> thing perhaps was possible.
>
> (Hopkirk, 1983: xv)

Therefore, we can see the firm delineation of the *realm of the true*
(those things which have material bases, and which accord
with our notions of what is 'scientific' and 'objective' – i.e.,
verifiable, tangible, provable) and the *realm of the fantastic*
(anything which lies outside this realm). The realm of the true
is located in Europe, and the realm of the fantastic is located in
Tibet. Western science, and, in fact, much western thought,
assert that anything which lies in the realm of the fantastic not
only is not 'true' (i.e., does not have power) but does not
actually exist. That is to say, we accept as 'natural' those events
which are considered 'true', and we do not analyse the
mechanics whereby the events become designated as 'true'.

There are several texts which have been instrumental in
constructing the Tibetan background in which David-Neel's
book appeared: some of them are 'fictional', and some of them
'factual'. Before the Younghusband expedition in 1903–4, there
were few written accounts of Tibet except those by explorers,
missionaries and government missions.[9] This expedition was
well publicised in Britain, and, because of the number of texts
which were published about Tibet in its wake, it started an
interest in Tibet which had been lying dormant since the
seventeenth century when British business interests had first
been roused to the possibility of a Tibetan market. From this
one expeditionary force emanated a great wealth of information and written accounts. Hopkirk remarks that the 'real' and
the textual become very close in this invasion, when he states
that Younghusband 'could easily have stepped from the pages
of John Buchan' (Hopkirk, 1982: 159). There were many
journalists and travel writers, such as Peter Fleming, who
accompanied the invasion, several of whom wrote accounts
afterwards which were highly influential in propagating and
circulating in Britain certain visions of Tibet. Thus, the textual

background to the emergence of David-Neel's book produced Tibet as a country which was concerned solely with mysticism and spirituality and which could be exploited by European trading interests. Tibet was constructed as an available signifying space for western writers. The textual background determines what the content of any text is to a great extent.

Writing within this atmosphere of suspicion of the validity of her claims led David-Neel to structure her text in certain ways. She faced the problems which all women travel writers confront in terms of the 'truth-value' of their writings, and thus included 'proofs' which might verify her claims. Certain elements are clearly included in the text only for the purposes of validation of the account. There are three main devices which are used to authenticate the text: foregrounded 'factual' material; a strong narrator figure – both in terms of physical strength and knowledge – and photographic evidence.

Because David-Neel was writing a book which was to be published as a travel book, she submitted to some of the generic conventions, such as the style of travel writing. There are two 'voices' within David-Neel's text: the first an 'objective' voice, and more obviously determined by colonial discourses, and the other, more personal and determined by the feminine discourses. For most of her text, David-Neel writes in a conventional 'factual' travel writing style, that is, a style which does not draw too much attention to itself as language, and which attempts to appear 'transparent' through its lack of foregrounded elements. The language items which are chosen are simple, common-core items, with all technical terms or foreign words being footnoted. For example, in the following extract the language seems to be drawn from reportage journalism, or from an encyclopedia entry:

> Thibetans prefer cremation to all other ways of disposing of dead bodies, and their great lamas are incinerated in a big cauldron filled with butter. But that kind of fuel is far too expensive for the common people, so in the barren regions, where wood is not available, the dead are placed on the hills and abandoned there to the vultures and other wild animals.
>
> (David-Neel, 1983: 13)

In passages such as the above, the style is of an 'objective',

136

dispassionate account, which gives her text greater authority. The present tense of 'facts' is used, and the repeated passives convey an air of 'scientificity'; the narrator's emotions and feelings about the event are not included.

The conventions of travel writing are drawn on, as in the following description of Norbu Ling, the Dalai Lama's residence in Lhasa:

> Norbu Ling is situated outside of the town in a large park which, owing to the lack of capable gardeners, is not much more than a wooded tract of land cut by a few avenues and parks. A miniature zoo is one of the attractions of the place.
>
> (ibid.: 265)

This type of description belongs to the conventions of guide books and travel writing in general. The description is specific as to the location and physical nature of the building, and gives information which is superfluous in terms of the rest of the account. Such a description is considered conventional in travel writing.

The second, more personalised voice is used to give the impression that the text was written without a great deal of planning, and was a simple transcription of events; for example, she begins a section 'However, before we begin our story', and digresses on to the subject of drunkenness, illustrating this with a Tibetan story. At the end of the story she writes: 'But enough! Thibetan stories about monks and the lamaist church are a rich mine of fine humour, and if we are once sunk into it we shall never get to the end of the chapter' (ibid.: 206). This seemingly 'random' juxtaposition of elements, and the calling attention to the lack of control of the narrator over the material leads the reader to assume that the text is being written without conscious planning or artifice. In this way, the text poses itself as unmediated and therefore 'true'.

At certain stages of the text, the reader is aware of the voice of the narrator being foregrounded. There are sections of dialogue between the narrator and various other characters which are recorded as if verbatim, and these add to the feeling of presence of the narrator's voice, and allow the reader to be *presented* with the wit and courage of the narrator, rather than being told of the fact. For example, in the following dialogue

137

with Tsering, a servant who has just stolen some of Yongden's (David-Neel's son) belongings and been discovered by the narrator:

> 'Tsering', I said with a stern voice, when he appeared, 'Three rupees are missing from Lama Yongden's purse. I have seen them under your head when you were lying down. Go and fetch them!' . . .
> *Jetsun Kusho rimpoche*,' he asked trembling, 'will the *Towo* kill me !'
> 'No,' I answered gravely, 'I shall do what is needed to spare your life.'
>
> (David-Neel, 1983: 232)

In this dialogue, the narrator asserts her superiority to Tsering, since he believes she has magical knowledge; at the same time she displays her skill to the reader since she has managed to trick Tsering who had previously been labelled as 'sceptical' about the narrator's powers (ibid.: 232).

There are also sections of free indirect speech, where the narrator's thoughts and feelings are presented; these invariably occur at moments of high tension, where there is a threat of discovery. This is a common 'literary' device, but one which is used in this context both to add to the suspense of the narrative and, more importantly, to personalise the narrator's voice. For example, when Yongden scouts around a monastery at night in an attempt to find an alternative route:

> Then I looked around me. Heavens! We were in a small courtyard . . . . We turned to the left without knowing why, climbed a steep winding path, and arrived at a village. Beyond it, higher up, we lost ourselves amongst irrigation canals and fields built terrace upon terrace. Where were we to go . . . ? Suddenly a dog barked above me and continued for a long time, tiring my over-strained nerves. Was the lama in that direction? Would he find the road? He did not come back. Several hours went by, as I could see by the radium dial of my small watch which I consulted again and again. What had happened to him? Far away big stones began to roll down . . . . What was that? A small landslide only, or an accident . . . ?
>
> (David-Neel, 1983: 82–3)

In this passage, the rhetorical questions are posed as if the narrator is in the position of not knowing what is to happen next. There is a constant switching between the 'objective' narrator, and the narrator as a character in the situation, as can be seen by such exclamations as 'Heavens!', 'What was that?' and by the depiction of uncertainty by the use of ' . . .'. At these points in the text, the language switches between the language of an objective narrator (i.e., written text-statements and common-core vocabulary) and that of a character (i.e., spoken text – with exclamation marks, rhetorical questions, etc.).

In writing a travel journal, David-Neel was constrained in the type of information which had to be included, because of genre expectations, but also because of the parameters which she set herself in writing the book. The book is not based on notes taken during the journey; all of the information is thus that which was remembered after the event; this information is structured according to the formal/conceptual rules of colonial discourse. The reader is struck in passages throughout the text by the extreme precision of the details which are given in the descriptions.

Since David-Neel could not include a great deal of the information which would normally be included in a travel journal for the purposes of authentification, as I have shown, the narrator figure has to bear the whole brunt of this task. The narrator is characterised by great physical and moral strength, for example, she states: 'People whose hearts are not strong and who cannot sufficiently master their nerves are wiser to avoid journeys of this kind. Such things might bring on heart failure or madness.' (David-Neel, 1983: 32). This figure seems to have been constructed within the tradition of accounts of early male travellers, such as Richard Burton and T.E. Lawrence for whom physical prowess and courage were essential attributes. Her power and courage are constantly referred to, for example, she says 'we relied on our robust constitutions and the strength of our will' (ibid.: 24) and 'I would find the pass; it was my duty. I knew that I would! There was no time for useless emotion' (ibid.: 129). The actions which are described call for great courage, for example, in an incident where a leopard comes to the camp-fire, she, rather than being afraid, talks to the animal and tells it gently to go away, since 'I was convinced that [leopards] would never harm me or those who were near me' (ibid.: 26).

The narrator figure in this text is determined by a long history of disguised westerners 'penetrating' eastern society, particularly travelling to places forbidden to foreigners, and fooling the 'natives'. Most notable amongst these accounts is Richard Burton's account of his journey to Mecca, and also William Lane's to Egypt.[10] The westerner in disguise is a figure of great textual power since it demonstrates great knowledge to a western audience, and at the same time it asserts even greater power over the people of the colonised country since they are represented as being fooled by the disguise. In David-Neel's text this tradition of a westerner in disguise militates against her drawing on the 'going native' tradition within women's writing. She produces a personalised account of her relation with the Tibetans, but the details she gives are not to demonstrate her allegiance to them, but rather her power over them, because of her disguise and knowledge.

Throughout the text the narrator's mystical power is often alluded to, and in one incident (which has become the focus of debate for many critics as to whether the text is 'true' or 'false') she relates how she practised the art of *thumo reskiang*, self-heating through meditation, in order to dry a flint to start a fire. She relates the incident in a very straightforward manner, giving the following information:

> *Thumo reskiang* is but a way devised by the Thibetan hermits of enabling themselves to live without endangering their health on the high hills. It has nothing to do with religion, and so it can be used for ordinary purposes without lack of reverence.
>
> (David-Neel, 1983: 133)

This matter-of-fact tone, which attempts to make *thumo* into a very mundane skill, is used throughout the description. She notes that, after a certain amount of thumo meditation, 'I saw flames arising around me' (ibid.: 133), and she reports that the ice near her was melted by these flames in the following way: 'A loud report awakened me. The ice on the river was rending. The flames suddenly died down as if entering the ground. I opened my eyes. The wind was blowing hard and my body burned' (ibid.: 133). These short, unemotional statements contrast markedly with the subject-matter of the passage.

There is great stress laid on the difficulties which faced her,

140

and yet most of the description is given over to the way that she overcame problems, such as the fasts she had to endure and the freezing temperatures in which she camped out on the snow. This relating of the physical hardships of the journey is conventional in women's travel writing as I mentioned in chapter 3. Although it is obviously a feature of all travel writing, women writers have to describe the physical difficulties of the journey, because they might run the risk of not being believed, with reference to discourses of femininity, that is, a text of what women are capable of. However, despite the frequent allusion to the hardships of the journey, there are repeated references to the narrator's ability to overcome them. She refers to the lack of suffering which she felt, for example: 'For nineteen hours we had been walking, without having stopped or refreshed ourselves in any way. Strangely enough, I did not feel tired, but only sleepy!' (ibid.: 131). She also refers to the six-day fasts that they were forced to endure without describing in detail the suffering this entailed. It is interesting that the only references the narrator makes to her gender are to present herself as an exception in relation to other females, for example: 'All sights, all things which are Lhasa's own beauty and peculiarity, would have to be seen by the lone woman explorer who had had the nerve to come to them from afar, the first of her sex' (ibid.: 259). Thus, gender is drawn attention to, but only for the purpose of showing that the narrator has transcended the norms of her sex, and is set apart from other women.

Because the account is written in the first person, the narrator often has recourse to other characters' views of her to construct her character as strong and powerful, for example:

> I ignored the danger of being overheard by travellers if any should happen to be on the road . . . . If anyone saw me forming the figures of the mystic dance and calling upon the gods and demons, he could but be convinced that I was a Thibetan *naljorma*, and, being struck with terror, would certainly not remain in the vicinity to ask idle questions.
>
> (David-Neel, 1983: 21)

Here, it is the effect she might have on a fictional, unwitting passer-by which allows her to present the narrator as a character capable of striking terror. In several passages, she characterises

141

the narrator as being seen by others as a 'khandoma' or goddess. She also refers to the fact that she is called Jetsunma by Yongden and others, which she footnotes: ' "Jetsunma" or "Jetsun Kusho": "Reverend lady" or "your reverend ladyship", is the highest honourific title of address for a woman belonging to the religious order' (ibid.: 132). Her power over other people and her ability to handle difficult situations is also reported in 'verbatim' conversations, for example, when Yongden states that he will attempt to placate the evil spirits, he then goes on to say:

> 'Let us see, then, if we can manage our business with [men] as cleverly as I have done with the folks of other worlds.'
> 'Have no fear about it,' I replied, seriously, 'I will look after that.'
> 'How will you do it ?' he asked.
> 'I will make them dream and see illusions, just as the *mi ma yins* did to us.' And I really did so, a few days later, when circumstances brought us before Thibetan officials.
> (David-Neel, 1983: 29)

An important element in the character of most travel narrators is their ability to handle difficult situations and not lose face. This is often a representation of the British as a civilised race triumphing over barbarians. Repeatedly throughout the narrative, the narrator is faced with situations where she has to use her wits. For example, when someone tries to lie to her so that they will not have to offer her accommodation, she takes pleasure in exposing the lie and reducing the person to tears (ibid.: 195). On another occasion, when faced with having to cross a river, she realises she cannot take off her boots because the whiteness of her legs, and hence her foreignness, will be exposed. Therefore, she asks one of the farmers to carry her across the river. She then realises that the western objects she is carrying (her revolver and gold) will press against the man's back and possibly give her away. Therefore:

> simulating the gesture familiar to all Thibetans, of one who (I beg your pardon, my readers!) feels uncomfortable on account of lice and looks for the unpleasant animals in his dress, I succeeded in pushing my automatic pistol under

my left armpit, the small bag of gold under the right one.
(David-Neel, 1983: 140)

Here the narrator manages to show herself quick-witted enough
to act within the Tibetan system of behaviour, whilst not losing
sight of the possible impropriety of such an action within the
western system. She even goes so far as to say, when stating that
she was not robbed in one of the regions in Tibet where robbers
are prevalent, 'Some will think I have been uncommonly lucky.
I shall not disagree; but luck has a cause, like anything else, and
I believe that there exists a mental attitude capable of shaping
circumstances more or less according to one's wishes' (ibid.:
142). There are many other occasions when she tricks Tibetans
into thinking she has supernatural powers when they attempt to
rob her, for as she says: 'No-one is ashamed to practise
[brigandage]. The shame is for the one who has been robbed,
who has not been able to defend himself by sheer strength or by
cleverness' (ibid.: 142). In this way, the narrator figure is seen
to be invulnerable to all attempts to make her lose face.

There are several characters or groups of characters against
which the narrator is measured, in order for her to be seen by
the reader as superior. The figure of Yongden, the adopted son,
is interesting for several reasons. His status as a lama and
'Thibetan' adds to the authority of the text.[11] He is portrayed as
a man of great learning, and yet he tricks the Tibetans, fore-
telling the future and muttering rites in 'broken Sanskrit'. He is
a member of the 'true' Buddhist faith, whilst the Tibetans as a
nation are portrayed as belonging to a corrupted form of
Buddhism which is tainted by the old Bön religion. His religious
position obviously gives status to the narrator. However, in
certain cases, Yongden is portrayed as superstitious, and this
information is filtered through the narrator's 'objectivity' and
mocked, giving the narrator a superior position of knowledge.
For example, Yongden suggests that certain blackbirds are, in
fact, evil spirits who caused them to see fires the previous night;
the narrator's comment is: 'I smiled at his imagination, but he
was quite in earnest' (ibid.: 22). And she makes the difference
between them explicit, when she says of Yongden: 'it is difficult,
even for one who had had a partly foreign education from
childhood, to give up entirely the ancestral notions of his native
land' (ibid.: 72). Thus, whilst the authority of the Yongden

figure adds to the authority of the statements in the text, this figure is constantly set in opposition to that of the narrator, with the narrator knowing more and being stronger. For example, she states:

> Had I been alone, I would have suffered no matter what agony and would have crept on my knees if I could no longer stand, rather than delay a single minute. But the exhausted lama's fatigue [Yongden] overcame prudence. Nothing could be done; he fell rather than sat upon the wet ground, and I went in search of fuel.
>
> (David-Neel, 1983: 12)

It is Yongden who suffers from hunger more than she does, who sulks and who becomes increasingly wrapped up in his own self-importance, and it is Yongden who has to be carried by the narrator when he sprains his ankle. Furthermore, there are several occasions when the narrator is forced to intervene in conversations with learned men, when Yongden does not appear to be sufficiently knowledgeable.

In addition to comparison with Yongden, the narrator is also contrasted to the Tibetans as a whole. The Tibetans are characterised as simple, gullible people, as in many colonial texts, and this depiction adds to the authority of the narrator, since very often she dupes them: 'Who could refuse these simple-minded ones the innocent illusion that meant so much to them?' (ibid.: 146) As well as comparing Tibetans to children, and sheep (ibid.: 184), their children are termed 'puppies' (ibid.: 150) and their behaviour is described as 'bovine' (ibid.: 199). However, as well as adding to the authority of the narrator, the representation of the Tibetans as stupid and 'credulous' (ibid.: 280) is essential for her disguise to be believed. Her disguise is not presented as convincing, for example, when she has to take off her hat on entering the Potala, thus exposing the parts of her hair which she had not dyed. However, not one of the Tibetans appears to notice, and, in fact, one of the crowd remarks that she must come from Ladakh in western Tibet. Despite this, on many occasions the narrator presents herself as fooling Tibetans with her disguise: in Lhasa she haggles in the market to fool a policeman, and he says to her 'You are a true *dokpa* [peasant/farmer], no doubt of that' (ibid.: 271), which seems rather a strange remark to make to a *dokpa*, but a reasonable remark to make to someone disguised as one. On another occasion, she meets a group of *dokpas* whose region she knows, and she talks to them in their dialect:

> they were convinced I was born in a neighbouring tribe. I have no doubt that with the quickness of imagination that is peculiar to them, they would, next day, have sworn in all sincerity that they had known me for a long time.
>
> (David-Neel, 1983: 272)

In fact, the reason she gives for leaving Lhasa is that, so much is she received as a Tibetan, that she is called as a witness in a lawsuit by her neighbours. Intelligent characters would have been able to see her as a western woman with blue eyes, yak pigtails, and dyed white skin who was speaking a foreign language.

The narrator's knowledge of Tibet is amply demonstrated by the use of footnotes throughout the text. In this way, she is able to include italicised Tibetan words in the body of the text, and then explain them in a footnote. The text is thus positioned within an academic framework, but it is also positioned within a framework of *knowledge*. Once a Tibetan term has been foot-noted, it is consistently used instead of the English word, and thus throughout the text *arjopa* – pilgrim, *dokpa* – farmer, are used, as are many other terms. This gives the reader the impression that the Tibetan terms are, in fact, the ones the narrator would normally use, adding to the impression of her great knowledge of the Tibetan language.

There are numerous occasions where the narrator adopts an 'objective' or sceptical position towards the information she presents in her text. Although unable to take precise geo-graphical measurements, she shows that she is working within a 'scientific' framework, something which many women travellers feel obliged to do in order to show themselves to be of the same status as male travellers. For example, she says:

> What might have been the exact level of the pass we had crossed I would not venture to tell, as I could not make any observation. Still, from the comparison of the plants and various other particulars, one who has tramped for years through many mountain ranges, in the same country, may make a rough guess. I had carefully looked at the lichens,

and observed a few other things; and I felt certain that the pass was about 19,000 feet.

(David-Neel, 1983: 131)

In this passage, the reader's attention is drawn to the fact that the narrator is aware of the convention in travel writing of the scientific measurement of passes. The narrator's qualifications for making an estimation of the height are presented (i.e., that she has travelled in similar regions), followed by the methods which are to be used, very much in the manner of a scientific report.

Other information in the footnotes is included to validate the account; for example, she gives precise details of the Dokar pass (ibid.: 8) which could only have been obtained from other texts, since, within the terms of the text, she had no method of measuring heights. This type of data is included because it is the sort of information which is given in many travellers' accounts. Furthermore, when she footnotes one item in the text, she frequently adds more information than is strictly necessary, for example, giving the masculine of a Tibetan noun form (ibid.: 145) where the additional information serves simply as a display of her knowledge of the Tibetan language. In some cases she shows her knowledge of not only the language, but also the appropriate usage: 'Thibetans do not shout "*lha gyalo*" after dark. I complied with the custom and threw only in six directions the old Sanskrit mantra, "*Subham astu sarvatagatam*" [May all beings be happy]' (ibid.: 130). Frequently the narrator draws attention to her own knowledge of the country, for example, statements are often prefaced by phrases such as 'Knowing Thibet and its people as I did, it would have been no surprise to me' (ibid.: 23), 'I have myself lived for several years, in caves or rough cabins in the grassy desert' (ibid.: 24), 'I was too well acquainted with Thibet to have the least doubt' (ibid.: 81), 'We had a sufficient experience of mountaineering in Thibet' (ibid.: 128) and so on. And she states that only a disguised traveller like herself could have obtained the information from the Tibetans: 'No traveller other than one who was really believed by them to belong to the same peasant stock could have gathered the same treasure of observations that I collected' (ibid.: 95).

The fact that she is interpreting a hitherto incomprehensible

146

race for a western audience is also alluded to, for example, she refers to the Tibetans as a 'strange people' (ibid.: 101) whom she, however, understands. She draws attention to the fact that there have been a great many misunderstandings of Tibetan life by westerners, which she attempts to resolve.[12] She even goes so far as to assert that she knows Tibet better than the Tibetans themselves, a common strategy in colonial discourse; for example: 'Thibet is essentially a monastic country . . . . [Monasteries] symbolize a lofty ideal but one little understood nowadays even by their inmates' (ibid.: 274). Implicit in this statement is the assumption that the narrator is one of the few who understands the 'lofty ideal'. In this way, she is in a position of knowledge superior to both Tibetans and westerners.

There are several occasions on which the narrator adopts the position of a sceptical traveller, simply observing strange events without any direct comment as to whether they are to be believed or not. For example, she recounts an incident which she prefaces with the following words: 'At the foot of the pass one of those mysterious and inexplicable incidents was to befall us, such as sometimes bewilders the traveller in Thibet' (David-Neel, 1983: 109). She states simply that the incident bewilders 'the traveller' without stating what her reaction to it was. Nor does she say whether she has any explanation for it whatsoever. In this way, she manages to report on mystical events without necessarily compromising her own position as an 'objective' westerner. For example, she says that during her visit to the north of Tibet as a lama 'I performed a few miracles, chance, the faith and the robust constitution of those who were benefited making it difficult to abstain from working wonders, and I had some gratifying success as an oracle' (ibid.: 35). This sets the narrator in a position of power over the people whom she cured, since she knows, as they do not, that she herself did not effect the cure. This ironic, sceptical tone also forces the reader into a position of collusion with the narrator.

The Tibetans are characterised as simple, child-like, un-educated people who lack western 'objectivity' for example, when Yongden performs a a mock rite for some farmers, she notes: 'The poor fellows felt as if in Heaven. The lama had spoken long and what he had said they could neither well under-stand nor remember, which meant that he was exceedingly

147

learned' (ibid.: 51). This is one of many occasions when the narrator laughs at the expense of the Tibetans. Throughout the narrative, a distance is created between the Tibetans and David-Neel and Yongden through the consistent telling of lies and the performing of mock rites. This distance between the gullible Tibetans and the narrator ensures that we accord an 'objective' position to her. She also mentions that the Tibetans are 'rather vague, if not fanciful' (ibid.: 118). It is therefore interesting to consider that all the information about directions was given to her by 'vague' Tibetans, whom she rarely acknowledges; instead, she uses a passive form, such as 'I had been told' (ibid.: 117), which centres on the narrator, rather than the information source.

There are various occasions when the narrator positions herself as a westerner, and thus shows her difference from the simple Tibetans. This, like the seemingly western 'objectivity', helps to distance her from some of the more far-fetched events in the text. For example, she has to accept all the food she is given as a beggar, and yet she does so reluctantly in some cases; when meat is cut on a cloth which has never been cleaned (David-Neel, 1983: 75), and also in an incident when she states: 'I should have to eat in the way of the poor, dipping my unwashed fingers in the soup and in the tea, to knead the *tsampa*, and to do any number of things which disgusted me' (ibid.: 76). She is disgusted from a position of western-ness. The most testing incident is one where she gives some money to a poor family, who are housing them for the night, to go and buy some meat. The husband returns with a stomach in which have been sewn the decaying entrails of the animal. She refers to this stomach as 'the horror', 'this filth' and 'this foul soup' (ibid.: 107–8), and whilst Yongden has to eat it since beggars do not refuse anything, she cannot bring herself to eat any of it and feigns illness, hence, in this behaviour, aligning herself with western values.

There are other occasions when she maintains western standards of behaviour:

The thing that proved most tiresome, and even at times became excessively difficult in the life I was now leading, was the part that I was always obliged to play in order to preserve my incognito. In a country where everything is done in public, down to the most intimate personal acts, I was forced to affect peculiar local customs which embarrassed me terribly. Happily, our way lay at times through large tracts of uninhabited land, and the greater freedom which I enjoyed there somewhat relieved my painful nervous tension.

(David-Neel, 1983: 106)

The fact that she performed these acts and yet presented them from a western perspective (even referring to them with western euphemisms), adds to the authority of the narrator.

The narrator is thus constructed firmly within the adventuring hero mould, and it is paradoxical, therefore, that the strength of the narrator figure is perhaps the main reason why David-Neel's work was called into question. The stronger the narrator figure is in a woman's text, it would seem, the more likely it is for the work to be considered 'false' or exaggerated, since it does not fit in with discursive models. However, there is one element which works against the full adoption of the hero model and that is the constant reference to fear of discovery throughout the text. There is an atmosphere of suspense which is maintained throughout the narrative. Since the reader knows from the title of the text that the narrator *does* in fact reach Lhasa (i.e., before starting to read), the suspense is rather a strange device, and results in the narrator stating at the beginning of the text:

Would I triumph, reach Lhasa, laughing at those who close the roads of Thibet? Would I be stopped on my way, or would I fail, this time forever, meeting death at the bottom of a precipice, hit by the bullet of a robber, or dying miserably of fever beneath a tree, or in a cave, like some wild beast? Who knew?

(David-Neel, 1983: 9)

The answer to this final rhetorical question is, of course, both the narrator and the reader, since both know the end of the narrative. However, this fictional device is used throughout to involve the reader in the process of the book, and to keep open the possibility of more obstacles to the progression of the narrative. It has an added effect of undermining the narrator's position of strength, since it seems to be drawing on the

149

feminine discourse of fear, a common feature of the discourses informing women's travel writing. There are several devices which are used to create this interest and which construct suspense in this text. Firstly, there is a complex representation of time, i.e., situating the narrator *in* the event, by using free indirect speech and the present tense or present perfect, for example, 'How many hours have I slept? I cannot guess' (ibid.: 151). The narrator is presented as if unaware of the outcome of events. By this means, the reader is presented with a series of obstacles which the narrator has to overcome, and the narrator is situated in the same position as the reader. The reader is also involved through the use of rhetorical questions. For example, when the narrator is talking to the *nepo* or master of the house:

'I have heard', said the *nepo*, 'that some *philings* [foreigners] have been to the Kha Karpo.'
Philings? . . . to the Kha Karpo! . . . Was it possible that rumours had spread about us on the direct roads to Lhasa, and that we owed our liberty solely to the devious route we had chosen? Who could tell? But if such was the case, they would be on the lookout around Lhasa, and would perhaps catch us near our goal.

(David-Neel, 1983: 147)

This speculation continues for another full paragraph. Here the narrator is placed in the same position as the reader, feigning ignorance of the outcome of the events ('Who could tell?'). Suspense is also maintained through simple events, such as the possible loss of her compass, which are transformed into events fraught with tension which might lead to her discovery. In addition, throughout the narrative there is a constant fear of her disguise being penetrated: she washes her kettle and her hands come clean, revealing her whiteness (ibid.: 54); her fingers are stained with ink from dying her hair and this drips into her food (ibid.: 79); she worries that a Tibetan will notice her blue eyes (ibid.: 55); and several of the characters suspect the narrator of being foreign (ibid.: 55). When actual problems do not present themselves, the narrator alludes to further dangers which *might* happen: the possibility of dying or injury in the difficult terrain, and of being robbed (this would also expose them as foreigners).

150

In addition to these devices used to develop suspense, a consistent atmosphere of suspicion is generated – each object is potentially dangerous, and could be animate, and each character who is introduced is depicted as a potential enemy. For example, at the beginning of the text, the narrator and Yongden have to walk throughout the night:

> Once I thought that we were approaching a hut built on the road and turned over in my mind what I would say and do if I met Thibetans. But the 'hut' turned out to be a passage between two great rocks.
>
> (David-Neel, 1983: 15)

As she states at one point she begins to see 'a spy behind every bush' (ibid.: 43). There are many occasions when frightening phenomena (like the fires in the night at the beginning of their journey) are not explained, but simply add to the atmosphere of the text (ibid.: 13). Added to this is the concentration in the text on the anguished emotions of the principal character: 'I felt as if needles were piercing my brain, so awful was the tension of my nerves. Did these men doubt us? That silence must be broken or something bad would come of it. What could I do?' (ibid.: 76). In this way, the undoubted strength of the narrator is nevertheless undercut by the suspense and by the concentration on the fearful emotions of the narrator.

She also includes some elements which seem determined by feminine discourses, which would not be appropriate in a male text. For example, despite the strength of the character, there are occasions when this figure is undercut through being the victim of several accidents, something which would not be possible in most male travel writing because of the problem of losing face. These accidents are treated in a humorous way which is quite common in women's travel writing, for example, when the narrator is descending a mountain:

> I tried to run straighter, avoiding the loss of time caused by the long windings. Then I suppose some invisible and compassionate little mountain fairy, seeing my trouble and wishing to do me a gracious service, pulled me by the foot. In the tenth part of a second I fell and slid just as in a toboggan race, yet with the noteworthy difference that I was myself the toboggan and its driver, all in one! I had

151

happily succeeded in grasping my staff low enough to use it
to steer. In such wise, dispensing with any 'tacking', I
passed Yongden with the speed of an express train and
pulled up far ahead of him.

(David-Neel, 1983: 155)

This self-deprecating humour can be traced in much women's
travel writing, as I show in the analysis of Mary Kingsley's text,
since there is a disparity between the acts that are performed in
their texts and what a female heroine is supposed to be able to
do within the discourses of femininity.

My Journey to Lhasa is thus a complex mixture of elements
determined by colonial and feminine discourses. Rather than
being a simple representation of an individual traveller, written
within the tradition of the bold adventuring hero, as it first
appears, there are many elements which undercut this. The
reception of the text determined that its meaning is more than
a simple analysis of the text in itself; the stress on exaggeration
and lying within women's writing in general determines the
context within which the text was produced and within which
we read *My Journey to Lhasa*.

6

MARY KINGSLEY: *TRAVELS IN WEST AFRICA* (1897)

In Mary Kingsley's account of her journey to West Africa in 1893–4, she describes travelling unaccompanied by European companions throughout the West African area, by boat and on foot, but accompanied by a group of Fan tribesmen, who were reputed to be cannibals. British and French trading involvement in West Africa meant that the narrator was able to stay with westerners and in Fan villages, and she was able to fund the journey by trading with the Fans she met. She collected large quantities of fish and beetles as specimens and in so doing found herself in many difficult and dangerous situations. Despite the serious nature of the journey (she discovered a new species of fish and described in some detail the fetish customs of the region), she terms it a 'lark', which is indicative of the textual and social constraints on women writers which leads to such self-deprecating 'feminine' statements. However, at the same time, the text works against some of the traditional 'feminine' discursive characteristics, for she does not include what she calls her 'bush journal': 'I am not bent on discoursing on my psychological state, but on the state of things in general in West Africa' (Kingsley, 1965: 101). And despite containing a strong critique of the exploitative nature of the colonial relation, which would seem to qualify the text as an example of 'going native', this critique is merely aimed at improving rather then dismantling colonialism. The book has been accepted as one of the classic 'eccentric' women travellers' texts, both by conventional critics and by feminists, albeit for very different reasons: the former finding it humorous and a 'good read', and feminists finding it an interesting representation of a determined and self-reliant female. Both readings are partial; the

153

text aligns itself both with colonialism and femininity at the same time as it undermines each alignment. In this chapter, I aim to explore some of the complexities of this position.[1]

Elizabeth Joyce considers Kingsley's *Travels in West Africa* (1897/1965), and compares it to Henry Stanley's *Through the Dark Continent* (1879), in order to consider the general problem of narrative voice in travel writing:

> travel books authenticate themselves by the authority of the first person narrative voice. This voice establishes a relationship with the reader . . . . It is the voice of experience, through which the explorer dramatises himself as the focus of events and their interpreter. His expertise is rooted in the undeniable fact of his presence.
>
> (Joyce, 1984: 101)

In Stanley's writing, there is little need to prove that he made the journey, since authentication of the text is achieved through the force of the narrator figure: 'his self-dramatisation and the vigour of his style together with the thrilling nature of the events, construct a tale whose authentication relies solely on Stanley's power to convince' (ibid.: 103–4). In Mary Kingsley's text, however, Joyce shows that there are two contradictory voices: one which follows the conventions of the explorer hero, and the other which undercuts this voice. Joyce states: 'Continually dramatising herself as female, she does not have available the option of authoritarian intervention' (ibid.: 110). It is this foregrounding of her femininity which differentiates the text and yet links it with that of David-Neel.[2] Joyce shows that, on numerous occasions, Kingsley has ample space for a heroic stance, yet instead uses a self-mocking ironic tone, occasionally resorting to parody; she even parodies the conventions, for example, she starts a section with the phrase: 'I grasped the helm, etc', where the 'etc' shows the narrator foregrounding and mocking the conventions whereby heroic travel accounts are written, and yet at the same time drawing attention to the fact that she is unable to adopt them. As Joyce notes:

> This choice of comic narrative voice liberates her in two ways: much of the comedy consists of accounts of her conspicuous failure to be intrepid or even competent in the face of Africa's perils, and as she continually reminds

the reader that she is a woman, the heroic role is simply not available to her. Secondly, by embracing the white observer of Africa within its comic scope the narrative voice liberates her from racial or cultural superiority.

(Joyce, 1984: 113)

Whilst I would agree that there are contradictory voices within the text, the situation seems more complex still, since Kingsley's text is certainly not wholly liberated from the positioning of the narrator as racially or culturally superior. I would like now to consider the two sets of discourses in turn to demonstrate that neither is unproblematically positioned within the hierarchy of conflicting voices in the text.

COLONIAL DISCOURSES

The way that Africa is presented is curiously contradictory, drawing on both the straightforwardly colonial and at the same time the feminine discourses, aligning with the colonial powers and aligning with West African people, at the same time as both positions are undercut through the use of irony. Consider this passage on the African forest:

> Unless you are interested in it and fall under its charm it is the most awful life in death imaginable. It is like being shut up in a library whose books you cannot read, all the while tormented, terrified and bored. And if you do fall under its spell, it takes all the colour out of other kinds of living.
>
> (Kingsley, 1965: 156)

The narrator is very aware of the problems of the possible 'illegibility' of the African forest to a European; however, it is to be assumed that she shares the latter view, that it is preferable to other environments and ways of living. Thus, she frequently locates a conventional colonial problem, only to undermine that problem or to take a contrary view.

Joyce suggests that Kingsley's narrator could not adopt the masculine adventuring hero position, but in many places in the text she does; it is simply that she cannot adopt only this voice since there are other voices which intervene (Joyce, 1984). The fact that the narrator is often termed 'he', and is referred to

155

throughout the text as 'sir' by the Fans, often creates a unsettling effect on the reader, especially when there are very
feminine presentations of the narrator in other sections of the
text. But this masculine stance seems to be entailed by entry
into the colonial situation. The narrator refers to herself as 'a
trader' and 'sea captain', and on several occasions she identifies
herself as male, for example, she says 'What the trader has got
to do, is to be a "Devil man". They always kindly said they
recognised me as one, which is a great compliment' (Kingsley,
1965: 312). Furthermore, the narrator presents herself reacting
to situations according to stereotypes of masculine behaviour
rather than feminine ones, for example, when there is a
problem about navigation she says 'I communicated my feelings
to the pilot, who did not seem to understand at first, so I feared
I would have to knock them into him with the paddle' (ibid.:
218). Like David-Neel, the narrator in Kingsley's text, at many
points, aligns herself explicitly with this male adventuring
tradition: when they come across a tidal swamp, she states:

> No need for an old coaster like me to look at that sort of
> thing twice to know what it meant, and feeling it was a
> situation more suited to Mr Stanley than myself, I attempted
> to emulate his methods and addressed my men.
>
> (Kingsley, 1965: 298)

She also refers to: 'the school of travellers of which DuChaillu,
Dr Barth, Joseph Thomson and Livingstone are past masters,
and of which I am a humble member' (ibid.: 368), and writes a
lengthy chapter praising the work of de Brazza:

> the man who . . . makes his long red line pass through great
> regions of choice spots . . . and attains power over their
> natives, and retains it, welding the districts into a whole,
> making the flag of his country respected and feared therein,
> he is a very great man indeed; and such a man is de Brazza.
>
> (Kingsley, 1965: 354)

Thus, at the same time that she aligns herself with male
travellers/colonisers, she also naturalises the colonial presence
in West Africa.[3]

She even adopts certain of the stances of this type of hero, for
example, she says when talking about 'natives': 'It is not necessary to treat them brutally . . . . Never let them become familiar,

never let them see you have made a mistake' (ibid.: 650). This seems to be drawing on the 'stiff upper lip' representation of British males in colonial situations.[4] Even the knowledges which she produces in this text are by and large within the heroic framework of Burton and T.E. Lawrence, that is, they consist of secret rites and information which it is difficult to obtain.[5]

She describes African women in a conventional sexualised way, for example, the Igalwa women are:

> the comeliest ladies I have ever seen on the Coast. Very black they are, blacker than many of their neighbours, always blacker than the Fans, and although their skin lacks that velvety pile of the true negro, it is not too shiny, but it is fine and usually unblemished, and their figures are charmingly rounded, their hands and feet small, almost as small as a high-class Calabar woman's and their eyes large, lustrous, soft and brown, and their teeth as white as the sea surf and undisfigured by filing.
>
> (Kingsley, 1965: 223)

She goes on to say: 'The usual statement that African women age – go off, I believe is the technical term – very early, is I am sure, wrong in many cases' (ibid.: 224), which, even whilst disagreeing with the male conventional knowledge still seems to naturalise that knowledge. An even stranger sentiment is expressed when she states: 'I chaperoned my men while among the ladies of Essoon – a forward set of minxes – with the vigilance of a dragon' (ibid.: 296), an extremely bizarre statement considering the position of women and chaperoning in Britain at that time.

In the above statements, the reader is addressed as if male; when the narrator describes women, she uses conventional descriptions used by male writers:

> The Fanny Po ladies . . . are not the most beautiful women in this part of the world. Not at least to my way of thinking. I prefer an Elmina, or an Igalwa, or a M'pongwe or – but I had better stop and own that my affections have got very scattered among the black ladies on the West Coast, and I no sooner remember one lovely creature whose soft eyes, perfect form and winning, pretty ways have captivated me than I think of another.
>
> (Kingsley, 1965: 72)

157

This is a straightforwardly male position addressing a male reader who will accept this information as 'natural' in a description.[6] In a similar vein, the narrator gives advice to a male reader:

> The ladies are divided into three classes: the young girl you address as 'tee-tee'; the young person as 'seester'; the more mature charmer as 'mammy'; but I don't advise you to employ these terms when you are on your first visit, because you might get misunderstood. For you see, by addressing a mammy as a seester, she might think that either you were unconscious of her dignity as a married lady . . . or that you were flirting, which was of course totally foreign to your intention, and would make you uncomfortable.
>
> (Kingsley, 1965: 21)

There is no similar advice addressed to female readers.

Adventure heroes in texts are generally presented in control of events, and not losing face, as I showed in chapter 3. Kingsley's narrator is no exception since her judgement is often proved to be correct in the narrative, for example: 'Dr Pelessier then insists on banging down monkey bread-fruit with a stick, to show me their inside. Of course, they burst over his beautiful white clothes. I said they would, but men will be men' (ibid.: 149). Similarly, when she and her bearers reach a bridge made of a tree trunk, all her bearers, through fear of falling, go through the water; Kingsley 'rushed it and reached the other side in safety' (ibid.: 280). As in David-Neel's text, the narrator measures herself against other characters in order to present an authoritative figure.

One of the surprising aspects of Kingsley's work is that she writes at length about the colonial situation in West Africa and even goes so far as to proffer advice to the government on the best way for the relationship to be developed, for example, saying: 'it is certain that the Congo Free State must soon be split up among the Powers in Africa' (ibid.: 361), a statement of assertion which displays a self-confidence which is more characteristic of books by male travellers. She considers 'that the trade of the West African Coast is its most important attribute' (ibid.: 631), and for this reason she adds an appendix to her travel text on the subject of trade. It is surprising that, in the travel

158

account itself, so much space is devoted to relating the situation of trade in the region. It is clearly in this sense structured by colonial discourse in that one of the ways in which travellers supported the colonialist venture was in describing possible markets or reporting on the state of mineral deposits (see Pratt, 1985). In this way she naturalises the colonial relation; it is presented as evident that such a relation should exist between Britain and West Africa.

She is very quick to point out the specificity of the colonial relation with Africa, for she says 'It is not an India filled with the accumulated riches of the past' (ibid.: 631), but rather it is rich in mineral wealth, and she is confident that 'the pacification of the country and the greater security of personal property to the native, which our rule will afford will aid him in bringing his goods to the coast' by a road which will also 'be valuable for military expeditions' (ibid.: 637). However, she is also critical of the British form of colonialism:

> I confess I am not an enthusiast on civilising the African. My idea is that the French method of dealing with Africa is the best at present. Get as much of the continent as possible down on the map as yours, make your flag wherever you go a sacred thing to the native . . . then when you have done this, you may abandon the French plan and gradually develop the trade in an English manner.
>
> (Kingsley, 1965: 639)

She considers the French form of colonialism better because they see the colonies as 'the employment of her martial spirits' (ibid.: 656) rather than as a commercial venture like the British did in West Africa. And she shows herself angry that, through British 'supineness and folly', it will now not be possible to have a belt of colonies running from north to south Africa (ibid.: 640).

In view of the account of her sympathy towards Africans in other parts of the text, it is surprising that in several sections she accepts the knowledge presented by colonial writers. Even though she states: 'I feel certain that a black man is no more an undeveloped white man than a rabbit is an undeveloped hare' (ibid.: 659), thus rejecting the notion that Africans are lower on the evolutionary scale to whites, there are numerous counter-examples of judging black people in this way, for example, she reproduces the colonialist 'knowledge' that Africans are nearer to apes than Europeans: 'when you are a Niger Delta native you have to be a little careful for fear of being taken for one of the lower animals' (ibid.: 477), and

> The mental condition of the lower forms of both races [Bantu and Negro] seems very near the other great border-line that separates man from the anthropoid apes, and I believe that if we had the material, or rather if we could understand it, we should find little or no gap existing in mental evolution in this old, undisturbed continent of Africa.
>
> (Kingsley, 1965: 458)

She goes on to assert: 'I own I regard not only the African, but all coloured races as inferior – inferior in kind not in degree – to the white races' (ibid.: 669). Similarly, she says: 'I do not believe that the white race will ever drag the black up to their own particular summit in the mountain range of civilisation. Both polygamy and slavery are, for diverse reasons, essential to the well-being of Africa' (ibid.: 680).[7] She goes on to reproduce the colonial views of African civilisations:

> they are notably deficient in all mechanical arts: they have never made, unless under white direction and instruction, a single fourteenth rate piece of cloth, pottery, a tool or machine, house, road, bridge, picture or statue . . . a written language of their own construction they none of them possess.
>
> (Kingsley, 1965: 439)

And she characterises 'African thought' as 'bad for the brain . . . the fascination of the African point of view is as sure to linger in your mind as the malaria in your body' (ibid.: 441). She even adopts the colonial conventions for describing black people, for example, she talks of black children being so attractive since 'their large mouths (are) not yet coarsened by heavy lips' (ibid.: 475), reproducing the view that Africans are deficient in relation to a western norm of beauty. The statements cannot be read as ironic as many of the adventure hero statements can, and they strongly work against many of the assessments of Kingsley's work as anti-colonialist which have so far been made (Joyce, 1984; Stevenson, 1985).

There are frequent discussions of cannibalism in Mary Kingsley's text, which is interesting since such knowledge would seem to be 'indelicate' for a 'lady' traveller. Hulme says about the word 'cannibal': 'No other word, except perhaps "sex" is so fraught with our fears and desires' (Hulme, 1986: 78). Kingsley travelled in the company of Fan tribesmen, supposedly notorious cannibals, and yet the narrator portrays them very much as individuals, not as the ridiculous caricatures of head-hunters which are found in much male writing on cannibalism. In a typically unsettling statement, she says:

> a certain sort of friendship soon arose between the Fans and me. We each recognised that we belonged to the same section of the human race with whom it is better to drink than to fight. We knew we would each have killed each other, if sufficient inducement were offered, and so we took a certain amount of care that the inducement should not arise.
>
> (Kingsley, 1965: 264)

Here, the narrator adopts the male adventurer hero model, who stresses his strength and ability to kill and drink hard, at the same time as asserting an alignment with the Fan – which is even more curious when this is compared to some of the feminine statements, as I discuss later (pp.167ff.).

Peter Hulme's discussion of cannibalism is enlightening in this respect but needs to be modified in the light of Kingsley's text because it seems that the text is not consistent in the way that the Fan are described. Hulme shows that, in male writing, there is rarely a description of a meeting with cannibals in the process of feasting; the remains of their feasts or reports of feasts are as near as most observers get to them in their text. This is very much the case with Kingsley, in that the narrator travels with one 'safe' Fan tribe, but they are constantly warning her of the cannibalistic practices of other Fan tribes in the vicinity. These warnings are acknowledged, but are also undercut with humour and irony by the narrator:

> The cannibalism of the Fans, although a prevalent habit, is no danger, I think, to white people, except as regards the bother it gives one in preventing one's black companions from getting eaten . . . . Man's flesh, he says is good to eat

joke re: cannibalism

. . . . Oh dear no, he never eats it himself, but the next door town does.

(Kingsley, 1965: 330)

There is a constant reference to her alarm at the thought of passing through cannibal country, even though these statements are undercut by humour:

'How are we going to get through that way?' says I with natural feminine alarm.
'We are not, sir' say Gray Shirt . . . my hair begins to rise as I remember what I have been told about those Fans.

(Kingsley, 1965: 238)

Here the 'natural feminine alarm' heightens the tension of situation, but it is also ironic since her situation is not one which demands 'feminine' behaviour, as I show later (pp.167ff). Added to this is the fact that her bearer calls her 'sir' creating a degree of tension in its coherence.

Like many of the male travellers' tales, she describes finding supposedly cannibalistic remains. When she is staying in a Fan village one night she finds some small bags hanging from the ceiling of her hut:

Smell

Waking up again I noticed the smell in the hut was violent, from being shut up I suppose and it had an unmistakably organic origin . . . . I tracked it down to one of those bags . . . . I then shook its contents out in my hat for fear of losing anything of value. They were a human hand, three big toes, four eyes, two ears and other portions of the human frame. The hand was fresh, the others only so so, and shrivelled . . . . I subsequently learnt that although the Fans will eat their fellow friendly tribesfolk, yet they like to keep a little something belonging to them as a memento.

(Kingsley, 1965: 274)

humorous re: cannibal.

This knowledge, which would normally be considered taboo within the 'feminine' discourses, is narrated in an ironic, humorous tone throughout. She describes the contents of the bag as if simply detailing something innocuous, not adopting either the straightforwardly 'scientific' descriptions usually favoured by male travel writers, nor the adventure hero mode of description.[8]

162

As Hulme shows, cannibalism is normally portrayed in texts as 'ferocious consumption of human flesh' (Hulme, 1986: 84), and it is this threat of violence which serves as a constant source of suspense in Kingsley's text, but which also serves to present these 'natives' as beyond the realms of the human. Hulme finds it interesting that cannibalism is only represented in colonial contexts. His explanation for this is that it is a projection of an embattled Christianity whose major rite consists of precisely this cannibalistic act. Cannibalism is thus something you accuse significant 'Others' of doing: as he says 'boundaries of community are often created by accusing those outside the boundary of the very practice on which the integrity of that community is founded' (ibid.: 85). However, this discourse of the cannibal was not produced in every colonial context, which would seem to undermine the generalisability of Hulme's statement. But his later statements begin to track down the specificity of the colonial relation, for he shows that the narratives of cannibalism 'have demonstrably less to do with the historic world of the mid-seventeenth century Caribbean than they do with the primary stuff of colonialist ideology – the European hero's lonely first steps into the void of savagery' (ibid.: 186). It would seem that this discourse develops in situations where the 'natives' are being constructed as lacking a civilisation. Kingsley's text presents precisely this vision of savages when the narrator enters a 'cannibal' village:

> I must say that never – even in a picture book – have I seen such a set of wild wicked-looking savages as those we faced this night and with whom it was touch-and-go for twenty of the longest minutes I have ever lived, whether we fought – for our lives, I was going to say, but it would not have been even for that, but merely for the price of them.
>
> (Kingsley, 1965: 248–9)

This is unusual, since only rarely in women's travel writing is danger from 'savagery' so clearly described. And, as with the other colonialist statements, her humour very often undercuts the threat of danger; she recounts that she was advised not to have too many Fans in her party as

> the Ajumba say that Fans will kill people, . . . and cut them up into neat pieces, eat what they want at the time, and

smoke the rest of their bodies for future use. Now I do not
want to arrive at the Rembwé in a smoked condition, even
should my fragments be neat.

(Kingsley, 1965: 252)

Thus, the narrator describes a situation which is clearly determined by colonial discourses, and yet at the same time she is unable to present it straightforwardly, undercutting its seriousness.
Some of the statements which appear at first sight to be
colonialist are undermined by the humour which pervades the
text. This humour seems to destabilise any fixed authoritative
position statements in the text might have. Humour is often
evident in those moments of the text when there is the
possibility of the most clearly colonialist statements being
produced, for example, she describes her encounter with a
crocodile which attacks her canoe, that would seem at first sight
to fall into the category of an adventure narrative:

I should think that crocodile was eight feet long; but don't
go and say I measured him, or that this is my outside
measurement for crocodiles. I have measured them when
they have been killed by other people, fifteen, eighteen
and twenty feet odd. This was only a pushing young creature
who had not learnt manners.

(Kingsley, 1965: 90)

Here, the adventure hero position is not adopted, since she
does not give 'scientific' descriptions of the crocodile, and her
humorous final phrase is rooted within the feminine discourses.
It is through this mocking tone that her text subverts the
position of the narrator figure, but also the stability of straightforward colonialist statements in general. For example, the
humour is directed at the male narrative voice of the genre
which needs to keep every situation firmly under control when
she says: 'I have seen at close quarters specimens of the most
important big game of Central Africa, and with the exception
of snakes, I have run away from all of them' (ibid.: 79). Not only
is she making fun of herself as a woman and as a westerner, but
also she is mocking the type of statement made by male writers,
where bravery, courage and not losing face are seen as para-
mount virtues.

164

There are numerous examples of the conventions of travel writing being undermined by her humour, and foregrounded as conventions, for example, one of her chapter headings is 'Concerning the way in which the voyager goes from the island of M'fetta to no one knows exactly where in doubtful and bad company' (ibid.: 257). She even states that she is aware of the conventions but cannot draw on them, for example, when she sees a herd of elephants:

> I know exactly how I ought to have behaved. I should have felt my favourite rifle fly to my shoulder, and then carefully sighting for the finest specimen, have fired. The noble beast should have stumbled forward, recovered itself, and shedding its life blood behind it crashed away into the forest. I should then have tracked it, and either with one well-directed shot have given it its quietus, or have got charged by it, the elephant passing completely over my prostrate body; either termination is good form, but I never have these things happen and never will.
>
> (Kingsley, 1965: 258)

And despite other statements which try to present her in a heroic light she says: 'In spite of my determination to preserve an awesome and unmoved calm while among these dangerous savages, I had to give way and laugh explosively' (ibid.: 260). In another incident, there is a similar mocking of the adventure hero:

> I ask Pagan [one of her party] whether there are many gorillas, elephants, or bush-cows round here. 'Plenty too much,' says he; and it occurs to me that the corn-fields are growing golden-green away in England; and soon there rises up in my mental vision a picture that fascinated my youth in the *Fliegende Blätte*, representing 'Frederich Gerstaeker auf der Reise'. That gallant man is depicted trampling on a serpent, new to M. Boulenger, while he attempts to club, with the butt end of his gun, a most lively savage, who accompanied by a bison, is attacking him in front. A terrific and obviously enthusiastic crocodile is grabbing the tail of the explorer's coat . . . . I do not know where in the world Gerstaeker was at the time, but I should fancy hereabouts.
>
> (Kingsley, 1965: 244)

In certain parts, the text also works against colonialist discourse since she describes not an undifferentiated mass of 'savages', but highly individualised groups of people:

> The Igalwas are a tribe very nearly akin, if not ethnically identical with the M'pongwe, and the culture of these two tribes is on a level with the highest native African culture. African culture, I may remark, varies just the same as European in this, that there is as much difference in the manners of life between say, an Igalwa and a Bubi of Fernando Po, as there is between a Londoner and Laplander.

(Kingsley, 1965:220)

Furthermore, many of the statements she makes which are of a colonialist nature are undermined by the stress she lays on fear: 'I was too frightened of the Fan, and too nervous and uncertain of the stuff my other men were made of, to dare show the white feather at anything that turned up' (ibid.:276).

In certain sections of the text she openly criticises the type of colonial relation in West Africa at a time when missionary presence was strong: 'I grieve to see thousands of pounds wasted that are bitterly needed by our own cold, starving poor' (ibid.: 664), and criticises the missionaries for providing Africans with useless knowledge, such as sewing, dress-making and clerking. She shows the way that religious teaching breaks down African traditions: 'the missionary fights a hard and losing fight for these souls against their inherited sensualism and sloth; they sink into a state that to my mind seems worse than they would have been in had they never seen a missionary' (ibid.: 214). She criticises the work of British women supporters of missionaries who send ill-fitting Hubbards to cover the nakedness of African women, and cites these clothes 'as one of the factors producing the well-known torpidity of the mission-trained girl; and they should be suppressed in her interest, apart from their appearance, which is enough to constitute a hanging matter' (ibid.: 221). She makes fun of the 'pious ladies' who spend their time making these clothes, especially since they make them as if 'the African figure [were] very like a tub' (ibid.: 221), and she continues to take a highly ironic tone: 'so I suggested that a few stuffed negroes should be sent home for distribution in working party centres, and

166

then the ladies could try the things on' (ibid.: 222).

She criticises government officials for not speaking the language of the country (ibid.: 206), and also for having preconceived notions on African behaviour; she says:

> Now polygamy is like most other subjects, a difficult thing to form an opinion on, if, before forming an opinion, you go and make a study of the facts and bearings of the case. It is therefore advisable to follow the usual method employed by the majority of people. Just take a prejudice of your own, and fix it up with the so-called opinions of people who go in for that sort of prejudice too. This method is absolutely essential to the forming of an opinion on the subject of polygamy among African tribes.
>
> (Kingsley, 1965: 212)

She also criticises the British for not regarding Africans as humans: she recounts that one official became very depressed when he thought he had been left alone in the jungle with 'a set of naked savages', but she shows that they are 'really good kindly Kru boys' (ibid.: 85). And she is quite clear that the so-called 'degeneration' of the African tribes is not due to their own laziness, but rather

> Nothing strikes one so much in studying the degeneration of these native tribes as the direct effect that civilisation and reformation has in hastening it. The worst enemy to the existence of the African tribe is the one who comes to it and says: – Now you must civilise, and come to school, and leave off all those awful goings-on of yours, and settle down quietly.
>
> (Kingsley, 1965: 315)

Because of these ironic, anti-colonialist statements, the narrator can certainly not be seen to be speaking for colonialism, yet nor can she be seen as arguing against it. The pressures from feminine discourses on any straightforward colonial statements lead to this complex conflict within the text.

FEMININE DISCOURSES

Like many of the other women writers, the narrator aligns herself at certain points with West Africans and seems to be taking the position of 'going native':

I confess the more I know of the West Coast Africans the more I like them. I own I think them fools of the first water for their power of believing in things; but I fancy I have analogous feelings towards even my fellow countrymen when they go and violently believe something that I cannot quite swallow.

(Kingsley, 1965: 500)

She refers to Africans frequently as her friends, includes dialogues with them throughout the text and names the Africans she stayed with, which is an unusual practice. She foregrounds this alignment when she says: 'The proudest day of my life was the day on which an old Fan hunter said to me: "Ah, now you see"' (ibid.: 102–3).

Frequently, the femininity of the narrator is foregrounded; there is constant reference to clothes, particularly her reasons for maintaining long skirts rather than trousers:

I am a most lady-like old person . . . . I hasten to assure you I never even wear a masculine collar and tie, and as for encasing the more earthward extremities of my anatomy in – you know what I mean – well, I would rather perish on a public scaffold.

(Kingsley, 1965: 502)

When she falls into a pit lined with sharp spikes she says:

It is at these times you realise the blessings of a good thick skirt. Had I paid heed to the advice of many people in England, who ought to have known better and did not do it themselves, and adopted masculine garments, I should have been spiked to the bone and done for.

(Kingsley, 1965: 270)

With such statements, she guards herself against accusations of 'mannish' behaviour at the same time as she adopts stereotypically masculine patterns of behaviour. She also signals to the reader that she respects British social dress codes, for example, she says: 'you have no right to go about Africa in things you would be ashamed to be seen in at home' (ibid.: 19). She even worries about the state of her clothing and the whiteness of her blouse. On a trip in a canoe to a mangrove swamp with Mr Fildes she says:

168

Mr Fildes lashing along first, I behind him, going like a clock, which was my one chance. When at last we reached the 'Boulevard' he wanted to reverse this order, but remembering the awful state that the back of my blouse got in at Fernando Po from a black boot lace I was reduced to employ as a stay lace, I refuse to go in front, without explaining why.

(Kingsley, 1965: 115)

This information is presented as if the reader will immediately understand the problem and consider it 'natural'.

She presents her behaviour as perfectly feminine in many respects, for example when she is recounting a journey to the Great Peak of the Cameroons she describes, rather than the adventure, the domestic difficulties which ensued:

My face and particularly my lips are a misery to me, having been blistered all over by yesterday's sun, and last night I inadvertently whipped the skin all off one cheek with the blanket, and it keeps on bleeding, and, horror of horrors, there is no tea until [the] water comes.

(Kingsley, 1965: 582)

She frequently mentions the difficulty of washing:

I hesitate on the bank . . . . Shall I make an exhibition of myself and wash here, or make an exhibition of myself by going unwashed to that unknown German officer who is in charge of the station? Naturally I wash here, standing in the river and swishing the mud out of my skirts . . . but what is life without a towel?

(Kingsley, 1965: 563)

When she arrives, and the German suggests that she have a bath, 'I decline. Men can be trying! How in the world is any one going to take a bath in a house with no doors and only very sketchy wooden window-shutters?' (ibid.: 563). It is this clear sense of what behaviour she should be reporting which structures her text, for example, women are supposed to be afraid of wild animals, and so she says that meeting tigers 'is not an unmixed joy to a person, like myself, of a nervous disposition' (ibid.: 543). 'I never hurt a leopard intentionally; I am habitually kind to animals, and besides I do not think it is ladylike to go

169

shooting things with a gun' (ibid.: 545) as if the rest of her account were 'ladylike'.

Even when reporting a story she will occasionally break off when she reaches a taboo subject, for example: 'There are stories about [goddesses] which I could – I mean I could not – tell you' (ibid.: 512), and when she describes the practice whereby twins are abandoned she refers to it as 'unpleasant little somethings that are not quite pleasant in African travel' (ibid.: 416). Similarly, she says when describing leeches:

> Knowing you do not like my going into details on such matters, I will confine my statement regarding leeches to the fact that it was for the best that we had some trade salt with us . . . . Of course the bleeding did not stop at once and it attracted flies and – but I am going into details, so I forbear.
>
> (Kingsley, 1965: 303)

The discourses of femininity allow the hero figure to admit to making mistakes, for example, when she sees a sickly child, she decides to amuse it by playing with the doll it is holding: 'The child regarded me with its great melancholy eyes pityingly' (ibid.: 473), since the doll is the image of its dead twin, kept beside him, so that the spirit might not call the remaining twin to follow it. She makes light of these errors, as she does of the times when she mishandles the boat: 'I hand over to Eveke, making it a rule, since I placed my bowsprit into a conservatory and took the paint off one side of a small-pox hospital, not to keep charge when approaching valuable objects' (ibid.: 426). She refers to an accident she had and the fact that she looked ridiculous;

> going through a clump of shenja, I slipped, slid, and finally fell plump through the roof of an unprotected hut. What the unfortunate inhabitants were doing I don't know, but I am pretty sure they were not expecting me to drop in, and a scene of great confusion occurred.
>
> (Kingsley, 1965: 134)

On another occasion where she has an accident, she again draws attention to the stupidity of the mistakes that she makes:

> 31st – Start out at 2.30 and walk through the grass country behind Baraka, and suddenly fall down into a strange

place. On sitting up after the shock consequent on an unpremeditated descent of some thirteen feet or so, I find myself in a wild place . . . . Are these sacrifice places, I wonder, or are they places where those Fan one hears so much about, secretly come and eat human flesh? . . . I investigate and find they are nothing in the world more than markers' pits for a rifle range.

(Kingsley, 1965: 117)

She goes on to say that if you are stuck in a boat in a mangrove swamp

if you are a mere ordinary person of a retiring nature like me, you stop in your lagoon until the tide rises again; most of your attention is directed to dealing with an 'at home' to crocodiles and mangrove flies . . . . On one occasion, the last, a mighty Silurian, as the *Daily Telegraph* would call him, chose to get his front paws over the stern of my canoe and endeavoured to improve our acquaintance. I had to retire to the bows, to keep the balance. (footnote: it is no use saying because I was frightened, for this miserably under-states the case.)

(Kingsley, 1965: 89)

As Joyce has shown, this contrasts markedly with male des-criptions, particularly of encounters with crocodiles. And instead of dealing 'manfully' with danger she often brings in rather ridiculous humorous elements, for when they are on a boat 'Eveke . . . handles the sail and I, when danger becomes imminent, energetically take soundings over the stern with my umbrella. It is magnificent, but not navigation, still it works well' (ibid.: 415).

She denies the scientific nature of her travels at times, stating that she merely found herself 'in possession of five or six months which were not heavily forestalled' (ibid.: 1). She refers to the endeavour as 'puddling about obscure districts in West Africa after raw fetish and fresh-water fishes' (ibid.: 8). In fact, her collecting of fishes is referred to only rarely, and then she frequently defers to authorities on the subject and quotes their work in full, refusing to give her opinion on matters she does not feel qualified to speak on. She even says that she does not understand standard geographical measurements:

171

Taking observations, surveying fixing points &c. These things I know not how to do . . . . I certainly have a dim idea that lunars are not a sort of pill; but I quite agree that they were unwholesome things for a man to take in West Africa.

(Kingsley, 1965: 101)

She mocks her own scientific ability, stating: 'I always get myself mixed up . . . in my attempts to "contemplate phenomena from a scientific standpoint" as Cambridge ordered me to do. I'll give the habit up' (ibid.: 141). And her scientific statements seem more like opinions than expressions of fact: 'I myself do not believe that this island was ever connected with the continent' (ibid.: 46), and she frequently starts statements with 'I am bound to own' and 'I may remark' rather than the simple statement of facts which is supposed to characterise colonial discourses. But she also mocks the scientific enterprise as a whole, with its obsession with measurements:

the last words a most distinguished and valued scientific friend had said to me before I left home was, 'Always take measurements, Miss Kingsley, and always take them from the adult male.' I know I have neglected opportunities of carrying this commission out on both banks, but I do not feel like going back. Besides the men would not like it, and I have mislaid my yard measure.

(Kingsley, 1965: 245)

This does more to satirise the measuring mania than it does her inability to adopt the scientific voice. These 'feminine' elements in the text position it as a text which is not asserting authority or claiming factual status. However, that non-assertive and conforming feminine character of the narrator is itself undermined by the more masculine behaviour of the narrator in other parts of the text, and also by humour. Even this 'feminine' voice, like the colonial voice, is undermined: she notes that while on board ship, members of the crew rush to the rail to see how far they are from the bank, and she says:

I confine myself to woman's true sphere, and assist in a humble way by catching the wine and Vichy water bottles, glasses and plates of food which at every performance are jeopardised by the members of the nobler sex starting off

172

with a considerable quantity of the ample table cloth wrapped round their legs.

(Kingsley, 1965: 193)

Here the irony surfaces in the phrases 'woman's true sphere' and 'the nobler sex', statements which cannot be taken at face value when read in the context of the rest of the book. She also ironises the restrictions which others try to impose on her because of being a woman, for example, a British official did not want to let her go on the rapids, but when she explains that a Mme Quinee has done it before her and he says that she had a husband with her, she tells him: 'neither the Royal Geographical Society's list in their "Hints to Travellers" nor Messrs. Silver in their elaborate lists of articles necessary for a traveller in tropical climes make mention of husbands' (ibid.: 167).

A final element which undercuts the straightforward authority of the text is the fact that the narrator frequently draws attention to the problems of writing, calling it 'well-intentioned word swamps' (ibid.: 154), and in her preface she says:

> To the reader: what this book wants is an apology, and a very brilliant and convincing one at that. Recognising this fully and feeling quite incompetent to write such a masterpiece, I have asked several literary friends to write one for me, but they have kindly but firmly declined, stating that it is impossible satisfactorily to apologise for my liberties with Lindley Murray and the Queen's English.

(Kingsley, 1965: xix)

There is a constant reference to the difficulty of keeping the text under control:

> The natives I have worked at, but as their fetish is of exceeding interest I have relegated it to a separate chapter, owing to its unfitness to be allowed to stray about in the rest of the text, in order to make things generally tidier.

(Kingsley, 1965: 73)

And she mentions that 'I will sketch the results of my observations here . . . because this has no pretension to being a connected work – a thing you possibly have already remarked' (ibid.: 42). She even draws attention to the problems of collecting material:

173

The state of confusion the mind of a collector like myself gets into on the West Coast is something simply awful, and my notes for a day will contain facts relating to the kraw-kraw, price of onions, size and number of fish caught, cooking recipes, genealogies, oaths (native form of) law cases and market prices &c, &c. And the undertaking of tidying these things up is no small one.

(Kingsley, 1965: 73)

In many ways Mary Kingsley transgresses both colonial discourse norms and the norms of femininity. Whilst arguing against practical changes to her feminine clothing, and stating that 'men are undoubtedly more gifted in foresight than our sex' (ibid.: 527), and 'A great woman either mentally or physically will excel an indifferent man, but no woman ever equals a really great man' (ibid.: 659), she nevertheless presents a strong subversion of the feminine and at the same time a subversion of the colonial discourses. Thus, Kingsley's text, rather than being a 'feminine' text or a 'colonial' text or for that matter a 'feminist' text, seems to be caught up in the contradictory clashes of these discourses one with another. No stable position can finally be given to the text.

7

NINA MAZUCHELLI: *THE INDIAN ALPS AND HOW WE CROSSED THEM* (1876)

Nina Mazuchelli's text, *The Indian Alps and How we Crossed them*, (1876), does not fit in with the conventional vision of the eccentric British spinster traveller figure which I have described in previous chapters. Mazuchelli rarely figures in accounts of women travel writers, partly because of this lack of congruence. She is, in many ways, the embodiment of the Victorian discourses of femininity: the narrator figure embraces the discourses of femininity wholeheartedly. However, despite this tendency towards the discourses of femininity there are still elements which are determined by the discourses of colonialism.

The full title of her book is *The Indian Alps and How we Crossed them: being a narrative of two years residence in the eastern Himalayas and two months tour into the interior, by a Lady Pioneer, illustrated by herself.* The text describes a journey to the Himalayas by Mazuchelli, her husband and a colleague who both worked for the colonial Indian administration, together with nearly 100 bearers.[1] For most of the journey, the narrator describes being carried in a dandy by bearers over very difficult terrain; the journey is presented as a simple excursion so that Mazuchelli can paint the 'alpine' scenery of the Himalayas. Towards the end of the account the expedition encounters difficulties because they run out of food and their guide deserts them. Despite this 'treachery' they eventually find their way back to the town where her husband is an administrator. The narrator is presented throughout as a frail, feminine creature, whilst at the same time being presented as a resourceful 'lady pioneer', able to command 'natives' to carry her and her belongings and to inspire them to continue when the situation becomes dangerous. The colonial context is not one which is foregrounded in the text by the narrator, but perhaps more than the other texts the colonial situation is very apparent to the reader: the narrator reproduces many of the knowledges constructed within the Indian situation, which because of her position as a memsahib, Mazuchelli can draw on, sometimes tempered by, sometimes reinforced by, the discourses of femininity.

DISCOURSES OF FEMININITY

The narrator presents herself as the archetypal image of femininity constructed within the discourses of colonialism. The text opens with a dedication: 'To my mother, these pages the substance of letters sent home to her during almost the only time we were ever separated are affectionately inscribed.' This sets out quite clearly what type of orientation and narrator figure this text is to adopt. The narrator frequently makes self-deprecatory remarks which sometimes have a more widespread destabilising effect, for example, after she makes a typically colonialist statement mocking the way that Bengalis speak English she goes on to say: 'But then on the other hand, we Anglo-Indians take our revenge by speaking execrable Hindustani, particularly my own sex' (Mazuchelli, 1876: 559). Here the feminine self-deprecating statement extends to other people within the colonial context. The text is presented in the form of letters rather than, for example, a scientific report:

> The following pages . . . make no pretension to a scientific character, the little band of travellers who ventured with me into the interior of the eastern Himalaya having done so, not for the purpose of scientific research, but simply to explore an almost unknown country, and to enjoy the incidents of travel. Neither do they pretend to give any adequate conception of the magnificence of scenery of that vast mountain region; for in truth its beauty and grandeur are alike beyond all powers of description. For the defects of this volume I may perhaps be allowed to plead the difficulties of a task which can never be more than imperfectly achieved . . . . I may mention that [the drawings] were painted in almost every instance with frozen fingers . . . . In laying them before the public I have yielded

176

to the earnest solicitation of my friends . . . . If the perusal
of these pages should prove a source of gratification to
others . . . . I shall not regret that I overcame the diffidence
I felt in giving publication to the book.

(Mazuchelli, 1876: viii)

There are several elements of note here: the narrator states that
the journey was undertaken simply for the pleasures of travel,
an ironic enough statement when the reader encounters the
numerous complaints in the text of the cold and lack of food.
Indeed much of the first half of the text is about the problems
of travelling. Furthermore, the reader is to presume that the
country into which Mazuchelli travels is an open space, which
presents no impediment to their journey; the reason why this
country is an open space is because of the British colonial
presence. But here the colonial presence is not hinted at; they
are simply travelling through beautiful countryside. The rest of
the passage draws attention to the 'feminine' qualities of the
narrator: she likes watercolour painting – a very lady-like pursuit
– and if the paintings are rather bad, or the reader thinks her
slightly arrogant in publishing the text, then it is clearly not her
fault. She foregrounds the fact that her friends have entreated
her to publish the book, thus obviating the possible suggestion
that she had chosen to publish the book herself.

The narrator goes on to present herself as a woman who is
unable to act on her own behalf, for example, she states 'I
remonstrate fiercely [at dirtiness] . . . in the most commanding
Hindustani I can muster on so short notice, but failing to make
myself intelligible I give it up in despair' (Mazuchelli, 1876:
118). Here it is only her own incompetence which prevents her
assuming a straightforwardly colonialist stance. She foregrounds her sensitivity when she states: 'I unfortunately am one
whom a crumpled rose-leaf would keep awake' (ibid.: 487),
positioning herself as feminine and she portrays herself as an
invalid throughout.[2] The narrator states that when they travelled
from India by train, her husband was concerned about her being
in a railway carriage on her own, and so he goes into it with her,
despite the fact that it was supposed to be a ladies-only carriage;
when he is discovered he refuses to leave: '"I can't" replies
F——, with some degree of truth; "my wife's an invalid and I
cannot leave her"' (ibid.: 14). During the journey this theme of

177

invalidism recurs frequently, since the narrator describes the difficult circumstances in which they find themselves, almost as an index of the degree of her femininity: 'My pulse beat fast . . . from misgivings lest, after all, the prophets of evil should be right, and I prove incapable of sustaining the fatigue of such a journey' (ibid.: 183). When she describes being carried by bearers she states:

> it is a greater marvel still how those dandy-wallahs manage to carry me, and perhaps greatest of all, how I contrive to keep in my dandy . . . but I seldom utter any word of complaint beyond Khabardar! (Take care!) and my poor men are cheerful and patient under all difficulties.
>
> (Mazuchelli, 1876: 269)

Thus, this exploitative method of being transported is presented simply in terms of the difficulties the narrator experienced, and the patience and forbearance – such feminine virtues – which she manages to exhibit. When they finally run out of food and the bearers are about to desert them, the narrator describes the way that she overcomes her own great fatigue and hunger, and gets out of the dandy to encourage them to stay loyal to the party. This very 'British' act of fortitude is a perfect representation of 'feminine', yet 'colonial' behaviour.[3]

As with Kingsley, there is a constant reference to the state of her clothes and hair, and the importance of keeping them in order and clean. She draws attention to her feminine appearance; because she is being carried she decides to wear embroidered mocassins rather than her boots, but she says: 'the bare fact of my ever consenting to wear them at all, does not manifest a total absence of female vanity, and a perfect indifference to external appearances' (ibid.: 214).

The feminine discourses determine that events are always presented in a positive way, for example:

> as the sun rises higher . . . Hatti [one of the bearers] exclaims in Hindustanee – with a pathos very touching, when I look around me, and observe the scanty covering of some of the poorest of my attendants – 'Oh, mem sahib! here comes the poor man's clothing!' and rapidly ascending, it soon sheds warmth and colour upon everything, and all is joy and gladness.
>
> (Mazuchelli, 1876: 265)

Thus, the poverty of her bearers is alluded to, but the scene is
represented through the 'feminine' view of the 'happy native'.
Later in the text she says: 'Whilst we partake of our rustic meal,
the people of our camp come straggling up; now pausing to
rest, or to gather herbs to flavour their simple food . . . now
toiling on again – but always merry' (ibid.: 267). Thus, at the
end of the book, despite the fact that she has represented an
expedition which nearly led to the death of over one hundred
people, she says: 'feeling very sad on the whole for on the
morrow we must bid farewell not only to this sweet idyllic life
. . . to the tents which have become little homes . . . to these
happy Arcadians . . . but to our kind host also' (ibid.: 603). The
events are suffused with this rosy, happy glow, even when the
subject-matter contradicts the tone.

There are many exclamations of horror at any ill-treatment
of animals, although she is prepared to eat the same animals,
once they have been killed by someone else. When a fowl is
eaten for breakfast it is 'usually run to earth at last beneath
one's very chair. Then succeeds the poor little captive's last
speech and confession' (ibid.: 27). Thus, the problem is not so
much with killing the animal, but having to be a witness to an
event which disturbs 'feminine' sensibilities. The narrator is
shown to be sympathetic to even the lowliest of animals, for
example: 'To me a pariah is the saddest thing in nature, and my
friendship for them has won me the proud title of the "pariah's
friend" ' (ibid.: 162). However, not all animals are the object of
her sympathy since she is 'terribly frightened' of a leopard she
sees, again a reaction structured by discourses of femininity.

Indeed, the narrator is often presented in mortal terror,
either of animals or of being in dangerous situations when she
is on her own:

> Now I have no wish to make myself out to be a heroine,
> being on the contrary the veriest coward; never *entre nous*
> having yet been able to go into a darkened room alone, or
> pass an open doorway at night, without seeing faces peering
> at me out of the darkness, but somehow I can go through a
> great deal for a picture.
>
> (Mazuchelli, 1876: 276)

When she decides to go sketching in the moonlight without
informing her companions she says 'The very beauty of the

179

scene made me afraid, it was all so supernatural' (ibid.: 277). Whilst she is walking towards a peak, the mist comes down: 'My position was by no means a dangerous one . . . I know that I had only to remain quietly where I stood, till the cloud had passed over . . . but my heart beat fast and thick notwithstanding' (ibid.: 279–80).[4] This is very reminiscent of the fear of accidents described in the advice book by Campbell Davidson, in chapter 3 (pp.99–103), where everywhere outside the home is a source of potential danger for women. In Mazuchelli's case, the most terrifying occasion is where:

> I became conscious of the appearance of a dark shadow or figure opposite; and on standing erect, a phantom of gigantic dimensions was before me. Terribly frightened, my heart this time stopped beating altogether, and a deadly faintness crept over me.
>
> (Mazuchelli, 1876: 281)

But soon she realises that 'The moon was shining obliquely *behind* me, and what I saw must be nothing more than my own shadow, greatly exaggerated, thrown upon the lake of white mist at my feet' (ibid.: 281). Thus this terrifying image is none other than herself. And, even though she has managed to decipher this monstrous vision, she still runs down the mountainside terrified, and spends the next day prostrate with nervous exhaustion.

It is in the description of the landscape that the narrator most clearly presents herself as a sensitive and deeply religious observer, and thus as 'feminine'. Much of the text is taken up with exclamations of wonder at the landscape, and particularly at sunsets, sunrises and the moon. Most of these exclamations are clichéd, for example, she remarks 'the moon rides majestically in the star-bespangled heavens' (ibid.: 125), and

> early as it was, the sun had sent upwards his avant-guard of crimson cloud, bearing, as on ensign armorial, all the blazonry of his pomp and splendour, and a curtain, like cloth of gold, suddenly spread itself over the Eastern sky.
>
> (Mazuchelli, 1876: 15)

She even draws attention to the problems of cliché in her writing:

All rivers are said to 'wind like a silver thread'. I wish I could say that mine did not. I wish I could say that the Teesta shot like a silver arrow, or wound like a green ribbon, or foamed like a mighty torrent – anything but the conventional simile, but I cannot.

(Mazuchelli, 1876: 145)

This foregrounds the fact of writing and representation, and an uneasiness with the conventions which is rarely foregrounded in the more 'seamless' texts by men in the colonial period.

Her statements about nature are often written in a lyrical, feminine mode: 'O scarlet poppies in the rich ripe corn! O sunny uplands striped with golden sheaves!' (ibid.: 4), and of Darjeeling she says: 'this fair Eden, oh joy! – we are to proceed' (ibid.: 9). Here she is concerned to present herself as a sensitive soul who responds to the minutest changes in nature. Nature becomes a gauge of her sensitivity, for example, she notices a snowdrop, 'lovely, pensive little flower, lowly but queenly in its beauty' (ibid.: 63), and she says she feels sadness when looking at flowers: 'Is it because they are so fleeting, so transient?' (ibid.: 64). This 'feminine' description is quite clearly very different to the botanical accounts of many other women travel writers, and seems to be confessing to and displaying a 'good' feminine subjectivity to the reader.[5] And yet it fits in with many of the conventions of manners and customs colonial discourses, since there is much more emphasis on the description of nature, moonlight on water, mountains in sunlight, than on the description of people.

And yet, at the same time, almost undercutting this feminine concern with small flowers, she displays a love of the passionate, which is determined by the sublime: 'To my mind and wild imagination, however, a love of the passionate in nature, the view from Darjeeling is never so grand and magnificent as after a storm' (ibid.: 65). This sublime element to her descriptions tends towards the melancholic, since the awe which landscapes inspire also reminds the narrator of death, for example, when watching a sunset she remarks:

We stood entranced, none of us breaking silence, our feelings too deep for utterance. As we watched the opal lights die out, one by one, that solemn, death-like pallor crept over them, which only those who have seen the sun

set on perpetually snow clad mountains, or stood in a
chamber visited by the 'beckoning angel', just when the
soul has passed away, can imagine. I shudder involuntarily,
for we seem surrounded by a pale world of death I
wander about the camp like an unquiet ghost.

(Mazuchelli, 1876: 227–8)

Pine trees 'seem to have been arrested . . . by death . . . . Oh,
how I love those haggard, lonely pines' (ibid.: 262). Nature is
presented here as a source of religious wonder 'we are going to
see His beautiful mountains and to learn more of Him and of
his greatness in the works of His hand' (ibid.: 181). In this way,
the Himalayas are presented as they have been throughout the
colonial period and onwards as the spiritual arena of the West,
as I noted in the discussion of David-Neel's work. Landscape
description becomes an opportunity to align the narrator with
the feminine position of religious feeling, for example, Mazuchelli states: 'plenty of "sermons" find we in this grand volume
of Nature' (ibid.: 255); and when attempting to paint moonlight, she says: 'I realised in an instant how utterly hopeless it
would be to attempt to portray it, and simply stood entranced,
losing for a while even my own individuality' (ibid.: 279).

Because of the Romantic conventions of representing sublime
awe in the face of nature, she states that she loves being alone,
'And is there *anyone* who does not enjoy days of solitude and
sweet home life, when one is completely alone? At any rate, I
do; but then I am an "anchoress", they tell me' (ibid.: 66). This
portraying of herself as a religious recluse does not fit in with
the events she describes where she is alone, as I mentioned
earlier (pp.179–80), which inspire utter terror. And there are
other contradictory elements in this depiction of nature, since,
later in the text, it is this same nature which threatens their
lives on several occasions.

The text as a whole orients itself towards Britain more than
many other women's travel writing: objects and people are
represented through a normative filter which is based in Britain;
events and landscapes are filtered through a clearly British
sensibility. This stress on nostalgia for Britain and home ratifies
the narrator within feminine discourses since 'a woman's place
is in the home' (even while that dictum is being violated), at
the same time as inscribing her within colonial discourses

whereby the other nation is seen as a poor substitute for the British landscape. For example, she notices 'oaks, birch and other trees which recall to memory one's native land' (ibid.: 36–7) and when she hears a cuckoo, that archetypally British bird which she terms 'blessed little thing!', she says:

> the plaintive vespers of the little creature, making me feel how many thousand miles we were away from our loved ones in England, caused the very inmost chord of my heart to vibrate, and brought a choking sensation in my throat, which I found hard to get rid of with undimmed eyes.
>
> (Mazuchelli, 1876: 43)

In this way, the text is not constructed as a surveying of this area for further British colonial exploitation, but rather the landscape serves as a series of catalysts for personal memories about Britain and home, revealing herself rather than revealing anything to the reader about the landscape. The Himalayas themselves are described as 'alps' and presented in much the same ways as the conventional 'sublime' Romantic descriptions of mountains, and yet at the same time the Himalayan landscape is frequently discussed in terms of death, and is strongly negatively marked. The specificity of the country is erased: 'Living day by day . . . with the Great Mother, one acquires an affinity with her and gets to find out her secrets' (ibid.: 246). Landscape becomes a more general description of nature in the abstract: nature is here simply a vehicle for the display of religious sentiment.

Most of the descriptions in the text are concerned with preparations for paintings and the views which were painted. Watercolour painting was considered a feminine pursuit for middle-class women, and a suitable pastime for women travel writers.[6] The illustrations fall into three categories: landscape paintings of a very conventional, stylised nature; the narrator herself, and the picturesque. The second category is particularly interesting since most of them represent Mazuchelli either being carried or being terrified (see figures 2, 3 and 4). For example, there are many illustrations of her in a variety of contexts being carried in a dandy. In several of the situations she is represented as frightened of insects or of frogs. In figure 5, she is depicted with a conventional look of horror on her face at the number of insects which have flocked into their tent

Figure 2   Illustration by Nina Mazuchelli, taken from page 382 of *The Indian Alps and How we Crossed them* (1876).

Figure 3   Illustration by Nina Mazuchelli, taken from page 249 of *The Indian Alps and How we Crossed them* (1876).

Figure 4   Illustration by Nina Mazuchelli, taken from page 220 of
The Indian Alps and How we Crossed them (1876).

because of the lamp on the table. Her male companions are
represented as unperturbed by the insects. In figure 6, she is
represented as having climbed on to furniture to escape from
three frogs in her tent. These representations fit in with the
feminine concerns mentioned above (pp.176ff.). However, the
third category of paintings, the picturesque, is very striking
since she often paints things which do not appear to fit in with
the 'feminine' concerns of the narrator. She does not paint
flowers and animals, but rather labour and dirt, for example,
she says: 'Sometimes the tired coolies may be seen resting their
loads . . . . Indeed, wherever one looks there is a subject for a

Figure 5   Illustration by Nina Mazuchelli, taken from page 201 of
The Indian Alps and How we Crossed them (1876).

Figure 6   Illustration by Nina Mazuchelli, taken from page 598 of
The Indian Alps and How we Crossed them (1876).

picture' (Mazuchelli, 1876: 212); and she also mentions the 'quaint looking loads' (ibid.: 117) of the bearers making a picturesque effect and she describes the 'men of our camp in "pictorial rags"' (ibid.: 208). Here the labour and poverty of the colonised people is only seen in terms of their potential for being quaint representations, in this way affirming colonial exploitation. At one stage in the narrative, when she goes to paint a village, she is scared away by some of the villagers because they suspect her of being a surveyor for British colonial interests; as she says 'they have a powerful and a *greedy* nation – as they think – on their borders' (ibid.: 563). Thus, even whilst distancing herself from the 'surveying' role, she is well aware of her involvement in that 'greedy' nation's designs on the country.

She portrays her painting expeditions as occasions for getting to know the 'natives' and their way of life:

> At one period of my Darjeeling career, I haunted the Bhootia Village . . . and I may say, in strictest confidence, that I became almost part of it myself, till the very pigs began to recognise and greet me as I sketched the dearest, raggedest, dirtiest of tumbledown tenements.
>
> (Mazuchelli, 1876: 58)

She states that because of these expeditions, the villagers accepted her as if she were one of them: 'But they never really annoyed me except when, in anticipation of my arrival at their village they attempted to tidy up the outside of their dwellings . . . sweeping away the delicious rubbish heaps . . . upon which I had set my artistic affection' (ibid.: 59). Her stated aim is to paint nature, but here the strangeness of her statements results from her wanting to paint the very filth that she so often objects to.

Because of her presentation of the narrator as 'feminine', she is shown to be sympathetic to 'native' women; indeed, she makes friends with one woman in particular, a Lepcha woman called Lattoo, who wants to come with her on the trip. The Lepcha woman is willing to go on the trip as her maid, but the narrator states: 'I believed I had no right to subject another woman to the hardships of the road and climate' (ibid.: 135). In this relationship with Lattoo, she presents the friendship as at once a relation between equals and as a relation between a mistress and servant; she says in stereotypical colonial terms: 'her mind was like a rich but uncultivated soil, whose depths I longed to open' (ibid.: 166). Yet when Lattoo dies she states: 'my shock was great . . . for in my affection for her all social inequalities had been forgotten and I felt that her nature and mine . . . were yet one' (ibid.: 606).

However, despite the strength of the feminine discourses within this text, there are still contradictory statements where the narrator remarks on the fact that her life in the Himalayas is less restricted than her life in Britain or in British India. She says 'There is a freedom inconceivable [here] . . . . No solemn garden parties or funeral dinners, no weary conventionalities of society, follow us here. We are children of nature' (ibid.: 245). And she goes on to say:

> How odd it will seem once more to return to the ways of civilisation and to home duties . . . to look spick and span and ladylike once more . . . . Our return to Darjeeling . . . is but a nail in the coffin of our departure from these hills altogether, a thought that even now pursues me like a terrible nightmare.
>
> (Mazuchelli, 1876: 604)

The text as a whole gives the impression of a narrator who is determinedly feminine, and this is supported and sometimes undermined by the pressure of the discourses of colonialism.

COLONIAL DISCOURSES

In many segments of the text, these discourses of femininity overlap with the representations of the feminine which occur within colonial discourse; Mazuchelli's narrator is very much modelled on the 'angel of the hearth' figure. However, there are moments when the discourses are in conflict, or seem to sit a little uneasily with one another; when, for example, the narrator makes a clearly colonialist statement – a statement of power which sits rather strangely with the other statements which signal the narrator's submission and passivity.

One of the ways that the narrator signals that she is a representative of the colonial project is that she fears nothing from the 'natives' by whom she is surrounded, and in fact does not consider them of human status; so much is this the case that she states: 'On this occasion, I take care to make my bearers keep well up with the gentlemen, for the gloom is painfully oppressive, and I would fain not be alone' (ibid.: 219). Her bearers here obviously do not constitute human company for her; to be in company means to be in English company.[7] Similarly, it is not the many 'natives' who surround her that she fears but rather a gloomy atmosphere. For the most part she treats the country as if it were empty; when she hears that there is another English traveller in the region she states: 'In my perverse character of "anchoress" I had hoped to have the beauteous valley all to ourselves' (ibid.: 101), suggesting that the 'natives' who inhabit the valley simply do not exist. She also replicates colonial 'knowledges' about 'natives':

> With our conventional notions concerning the bearing of the lower classes to the upper . . . it takes some little time to accustom oneself to the familiarity of these hill men . . . but one soon learns to regard them as so many over-grown children.
>
> (Mazuchelli, 1876: 221)

In this way, the threat of over-familiarity which could lead to sexual threat is lessened, since these are no more than children. The fact that a seemingly frail woman can consider these grown men as children reaffirms many of the conventions for representing 'natives' at that time. In fact, these childlike 'natives' are often portrayed not as servants, but as children who are willing to please and who are performing their tasks not because they have to, but because they want to; for example, 'when the path led over very dangerous places, Hatti, [one of her bearers] proud of his great strength, would insist on being the one to carry me' (ibid.: 248). In this way the colonial relation between Hatti and herself is glossed over. Even the wider colonial relationship between Britain and India itself is described in this way, for she says that Darjeeling became British without conflict but rather 'out of friendship' (ibid.: 51).

Like many of the women travellers she gives her bearers and servants English nicknames: 'I have surnamed (him) Rags, as his own name is utterly unpronounceable . . . . Most of their names however are pretty much alike' (ibid.: 222). In this way, the 'native' is presented as an object to be named by the colonial representative.[8]

189

She often portrays the 'natives' in a negative light, for example, suggesting that they are unable to sing in the same way that English people do, or even to speak a real language, for example, she says: 'Groans and grunts do escape them sometimes, but even these are relieved by scraps of song, with which bidding defiance to every laws of harmony, they endeavour to beguile the tedium of the way' (ibid.: 269). The grunts and groans and the scraps of song issue from the bearers who are carrying her, it must be remembered. She represents their art in a similar way, for example, when she goes to sketch monks and sees the pictures which they use to adorn their monasteries: 'To attempt to analyse them would have driven one to the borders of insanity. The truth is that we are dealing here with art which at best must be called semi-barbarous' (ibid.: 530). And she represents the language that is spoken as meaningless, 'jabbering persuasion . . . beyond everything annoying to the ear' (ibid.: 21). Although she admits that she speaks very little Hindustani she states, with perfect colonialist assurance: '"Hoga" forms the vague and indirect answer to nine out of every ten questions you may ask a native, embracing as it does the past, present and future tenses, as well as the conditional and potential' (ibid.: 49).

Very frequently, she uses the classic Orientalist trope of casting the other country in a European past, for example, she remarks on a carriage that 'you feel sure [it] must have been in use at the time of the Pharoahs' (ibid.: 20), and the drivers 'all look . . . as if they had come straight out of the land of Canaan' (ibid.: 24). On another occasion she says 'We were probably witnessing a scene similar to that upon which Alexander himself may have gazed' (ibid.: 534). In this way the situation is portrayed as unchanging, in contrast to British progression through time.

There are several incidents, particularly at the end of the book, where the group run into difficulties in obtaining food. The 'native' is here portrayed as inherently deceitful, since although they were promised food, the food was not sent. Furthermore, the person who was supposed to be guiding them made a mistake and guided them in the wrong direction; it is assumed he did this on purpose, since he then disappeared during the night. These incidents lead to some straightforwardly colonialist negative portrayals of the 'native' who is unable to be trusted. At the same time, Mazuchelli devotes some space to justifying the fact that her husband and his colleague should not be considered to be stealing from the villages they plunder when they run out of food. She states that they simply had no choice. Food certainly deserves especial consideration in an analysis of Nina Mazuchelli's text, since although food and appetite within the discourse of femininity is supposed to play a very small role, in fact here it looms large. *food* She is quite adamant that Indian food is unpalatable, and thus her descriptions of food fall into the standard colonialist mode: the chupatee is 'an odious leathery, indigestible compound, apparently made of equal proportions of sand and flour' (Mazuchelli, 1876: 26–7); ghee is 'a disagreeable looking substance' (p.73) and they thus survive in the main on wildfowl which have been shot, eating these for all three meals. Having established the inedibility of the food of the country in which she is travelling, it is interesting that this is where the colonial journey is at its most vulnerable.[9] When they have their most serious problems of food shortages, the text aligns itself quite clearly with the colonial *status quo*; the colleague of her husband who is accompanying them discovers that he has many tins of food. However, they decide to keep the tins for themselves and ration the food for the 'natives', since she feels that, divided between many people, the food would not go very far.

In the presentation of the narrator figure, despite the feminine representations mentioned above, she draws on some of the narratives of adventurer heroes, for example, when she calls herself a 'lady pioneer', and she goes on to say 'Few Europeans and no lady had hitherto attempted to explore the eastern Himalaya' (ibid.: 80), thus setting herself firmly within the adventurer mode. She stresses that the journey was entirely her idea, and she details the persuasion and guile she has to use to force her husband to agree to the trip. She details the dangers and inconveniences of the journey, for example, the tigers, scorpions, dacoits and malaria which all threaten their party. However, even though 'the [inhabitants] appear not a little hostile, some experience of their harmless habits [is] necessary before one can feel altogether at ease in living amongst them' (ibid.: 52). It is this feeling of ease which confirms colonialism most, since the potent fear surrounding the representation of a frail, feminine, woman being in a

191

country full of potentially hostile 'natives' is assuaged by her coming to no harm whatsoever, even in the most difficult of circumstances. In fact, very often the journey is portrayed simply as a 'tour', for example, when she says 'we try to comfort ourselves . . . by the consideration that we are "doing" Bhootan' (ibid.: 153).

Although the narrator herself has little status, she plays on the status of her husband and his colleague, portraying it as a full colonial expedition with many servants, 'coolies' and bearers. However, at the same time, rather than these two male figures being cast as noble adventurers, they are presented as rather ridiculous figures who collect butterflies and yak tails. When they all attend a Buddhist ceremony, the colleague 'abstained from being present at their Service on religious grounds' (Mazuchelli, 1876: 535), and she portrays this behaviour as insulting to their hosts. She also criticises her male companions for shooting animals when they are in the vicinity of a monastery, and when they have been requested to stop by the lamas. She is quite critical of her husband, since 'F. has little respect for the creed . . . I am afraid, and of all things, likes to interrupt them when engaged in their religious exercises' (ibid.: 577), because, if interrupted, they have to start their rituals from the beginning. A further way in which the colonial discourses inform the text is that the religious elements which surface throughout the text seem to be used to justify the colonial situation; she states that Christianity is a better religion than the one practised in this country: 'I realised . . . there is none so suited to the wants of poor humanity as that of the Christian' (ibid.: 537). For her Christianity is self-evidently superior.

Occasionally, there are references which remind the reader that she is travelling through a country which is subject to a colonial relation, for example, she draws attention to the exploitation of the country for tea-planting by the British, and she notes that 'the glorious forest trees have been cut down to make way for the cultivation of the tea bush . . . a tea plantation is eminently unpicturesque and only interesting, I should imagine, to the eye of the planter' (ibid.: 39). She goes on to say:

In the manufacture of the 'cup that cheers' there certainly

192

is not lack of *manual* labour, and I think, as a tea-lover, I
half-regretted having witnessed the process, for it is one of
those many cases in which ignorance is bliss.

(Mazuchelli, 1876: 42)

She is aware that the tea-trade is one of the reasons for a
colonial presence, but would rather ignore the presence.
Instead, she concentrates more on 'how our faces and hands
were scratched, and my riding habit torn by encounter with its
treacherous brambles' (ibid.: 43). She also notes that as part of
the colonial enterprise there are 'already deep schemes and
dark designs . . . being laid for a railway' (ibid.: 125), which she
portrays with regret because it will mar her sole enjoyment of
the area.

However, as with the feminine discourses, she does not
present a simple adoption of the colonial discourses. For
example, she says:

It must be remembered that Hindustan was the cradle of
the arts and sciences, and these people – 'Niggers' as I have
often heard them contemptuously called – were in possession of both, when even the Greeks lay in obscurity, and
the Britons, too oft their despisers, were – humiliating
thought – barbarians!

(Mazuchelli, 1876: 17)

In this passage there is a pull in both directions: she is sympathetic to the 'natives' and wishes to show that British people
are wrong to make negative comments about them, and yet she
is very patriotic, and therefore it is a 'humiliating thought' to
think of Britons as barbarians, especially now when they are at
the height of the imperial progress.

In her tone this problematic status is often signalled by irony,
where the reader is unsure whether irony is in fact the best way
to interpret the text. For example, the title for chapter 5 is 'We
make our triumphal entry into Bunkahbaree'; there is an
obvious irony here, but where does it spring from – the
statement is colonial in nature and yet it is not possible for the
narrator to adopt the serious colonial voice with any ease,
because of the self-effacement which has been so strongly
stressed in other parts of the text.

There are discursive conflicts in this text, although the

nature of the clashes is slightly different to the other travel accounts considered. Mazuchelli is quite clearly transgressing so many of the codes of femininity, even whilst she is being carried along in her 'invalid carriage' – an archetypal feminine form of travel. In this way, Mazuchelli's text, although tending far more towards the feminine discourses than either Kingsley's or David-Neel's, is still written within the framework of the clashes and reinforcements of these discourses.

8

CONCLUSION

It has been the aim of this book to bring together various theoretical frameworks, in order to develop a form of analysis which would account for the similarities and diversity of women's travel writing within a particular historical and political period. I have shown that Foucauldian analysis can be grafted on to feminist analysis to produce a gendered colonial discourse study. Whilst aware of the difficulties of using the work of a male theorist, it is clear that Foucault's work is now part of feminist theory, because of the work of theorists like Morris, Weedon and Haug (Morris and Patton (eds), 1979; Weedon, 1987; Haug (ed.), 1987). A feminist study of colonial discourse is concerned with gender issues, but sets those issues within other discursive frameworks and conflicts as critics like Gayatri Spivak and Trinh Minh-ha have shown (Spivak, 1987; Minh-ha, 1989). This type of framework can describe each text in its specificity without having to resort to the biography of the author (yet another text) to explain those elements which are peculiar to that text. Although each text *is* different from other texts, as is clear from the analyses of the texts by David-Neel, Kingsley and Mazuchelli, these differences occur within larger discursive frameworks. This type of discourse analysis enables the reader to examine the whole text in its complexity, rather than offering more cohesive but partial readings. The reading which is produced is more unwieldy, each assertion being constantly modified by other evidence, and ultimately it is more difficult to make generalisations about texts. However, it is hoped that it holds potential for the analysis of other types of texts, both literary and non-literary.

One of the advantages of this type of analysis is that because of a concern to simply describe as accurately as possible the discursive frameworks within which the text was produced and received, the reader is freed from having to make evaluative judgements about the feminist or anti-colonialist nature of the text. Although for strategic purposes it is necessary to distinguish between those texts which are progressive and therefore useful and those which are not, such value-judgements have little theoretical use. Much of the feminist work on women's travel writing has been marred by a tendency to privilege one text over another in an effort to trace proto-feminism or anti-colonialism. Rather than the simple reading of the texts as inspiring examples of women's bravery, I have found it necessary to analyse the way that the texts are determined by elements other than the author's personal wishes or actions, and it is clear to me that the texts I have analysed are far more complex than most critics have described them. Texts written within the colonial situation cannot be analysed without an examination of the effect that context has on the way the text is structured, even though, by doing so we make the analysis and the theoretical framework less neat and clear-cut. Feminists such as Dale Spender have suggested that when we read texts from the past by women, we should 'leave out' the elements which do not appeal to us as twentieth-century feminists (Spender, 1986). I hold quite the opposite position; the texts have to be considered in their entirety, both those elements which we find unattractive, as well as those elements which are more enjoyable, and works should not be judged against our present feminist standards. We should be aware of the extent to which our readings are determined by discursive frameworks. There will never be a 'pure' and 'total' reading of any text.

A further factor which has great potential for colonial discourse analysis is that rather than asserting a homogeneity for texts written within the colonial context, such an analysis makes it possible to map out the discursive specificity of each set of texts. Thus, the discourses which are generated within the Indian colonial situation are here clearly different from those developed in West Africa. Because of the differences of colonial rule – in India a long-established settlement, and in West Africa, a trading relation with only sporadic settlement and missionary involvement – there are different ranges of discursive possi-

196

bilities. India is often seen as a 'natural' part of Britain, whereas the relations with West Africa are seen as much more open to change and development. India, at various periods, is represented as an ancient civilisation which degenerated, whilst Africa is often represented within this period as simply barbaric. Britain's colonial role was seen as mainly to civilise India and help the country to function; West Africa was represented as more of a rich resource which the British could take advantage of. Tibet has a very different colonial narrative to either area, in that it is represented as being the site of political struggles between Britain and other countries. At the same time, texts often represent Tibet as a spiritual haven and this has a profound effect on the type of discursive frames which are drawn upon. The difference in colonial situation has implications for the type of texts which are produced, since there is a range of narrative roles that members of the colonial country can adopt which are determined by these larger economic and social distinctions.

Particularly for women's travel writing there are important discursive roles which are available in India but not available in other contexts. The memsahib role can be drawn on instead of the adventure hero model which is often the dominant role in Africa and Tibet. This memsahib role is reinforced and at the same time undercut by other elements of colonial discourses which the text contains. In all of the texts considered, the differences between the texts are more the product of the difference of colonial context than the result of the difference of the individual author, as is usually asserted.

A further element in this type of analysis is the notion of subversion of discourses, since it denies a stable position to the text as a whole. Although we often read texts as having unitary effects (and in many ways the dominant readings of texts are unitary), it is possible to trace the instability of individual statements when read against other sections of the text. Each discursive position is undermined or called into question by other elements within the text, and while some elements may be dominant, there are sections of the text which temper a straightforward position being offered. This is particularly true of women's texts produced within this period of colonial history, because of the complexity of the way that women are constituted as producers of texts. However, this discursive instability must also be the case with texts produced within other contexts. This lack of a stable position enables us to read these texts less as simply replications of or reaffirmations of colonial rule, but rather as symptoms of the contradictions inherent in that power relation. However, it is necessary to analyse this instability in more detail, since the contradictions are only apparent at certain points in the text. For example, in the analysis of women's travel writing, irony and humour seem to surface at key points of the text, where difficult transitions are being made. There are a great number of statements which are not undercut by irony or humour. Thus, some of these women writers seem quite able to give accounts which draw on racist discourses, but are unable to adopt narratorial positions which are traditionally seen as masculine. Further work will reveal the regularity of the nature of the occurrence of these signs of the instability of the text, and will examine why certain statements can be made in an unmodified way and other statements need to be undercut.

I would argue that the models of colonial discourse analysis which have been developed should be re-examined because of their ignoring gender as an issue in the production and reception of texts, and also because of their ignoring of women's texts. As I mentioned earlier (pp.47ff.), it is not enough that women's texts now begin to be considered by colonial discourse theorists (although, of course, that must be done). What is needed is that the theoretical models of colonial discourse should be reformulated to account for the differences of women's texts; models of colonial discourse which cannot account for the difference of women's texts need to be revised. Furthermore, gender issues should be analysed in men's texts: the masculinist nature of imperialism should not be simply accepted but should be subjected to greater scrutiny.[1] The eliding of colonial conquest and sexual conquest needs to be analysed in greater detail, instead of simply being described as a common textual strategy. This is not a call for more analysis of the 'images of women' in male colonial texts, but rather a call for a fundamental analysis of the way that gender, amongst other factors, structures texts in both their production and reception.

I have been careful in this book not simply to consider women's writing in isolation, since it is very easy to make judgements about the difference of women's work when, in fact, similar elements can be found in men's writing. However, as I have noted, even when similar elements are noted in both types of writing, there may well be a difference in the way that these are received. It is the complexity of the process by which these texts acquire their meaning which I have been concerned with here, both for us as 1990s' readers and for the readers in the time that the texts were published. Any archaeological work is necessarily a partial interpretation, unable to come to grips with the past; however, perhaps it is this which comes through the analysis: that these are not the simple texts that they have been described as. Their meaning cannot be deduced from an analysis of the text itself; the writing has to be considered within the discursive frameworks within which it was produced and received. This is why it is important to consider both the production and reception of the texts, since the way we read is largely a product of discursive frameworks. The division male/female is obviously not a satisfactory way of describing differences between texts, as many women write within the same discursive frameworks as men; however, the differences may be the result of judgements made about their texts rather than any intrinsic differences. The travel writing by women considered here does not in any way form a coherent grouping of characteristics; rather the aim of the book has been to define the discursive parameters within which the texts might have been produced and received.

With a few exceptions, women within the colonial period have been regarded as outside the colonial system, and women's travel writing has been analysed as if it were simply accounts of the lives of individual women. It is to be hoped that this book will contribute to the growing body of work on colonial discourse, and bring about a movement away from the praising or blaming of individual writers. It is hoped that women's role within the colonial system will be more thoroughly examined to analyse the way that women's writing contributes to and subverts the maintenance of the discursive frameworks of the period.

199

NOTES

INTRODUCTION

1 I have not considered the writing of British women about European countries, since this is qualitatively different both in its production and its reception. Although certain similar strategies can be seen at work in the production of this writing, it is the specificity of the colonial context which interests me here.

2 See bibliography for full details of their work.

3 See the work of Alexandra Allen, Maria Aitken, Leo Hamalian, Dorothy Middleton, Luri Miller, Dea Birkett, Shirley Foster, Joanna Trollope, Mary Russell, Catherine Stevenson, Caroline Oliver. The bibliography gives full details of their work. Much of this work provides biographical descriptions of women travellers. I have not included photographs of the women travellers for that reason, and because I would like to concentrate on an analysis of their writing rather than reading these books as straightforward 'truthful' accounts of their travels to other countries. Although it is not possible to dispense with the notion that these texts were written as accounts of a journey which was undertaken, the notion that the account only gives an account of factual events must be dispelled. It is the fictionalising possibilities within the discursive frameworks circulating at the time that these texts were produced and received which will be my focus of attention and not the female authors who produced the books.

4 For example, in her book, *The Wilder Shores of Love*, Lesley Blanch includes amongst women travellers even women who have been kidnapped and forced to travel against their will: for example, Isabella DuBucq Rivery, who was kidnapped by Turkish pirates and spent her days in a harem (Blanch, 1974). A similar process is at work in Mary Russell's *The Blessings of a Good Thick Skirt*, where a woman who was forcibly carried up Mont Blanc against her will for a publicity stunt is considered as a woman mountaineer (Russell, 1986).

5 Some of the work which has been undertaken by the contributors to the journal *Inscriptions* is an example of the value of feminist theory in the analysis of colonial discourse.

6 As I show in chapter 3, Foucault wrote specifically against the proliferation of 'readings' as such, locating this practice within what he calls 'commentary', which for him is a form of repetition of the text. (See, for example, Foucault, 1981b.)

7 The attempt to describe Foucault's work in stages is further complicated by the fact that he was concerned to undermine notions of continuity and progress. Despite this, the events of May 1968 in France can be taken as marking a distinct break in Foucault's work and a more clearly articulated political position which makes his later work of particular importance in this context. After this period and his involvement with the Groupe d'Information sur les Prisons, power becomes one of the prime determinants of events and texts and the focus of attention in his theorising. Groupe d'Information sur les Prisons was a group which Foucault, amongst others, set up during the French prisoners' strikes in 1972 to create a space from which prisoners could speak. This is part of Foucault's revised views on the status and position of the intellectual which he describes in 'The political function of the intellectual' (Foucault, 1977b).

8 The statement seems very similar to the speech act in many respects, and although Foucault at first asserts that the two terms are entirely different, in that several statements can make up a more complex statement which he thought speech acts could not do, when challenged by Searle he was later to admit that the distinction was based on a misapprehension (cited in Dreyfus and Rabinow (eds), 1982: 47).

9 There are many other problems in using psychoanalytic theory to analyse colonial discourse, in that colonialism may appear to be reduced to a simple case of the psyche's attempt at mastery.

10 There has been a shift in recent years to analyse non-fictional writing (see, for example, Elspeth Graham and others on autobiography, *Her Own Life* (1989)). This is particularly a move with women's writing, where so much non-fictional and non-canonical writing by women exists in earlier periods. Using literary theoretical frameworks to read those texts which have been defined as non-literary can be very productive.

11 In fact in some of the later volumes of *The History of Sexuality* Foucault could be seen as positively unhelpful for feminist work.

12 Frigga Haug (ed.) (1987), Chris Weedon (1987), Diane Macdonell (1986) and Diamond and Quinby (eds) (1988) are some of the feminists who have found his work useful. Haug's work is excellent in that it provides a working model for the analysis of femininity using a Foucauldian framework, and Diamond and Quinby's collection displays the wide range of possibilities for feminist appropriation of Foucault's work, at the same time as stressing the difficulties encountered.

13 In discussions with German feminists at a British Council conference at Hanover in 1989 it was suggested that feminism is primarily a position of critique rather than constituting a theo-

retical position in its own right. Gloria Bowles and Renate Duelli-Klein, in *Theories of Women's Studies* (1983), explicitly contest such a claim.

14 Lacan and Althusser have both appropriated the theoretical work of others. However, their work is not considered to be simply critique, but is classified as theory in its own right. It is more productive to ask what theoretical work consists of apart from appropriation and also to analyse how feminist theory is different to theorising by men.

15 See Rosalind Coward (1983) for a discussion of models of patriarchy, and also Sylvia Walby (1990).

16 Although there are moments when the authors are mentioned by name, I do not intend to use the texts to construct a unified author–subject; what I am concerned with is the texts themselves within their historical context and within the context of the 1990s.

Part I Critical Responses to Women's Travel Writing

1 FEMINIST WORK ON WOMEN'S TRAVEL WRITING

1 Margery Kempe's *The Book of Margery Kempe* 1436–8 (1985) is the earliest recorded travel book I have encountered. See Elaine Hobby's *Virtue of Necessity* (1988) for an account of some of these earlier women's travel writing. Especially in the eighteenth and nineteenth centuries there were many hundreds of women's travel accounts.

2 Despite the large number of women travel writers, as I have noted, their work has been largely ignored by male theorists, and they have generally not been included in anthologies of travel writing. There are few, if any, women whose work has been considered of 'literary' merit, as I noted in my Ph.D, 'A Foucauldian perspective on literariness and fictionality in travel writing' (1988b). It is only the female theorists who have concerned themselves with an analysis or description of women's travel writing.

3 Ken Parker in a paper on Dorothy Osbourne, at the University of Strathclyde, English Studies research seminar, in February 1990, argued that it is very important not to characterise women writers as simply capitulating to prevailing ideologies; in some writers' work it is possible to see strong resistance to these ideologies. In his analysis of Osbourne's private letters, he shows that she, and many other women, did not simply accept their role within society.

4 It is tempting to read women's texts as unified in this way, but Gilbert and Gubar's notion of female affiliation shows clearly that not all women writers are feminist writers. Some of them actively align themselves with a male tradition.

5 See, for example, A. Diamond and L. Edwards (eds) (1977). Toril Moi discusses this mode of criticism in her book *Sexual/Textual Politics* (1985).

6 See, for example, the discussion by Percy Adams, in *Travellers and Travel Liars* (1962), and my thesis on 'A Foucauldian perspective on literariness and fictionality' (1988b).

7 Although I find this work very difficult because it is untheorised in my terms, I do not simply want to dismiss it as worthless. Many of these texts introduce the writing of women travellers to other women, and they therefore serve a very useful function. I discuss the notion of accepting authentic realist critical positions for strategic purposes in *Feminist Readings/Feminists Reading* (1989: 51–82). I am grateful to Elaine Hobby for this observation.

8 The critics' stance towards the women travellers they describe is also quite different from the male critics, since they often refer to the women writers by their first names, a common practice amongst critics of female writers, which diminishes the distance between the critic and writer, but also sets the writer in an inferior position, almost like that of a child (see, for example, Russell, 1986).

9 This bears striking resemblances to Mikhail Bakhtin's notion of the polyphony of texts – that there is not one monologic utterance in the text, but a series of 'voices' struggling for dominance (Bakhtin, 1981).

10 See Roland Barthes, 'The death of the author' (1986a) and Michel Foucault, 'What is an author' (1980b).

11 I will deal with the constraints on the process of reception more fully in chapter 3.

12 See Jane Spencer (1986: 25) for an account of Katherine Phillips, and also Mary Brunton's situation described by Elaine Showalter (1977: 18), where she states in a letter to a friend 'my dear, I would sooner exhibit as a rope-dancer' rather than have her works published.

13 I do not wish to present male writing as therefore free of all discursive pressures. In fact, it is constructed within the discourses of masculinity, which are intimately tied in with colonial discourse.

14 See my article 'The male sentence' (1987) which attempts to challenge the notion that there is a distinction at the level of language between women's and men's writing.

15 Although in my work I use the term feminine discourses, I would like to distance myself from a Kristevan definition because the 'feminine' is used by Julia Kristeva to describe a position which seems to have greater access to the semiotic, which can be adopted by both females and males. When I use the term feminine discourses, I mean to refer to those discourses which are precisely not open to men; they do not act at all on men directly, although of course they do act on them indirectly and enable them to formulate their own ideas about women's position in relation to them. It is important to realise that feminine discourses act upon

women and they resist or adopt them. However, it is important also that we do not elide the female and the feminine, because female is a biological essence and feminine is a discourse which acts upon and partly constitutes the feminine subject. The two may at times be almost indivisible, but the female is constituted from other elements than the feminine. This is what enables us to describe women who have other elements in their writing than those qualities which are viewed as feminine.

2 GENDER AND THE STUDY OF COLONIAL DISCOURSE

1 It should be noted that the term, colonial discourse, itself is problematic; in North America, there is much debate about the use of the word, since some assert that it is a depoliticised term; that is, by using discourse in the Foucauldian sense it is felt that the very colonial nature of these texts and their imperial context tends to be minimised, and analysis is restricted to description of surface regularities. For a discussion of this question see the editorial in *Inscriptions*, 3–4 (1988) on *Feminism and Colonial Discourse*.
2 Said does not specify what status 'the Other' has as a term; whether he is in fact referring to a psychoanalytic or philosophical Other.
3 There is a similar theoretical problem in the field of critical linguistics as practised by such writers as Fowler, Kress, Hodge and Trew, particularly in their work *Language and Control* (1979), where formal features are mapped on to semantic features. This work has recently been subjected to a critique where the relation between the features has been questioned. See, for example, Michael Clegg's unpublished dissertation on 'Critical language analysis' (1990).
4 Kristeva described this descriptive framework in 'Women's time', *Signs*, 7: 1 (1981) and it was popularised by Toril Moi in *Sexual/ Textual Politics* (1985).
5 Whilst acknowledging that at the time when they were published these approaches were very useful, as books like Millett's *Sexual Politics* opened up new ways of analysing male texts, it soon became apparent that this was not sufficient; this type of analysis could only really work on male texts and was essentially negative; within its own terms, all that could be suggested was further criticism of male texts (Millett, 1977).
6 As in early feminist work, in this type of criticism anger is a key element, and Said's recent attacks on Orientalist writing have displayed an amount of vitriol which is only equalled by early feminist writing.
7 This is one of the problems of Kristeva's framework, because it seems as if these are simply stages towards the final deconstructive phase. However, there is no sense in which there is a *necessary*

forward progression towards the deconstructive phase, and even Moi states that all of the these phases have to be worked on at the same time (Moi, 1985).

8 For example, see the work of John McBratney in the special issue of *Inscriptions* (1988).

9 Consider, for example, the wide readership of writers such as Flora Annie Steel and Maud Diver, who are rarely mentioned in work about literature of the colonial period. See Saros Cowasjee's *Women Writers of the Raj* (1990); see also Jane Haggis (1988) on women's conceptual absence in colonialism.

10 See John McBratney (1988); and also Malek Alloula (1981), Rana Kabbani also has an interesting section on the differences between the representations of British and 'native' women in her book *Europe's Myths of Orient: Devise and Rule* (1986). Both of these types of representational practice affect women's writing in that they may constrain the choice of narrator figure.

11 This representation of the British woman as chaste was remarkably prevalent within the colonial period and surfaces in popular cultural forms such as advertising, where the figure of the chaste white woman seems to come to represent the imperial spirit itself. See, for example, John Mackenzie (ed.) (1986).

12 It should be noted that Said does include in his account Gertrude Bell. However, he does not discuss her gender and the possible difference this might make to the way her text was produced and received.

13 But it is also important to refute the notion that there were very few women writers during the colonial period. In my limited study I have discovered literally hundreds of these women writers: a global account of their work would not be possible precisely because of this problem of numbers.

Part II   Constraints on Production and Reception

3   FOUCAULT AND CONSTRAINTS ON THE PRODUCTION OF TEXT

1 I consider constraints on reception in chapter 4.

2 Bettina Selby, *Riding the Mountains Down* (1984); Dervla Murphy, *Full Tilt* (1965); Robyn Davidson, *Tracks* (1982).

3 A shorter version of part of this chapter appeared as Mills (1990a).

4 See the section on reception and dominant readings in chapter 4.

5 I consider this aspect of Steedman's work in more detail in an article on Flora Thomson's *Larkrise to Candleford* which is reprinted in Humboldt University's conference proceedings: see Mills (1990b).

6 See, for example, the campaigns around rational dress, which

resulted in the movement to adopt bloomers. For an account of this see Gattey (1967).

7 Foucault discusses Bentham's invention of the panopticon, which he considers the paradigm of control. The panopticon was a mechanism whereby a large number of people could be watched and guarded at the same time by one person. At the same time, information is amassed about these people (Foucault, 1979).

8 See the anthology of travel writing, Carrington (ed.) (1949: 339).

9 Cited in Batten (1978: 102).

10 See, for accounts of this, Margaret Alic (1986); and also Brian Easlea (1981).

11 Mary Kingsley (1897/1965); Fanny Bullock Workman (1895); Isabella Bishop-Bird (1880/1984).

12 See for an account, C. Morris (ed.) (1982), of Celia Fiennes' journeys in 1682–1712, which are in marked contrast to Romantic views of wasteland.

13 In the twentieth century this has become increasingly popular, since travelling to distant places has become relatively easy: for example, by donkey, Dervla Murphy's *Full Tilt* (1965); by bicycle, Bettina Selby, *Riding the Mountains Down* (1984); or on a camel and on foot, Robyn Davidson, *Tracks* (1982). One recent development in the genre is the annexation by travel writing of photo-reportage: in this case, it is not a place which is visited and described, but the socio-economic and political situation of a whole country. The countries which are now described are the ones which are in the midst of political turmoil, and this is thus how 'place' is defined. Issues 10 and 20 of *Granta* are good examples of this tendency, as is Salman Rushdie's account of Nicaragua in *The Jaguar Smile* (Picador, London, 1986).

14 This distinction is of especial interest in relation to Mary Kingsley's work, which I discuss in chapter 6.

15 It is important that this form of Othering is not simply seen as an inbuilt psychological mechanism, but a strategy for dealing with nations in conflict.

16 Jane Root (1984) describes a similar process at work in pornography.

17 For a full discussion of this, see Patrick Williams (1989).

18 However, there are many exceptions where women travellers write explicitly about colonial involvement, for example Mary Kingsley wrote an appendix on trade and labour in West Africa which is a direct address to the government to change its colonial policy in the region. I am not suggesting that women travellers never wrote about the colonial context but rather their adopting of a scientific, colonial voice was problematic, and often they modified such 'truth'-claims.

19 For a discussion of the different models of femininity, see Paulina Palmer (1989).

20 There is a clear class divide in the discourses of femininity in the nineteenth century, as Ehrenreich and English have shown (1973,

1979); however, many of these elements filtered through to working-class models of femininity.

21 See Martha Vicinus (ed.), *Suffer and Be Still* (1972) and *The Widening Sphere* (1980).

22 See Ehrenreich and English, *For Her Own Good* (1979). Dea Birkett (1986) describes the way that women travellers often had to, like Isabella Bishop-Bird, succumb to debilitating illnesses when at home, in order to be 'forced' to travel to far off places.

23 The first *Married Women's Property Acts* were passed in the USA in 1839, and in 1857 in Britain: because of the doctrine of coverture, for women, marriage was, until reform, civil death; the few rights women possessed when single were forfeited on marriage.

24 As Palmer (1989) shows, it is more productive to discuss femininity, not as monolithic and negative, but composed of elements such as passivity and hesitancy which are disenabling and compassion and concern for relationships as enabling.

25 See, for a more detailed discussion, Dale Spender (1986); Jane Spencer (1986); Peggy Kamuf (1980); and chapter 2 in this book.

26 See, for a discussion of the importance of the relationship and its role in the construction of femininity, accounts by Rosalind Coward (1984); and also Tanya Modleski (1984), where she describes the way that women learn to 'read' other people and see that as one of the elements which define them as women.

27 See Rosemary Betterton (ed.) (1987) and also Frigga Haug (ed.) (1987).

28 This bears comparison with some of the work going on in feminist anthropology, where anthropological accounts written by women have been seen to constitute an alternative anthropology: see, for example, Deborah Gordon (1988); and also Kamala Visweswaran's attempt to formulate a woman-centred ethnography, 'Defining feminist ethnography' (1988).

29 The Network feminist theory meeting in November 1989, at Leeds University, on the subject of courtesy and conduct literature proved very illuminating for this discussion of congeneric texts, especially Margaret Beetham's paper on Sarah Stickney Ellis and discussion about conduct literature in the nineteenth century.

30 There are many texts directed towards advising male travellers, as I mentioned in chapter 2, starting with V. Knox's *On the Manner of Writing Voyages and Travels* (Dilley, London, 1784), but they are generally concerned with how to present material and how to develop adequate classificatory systems. Charles Batten (1978) discusses this aspect of travel manuals.

31 The growth of this tendency to advise women in the nineteenth century has been noted by Ehrenreich and English (1979).

32 For an account of the New Woman and its textual manifestations see Penny Boumelha (1982).

33 See Patrick Williams (1986) for a brief analysis of the way that the female members of the Kipling school negotiated their position in relation to colonial discourse in quite a different way.

NOTES

4 CONSTRAINTS ON THE RECEPTION OF WOMEN'S TRAVEL WRITING

1 Extract from *New Statesman* review of *Granta*, included on the dust-jacket of the issue (Buford (ed.), 1984).
2 *Granta*, 20 (1986), 70. The present-day reading public for travel writing is again being reconstructed, since there have been reissues of women's travel writing and the more 'literary' texts such as Doughty's *Passages from Arabia Deserta* (1888/1931).
3 Information from the dust-jacket of Leigh Fermor, *Between the Woods and the Water* (1986).
4 Virago catalogue (1987), p.17.
5 Pamphlet issued by Thomas Cook, 1987.
6 A term popularised by Robyn Lakoff in *Language and Woman's Place* (1975), but heavily disputed by writers such as Deborah Cameron in *Feminism and Linguistic Theory* (1985).
7 Powerless language displays much the same features as Lakoff's 'women's language', that is, such features as disfluency, hesitation, over-modification and overuse of modal verbs.
8 See Alexandra Allen (1980) where two derogatory terms – lady and adventuress – are employed. Also, consider Dea Birkett's book entitled *Spinsters Abroad* (1989).

Part III   Case Studies

5 ALEXANDRA DAVID-NEEL: *MY JOURNEY TO LHASA* (1927)

1 The book was originally published in French as *Voyage d'une Parisienne à Lhasa*. The English version of this book, out of print since 1940, has recently been reissued by Virago.
2 She is often referred to as an authority on these subjects, for example in Adyar's catalogue in 1962 it was stated that she was 'L'auteur français le plus autorisé à traiter les sujets touchant le lamaïsme', and it goes on: 'Ses écrits font autorité'. The fact that she was awarded several state distinctions adds to her authority, since she was awarded the Légion d'Honneur and the Médaille d'Or from the Société de Géographie. There are schools and streets named after her in France, and there are frequently television and radio programmes devoted to her and to those who have retraced her footsteps into Tibet. In Digne there is a Tibetan cultural centre, the Fondation Alexandra David-Neel, based at her house, which many thousands of tourists have visited. Her books on travel and on Buddhism have been published and reissued in many languages.
3 It is interesting that it is often on the subject of mysticism and

spirituality that women are permitted to write authoritatively. On more strictly doctrinal matters, women have been rigorously excluded; yet there is a great wealth of female mystical writing within the Christian church. In many ways, spirituality is considered a harmless outlet for females, an overflowing of their 'natural' emotionality. Yet again, mysticism sets women at the margins, rather than at the centre of religious debates. Thus, it is not unusual to find a woman writing about spirituality, and some of the authority of David-Neel's text derives from her position within this tradition. However, it is unusual to find a woman writing authoritatively about a religion other than Christianity, and claiming mystical and supernatural powers for herself. This is obviously not easily recuperated within the west's 'regime of truth'.

4 A great deal has been written on this subject, most notably, Jeanne Denys, *Alexandra David-Neel au Tibet* (1972) (the translations from the French are my own). But see also Frétard (1985); Hopkirk (1983); Norwick (1976).

5 It should be noted, however, that David-Neel does refer to other traveller's writings (within her introduction she refers to eighteen of the travellers who went to Tibet before her), and adheres to the academic practice of footnotes, but for Denys this is insufficient. Once having decided that the text is a 'false' account, she is forced to read the text in a certain way (just as, for that matter, those readers who decide that the text is 'true' are led to read the text in a particular way).

6 Although here it is interesting that David-Neel is described as both frail *and* overweight. Denys even goes so far as to calculate the average daily mileage of male travellers in Tibet and compares them to the daily averages which she calculates David-Neel must have attained to reach Lhasa when she claimed she did. Unable to believe that a woman could attain these averages, she then accuses David-Neel of travelling by sea from Yunnan to Gyantse.

7 It should be noted that because of these accusations David-Neel's secretary, Mme Peyronnet, has amassed many items of proof and exhibited them in the Fondation Alexandra David-Neel, in Digne. Some of these proofs relate very closely to the text, for example, the hat which forms part of a textual incident on page 62 of the text is preserved in a glass case, and her goggles and cooking-pot which were mentioned in the text are also preserved. However, there are also written testimonials from various dignitaries, such as Prince Pierre of Greece, Captain Perry, commander of the guard at the British Trade Mission at Gyantse, and the French Ambassador of China, attesting to the truth of her account. Hopkirk notes that her account should be considered true because she did not include scientific information: these were 'details which Alexandra, who was neither geographer nor explorer, must have considered of minor importance. Her explorations were of the Tibetan mind rather than of the terrain' (Hopkirk, 1982: xv). Thus the book is allowed to be 'true' but only a very 'feminine' 'truth'.

8 For example, Sir T. Holdrich, *Tibet the Mysterious* (1906); F. Maviani, *Secret Tibet* (1954); A. Waddell, *Tibet and its Mysteries* (1905).

9 This expeditionary force was sent into Tibet as part of the 'Great Game', whereby Russia and Britain attempted to gain dominance in areas around northern India. Members of the British government suspected that there had been Russian infiltration into the Lhasa administration, and sent a small army to assert British dominance. As well as establishing military control (there was a bloody battle at Guru, where many hundreds of Tibetans were massacred), a trading relationship was established.

10 See Williams (1989) for a discussion of male travellers in disguise; and also Said (1978a) on William Lane and Richard Burton. See also Dekker and van de Pol (1989); and Wheelwright (1989) for descriptions of women in disguise. For other female disguise travel texts see Hobson (1973).

11 He is presented in the text as Tibetan although it is stated at the beginning of the text and in other texts that he is Sikkimese.

12 For example, she remarks in a footnote that 'tulkus' have been termed by westerners 'living buddhas' which is a mistake (David-Neel, 1983: 192); she also remarks on the incompleteness of western knowledge of Tibetan geography (ibid.: 119) and the fact that certain towns are named by westerners with names which are not recognised by Tibetans (ibid.:191).

6 MARY KINGSLEY: *TRAVELS IN WEST AFRICA* (1897)

1 At the same time as analysing the text, it is necessary to remember the way that, as I mentioned previously, Mary Kingsley was forced to revise and exclude certain descriptions which publishers found to be unbelievable. This has some bearing on the final form of the text and should make the reader sceptical that the text is a simple autobiography.

2 Joyce asserts that it is the foregrounding of the female which undercuts the colonial voice, but it seems to be more femininity which is stressed throughout Kingsley's account.

3 This alignment is ironic since the Royal Geographical Society adamantly refused to allow women travellers to be accepted as fellows until after a great deal of protest.

4 For Catherine Stevenson (1985) this adopting of a male persona is evidence that Kingsley herself wanted to be a man, as I showed in chapter 3. However, it is clear that this heroic role is already gendered. It would thus be surprising if Kingsley had written drawing on a persona of the type she describes without at the same time presenting the figure as male. However, David-Neel does present herself within this model without presenting herself as male; instead she foregrounds her exceptional nature as a woman. As I go on to note in this chapter, this adoption of the male

persona in Kingsley's text is undercut by the dramatising of the narrator as feminine.

5 This probing into the secrets of a colonised country is particularly noted in the treatment of the harem, as Alloula (1981) has shown. Fanny Parks's *Wandering of a Pilgrim in Search of the Picturesque* (1850) gives an account of her 'penetration' of the harem which is also fascinating for the reproduction of colonial strategies of uncovering the secrets of the colonised society. It is especially interesting because the secrets disclosed – women addicted to opium and *pān* – were taboo subjects for a Victorian woman to write about.

6 At a meeting of Northern Network in 1989, where I discussed this material, it was suggested that this material could be read as a lesbian text.

7 This type of racist statement is typical of the discursive structure of the African situation in the nineteenth century, within the framework of ideas expounded by Arthur de Gobineau (1853–5). See Michael Biddis (ed.) (1970), where his essays on race are collected. That is not to say that Gobineau was the originator of these ideas, but his work can be seen as a crystallisation of many of the discourses on race and Africa which were being constructed at that time.

8 It is interesting that Fanny Parks, in her account of travel to India, also gives accounts of Thugs and their repression by the British in India (Parks, 1850). Some of the accounts are very graphic and would normally be considered 'unladylike': in Parks's text the sections on Thugs are presented as unedited letters from a male friend who was involved with the elimination, thus distancing the knowledge from the narrator herself.

7 NINA MAZUCHELLI: *THE INDIAN ALPS AND HOW WE CROSSED THEM* (1876)

1 Emily Eden's account, *Up the Country* (1866/1983), is very similar in this respect since she describes travelling with a full retinue of servants and soldiers, as she travelled with her brother who was the Governor-General of India. Much of the description is taken up with the day-to-day routine of life in their 'city' of tents, the mundane details of jewellery and presents which they are offered by the 'native' rulers and minute descriptions of the dress and appearance of the rulers. Little description is given of the political crisis in Afghanistan which was on the verge of exploding at that time and for which her brother was responsible. Eden, like Mazuchelli, gives extensive descriptions of her own paintings. Both seem to affirm both the discourses of femininity and colonialism.

2 For an account of the invalidism of British middle-class women of the nineteenth century, see Ehrenreich and English (1979).

3 It is interesting that the feminine is not entirely passive, as I have

noted in chapter 3, and that within the colonial context courage is still expected, even of the 'weakest' subjects. See, for example, some of the representations of women's resistance in the moments of colonial crisis, such as the Indian Mutiny and the Afghanistan Crisis.

4 This passage is interesting especially in the light of descriptions in Mary Kingsley's text of expeditions alone at night. Kingsley describes the way that, in a 'cannibal' village, she borrows a canoe and paddles in the moonlight since she finds she cannot sleep. She says: 'While engaged on this hunt [for glow-worms] I felt the earth quiver under my feet and heard a big soughing sound, and looking round saw I had dropped in on a hippo banquet (Kingsley, 1965: 253). Here, instead of the night journey being a source of terror, it is the source of humour.

5 See, for example, Isabella Bishop-Bird (1880/1984) for extremely full botanical descriptions.

6 Many of the more 'feminine' travel writers illustrate their texts in a similar way, for example, with portraits of 'natives' and landscapes, like Emily Eden (1866/1983), but it is rare to represent the narrator herself to the extent that Mazuchelli does.

7 Freya Stark also makes a similar statement when she escapes from the company of her British archaeologist friends, with whom she has travelled; in the company of many tribesmen who are guiding her she states 'At last I was alone' (Stark, 1940).

8 Mary Kingsley and Mildred Cable both give their servants and bearers ludicrous nicknames.

9 Peter Hulme (1986) discusses this vulnerable position of the colonial project through its over-dependence on being supplied with material and food by the very people who are being subjugated.

8 CONCLUSION

1 Ronald Hyams, in *Empire and Sexuality* (1990), gives a rather nostalgic account of male British sexuality in the colonised countries. Other sexualities are not dealt with, and there is no analysis of the role of power relations in male sexuality in this context.

BIBLIOGRAPHY

Adams, P. G. (1962) *Travellers and Travel Liars: 1600–1800*, University of California Press, Berkeley.
——(1983) *Travel Literature and the Evolution of the Novel*, University of Kentucky Press, Kentucky.
Aitken, M. (1987) *A Girdle Round the Earth*, Constable, London.
Al Azm, S.J. (1981) 'Orientalism and Orientalism in Reverse', pp. 5–26 in *Khamsin*, 8.
Al-Debbagh, A. M. (1988) 'Orientalism and literary orientalism: preliminary observations', discussion paper, Salahadine University, Iraq.
Alic, M. (1986) *Hypatia's Heritage: A History of Women in Science from Antiquity to the Late Nineteenth Century*, Women's Press, London.
Allen, A. (1980) *Travelling Ladies: Victorian Adventuresses*, Jupiter, London.
Allen, R. (1986) *Women and Literature*, Open University, PU 712, Open University, Milton Keynes.
Alloula, M. (1981) *The Colonial Harem*, trans. M. and W. Godzich, Manchester University Press, Manchester.
Althusser, L. (1984) *Essays on Ideology*, Verso, London.
Anderson, L. (1987) 'At the threshold of self: women and autobiography', pp. 54–71 in M. Monteith (ed.) *Women's Writing: A Challenge to Theory*, Harvester, Brighton.
Ardener, S. ed. (1981) *Women and Space: Ground Rules and Social Maps*, Croom Helm/Oxford University Women's Studies Committee, London.
Armstrong, N (1987) 'The rise of the domestic woman', pp. 96–141, in N. Armstrong and L. Tennenhouse (eds) *The Ideology of Conduct: Essays in Literature and the History of Sexuality*, Methuen, London.
Armstrong, N. and Tennenhouse, L. (eds) (1987) *The Ideology of Conduct: Essays in Literature and the History of Sexuality*, Methuen, London.
Ashcroft, B., Griffiths, G. and Tiffen, H. eds (1989): *The Empire Writes Back: Theory and Practice in Post-Colonial Literatures*, Routledge, London.

Assad, T. (1964) *Three Victorian Travellers: Burton, Blunt, Doughty*, Routledge & Kegan Paul, London.

Bakhtin, M.M. (1981) *The Dialogic Imagination*, trans. C. Emerson and M. Holquist, Texas University Press, Austin.

Balibar, R. (1978) 'An example of literary work in France', trans. J. Coombes J. pp. 134–47 in F. Barker (ed.) *1848: Proceedings of the Sociology of Literature Conference*, July, University of Essex, Colchester.

Barbour, P. L. (1963) 'Fact and fiction in Capt. John Smith's "True Travels" ', pp. 101–14, in W.G. Rice (ed.) *Literature as a Mode of Travel*, New York Public Library, New York.

Barker, F. ed. (1982) *The Politics of Theory*, Proceedings of the Essex Sociology of Literature Conference, July 1982, University of Essex, Colchester.

——(1984) *Europe and Its Others*, vol. I, Proceedings of the Essex Sociology of Literature Conference, July 1984, University of Essex, Colchester.

Barr, P. (1976) *The Memsahibs: the Women of Victorian India*, Secker & Warburg, London.

Barrows, H. (1963) 'Convention and novelty in the Romantic generation's experience of Italy', pp. 69–84 in W.G. Rice (ed.) *Literature as a Mode of Travel*, New York Public Library, New York.

Barthes, R. (1977) *Image, Music Text*, trans. S. Heath, Fontana, London.

——(1982) 'Le Degré zero de l'ecriture', pp. 31–61, in S. Sontag (ed.) *Barthes: Selected Writings*, Fontana, London.

——(1986a) 'The death of the author', pp. 49–55, in R. Barthes *The Rustle of Language*, Blackwell, Oxford.

——(1986b) *The Rustle of Language*, Blackwell, Oxford.

Bartkowski, F. (1988) 'Epistemic drift in Foucault', pp. 43–58, in Irene Diamond and Lee Quinby (eds), *Feminism and Foucault: Reflections on resistance*, North Eastern University Press, Boston.

Bartky, S L. (1988) 'Foucault, femininity and the modernisation of patriarchal power', pp. 61–86 in I. Diamond and L. Quinby (eds), *Feminism and Foucault: Reflections on resistance*, North Eastern University Press, Boston.

Batten, C. (1974) 'Humphry Clinker and eighteenth century travel literature', pp. 392–408, in *Genre*, 7.

——(1978) *Pleasurable Instruction: Form and Convention in Eighteenth Century Travel Literature*, University of California Press, Berkeley.

Battersby, C. (1989) *Gender and Genius: Towards a Feminist Aesthetics*, Women's Press, London.

Beer, G. (1989) 'Representing women: re-presenting the past', pp. 63–80, in C. Belsey and J. Moore (eds) *The Feminist Reader*, Macmillan, Basingstoke.

Berger, P. L. and Luckman T. (1966) *The Social Construction of Reality*, Penguin, Harmondsworth.

Bersani, L. (1977) 'The subject of power', pp. 2–21 in *Diacritics*, fall, 7:3.

Betterton, R. ed. (1987) *Looking On: Images of Femininity in the Arts and Media*, Pandora, London.

Bhabha, H. (1983) 'The other question', pp. 18–36, in *Screen*, Nov.–Dec., 24.

Biddis, M. ed. (1970) *Gobineau: Selected Political Writings*, Jonathan Cape, London.

Birkett, D. (1986) 'The invalids at home, the Samsons abroad', pp. 18–19 in *Women's Review*, April, 6.

——(1989): *Spinsters Abroad: Victorian Lady Explorers*, Oxford University Press, Oxford.

Birtles, D. (1985) *North-West by North*, Virago, London (f.pub. 1935).

Bishop-Bird, I. (1984) *Unbeaten Tracks in Japan*, Virago, London (f.pub. 1880).

Bitterlee, U. (1989) *Cultures in Conflict: Encounters between Europe and non-European Cultures 1492–1800*, trans. R. Robertson, Polity, London (f.pub. 1986).

Blackburn, J. (1979) *The White Men : The First Response of Aboriginal People to the White Men*, Orbis, London.

Blanch, L. (1974) *The Wilder Shores of Love*, Panther, London.

Boumelha, P. (1982) *Thomas Hardy and Women: Sexual Ideology and Narrative Form*, Harvester, Brighton.

Bowen, E. S. (1956) *Return to Laughter*, Victor Gollancz, London.

Bowles, G. and Duelli-Klein, R. (1983) *Theories of Women's Studies*, Routledge & Kegan Paul, London.

Brée, G. (1968) 'The ambiguous voyage: mode or genre', pp. 87–96 in *Genre*, 1.

Brownmiller, S. (1986) *Femininity*, Paladin, London.

Buford, B. ed. (1984) *Travel Writing*, Granta 10, Penguin, Harmondsworth.

——(1986): *In Trouble Again: A Special Issue of Travel Writing*, Granta 20, Penguin, Harmondsworth.

Butor, M. (1974) 'Travel and writing', pp. 1–16 in *Mosaic*, fall, VIII, part 1.

Cable, M. and French, F. (1927) *Through Jade Gate and Central Asia*, Hodder & Stoughton, London.

——(1942) *The Gobi Desert*, Hodder & Stoughton, London.

Cameron, D. (1985) *Feminism and Linguistic Theory*, Macmillan, London.

Campbell, J. (1984) 'Going native', pp. 38–9, in *New Statesman*, 5 October.

Carrington, D. ed. (1949) *The Traveller's Eye*, Pilot Press, London.

Carroll, D. (1978) 'The subject of archæology or the sovereignty of the episteme', pp. 695–722, in *Modern Language Notes*, May, 93: 4.

Chalon, J. (1985) *Le Lumineux Destin de Alexandre David-Neel*, Perrin, Paris.

Clegg, M. (1990) 'Critical language analysis', unpublished MLitt. dissertation, University of Strathclyde.

Clifford, J. and Marcus, G.E. (1986) *Writing Culture: The Poetics and Politics of Ethnography*, University of California Press, Berkeley.

Colls, R. and Dodd, P. (1986) *Englishness: Politics and Culture 1880–1920*, Croom Helm, London.

215

Couzens-Hoy, D. (ed.) (1986) *Foucault: A Critical Reader*, Blackwell, Oxford.

Coward, R. and Ellis, J. (1977) *Language and Materialism: Developments in Semiology and the Theory of the Subject*, Routledge & Kegan Paul, London.

Coward, R. (1983) *Patriarchal Precedents: Sexuality and Social Relations*, Routledge & Kegan Paul, London.

——(1984) *Female Desire: Women's Sexuality Today*, Paladin, London.

Cowasjee, S. (1990) *Women Writers of the Raj*, Grafton, London.

David-Neel, A. (1929) *La Lama aux Cinq Sagesses*, Plon, Paris.

——(1931) *Initiations and Initiates in Tibet*, Rider, London.

——(1976) *Journal de Voyage: Vols I-II*, Plon, Paris.

——(1977) *Buddhism*, trans. H.N.M. Hardy, Bodley Head, London.

——(1983) *My Journey to Lhasa*, Virago, London (f.pub. 1927).

——(1984) *Magic and Mystery in Tibet*, Unwin, Hemel Hempstead, (f.pub 1967).

Davidson, L.C. (1889) *Hints to Lady Travellers at Home and Abroad*, Iliffe & Son, London.

Davidson, R. (1982) *Tracks*, Paladin, London.

Davies, K. (1985) *Women Explorers*, Macmillan Educational, Basingstoke.

Davies, M. and Jansz, N. eds (1990) *Women Travel: Adventures, Advice and Experience*, Harrap, London.

Davin, A. (1989) 'Imperialism and motherhood', pp. 203–35 in R. Samuel (ed.) *Patriotism: Making and Unmaking of British National Identity*, vol. I, *History and Politics*, Routledge, London.

Davis, L. (1983) *Factual Fictions: The Origins of the English Novel*, Columbia University Press, New York.

Dekker, R.M. and van de Pol, L.C. (1989) *The Tradition of Female Transvestism in Early Modern Europe*, Macmillan, Basingstoke.

Denys, J. (1972) *Alexandra David-Neel au Tibet: Une supercherie dévoilée*, La Pensée Universelle, Paris.

Desai, A. (1977) *Fire on the Mountain*, Penguin, Harmondsworth.

Diamond, A. and Edwards, L. eds (1977) *The Authority of Experience: Essays in Feminist Criticism*, University of Massachusetts Press, Amherst.

Diamond, I. and Quinby, L. eds (1988) *Feminism and Foucault: Reflections on resistance*, North Eastern University Press, Boston.

Dodd, P. ed. (1982a) *The Art of Travel: Essays on Travel Writing*, Cass, London.

Dodd, P. (1982) 'The views of travellers: travel writing in the 1930s', pp. 127–36, in P. Dodd (ed.) *The Art of Travel: Essays on Travel Writing*, Cass, London.

——(1986) 'Englishness and national culture', pp. 1–28, in R. Colls and P. Dodd (eds) *Englishness: Politics and Culture, 1880–1920*, Croom Helm, London.

Doughty, C. M. (1931) *Passages from Arabia Deserta*, Penguin, London (f.pub. 1888).

Douglas, M. (1966) *Purity and Danger: An Analysis of Concepts of Pollution and Taboo*, Routledge & Kegan Paul, London.

Dreyfus, H. L. and Rabinow, P. eds (1982) *Michel Foucault: Beyond Structuralism & Hermeneutics*, Harvester, Brighton.

Duff-Gordon, L. (1983) *Letters from Egypt*, Virago, London (f.pub 1865).

Durham, E. (1985) *High Albania*, Virago, London (f.pub.1909).

Duyfhuizen, B. (1986) 'Diary narratives in fact and fiction', pp. 171–8 in *Novel*, winter.

Eagleton, T. (1979) 'Ideology, fiction, narrative', pp. 62–80 in *Social Text*, 2.

Easlea, B. (1981) *Science and Sexual Oppression: Patriarchy's Confrontation with Women and Nature*, Weidenfeld & Nicolson, London.

Eberhardt, I. (1987) *The Passionate Nomad*, Virago, London (f.pub. 1905).

Eden, E. (1983) *Up the Country*, Virago, London (f.pub. 1866).

Edwardes, M. (1967) *Glorious Sahibs*, Eyre and Spottiswoode, London.

Edwards, A. (1986) *Untrodden Peaks and Unfrequented Valleys*, Virago, London (f.pub 1873).

Ehrenreich, B. and English, D. (1973) *Complaints and Disorders: The Sexual Politics of Sickness*, Writers and Readers, London.

——(1979) *For Her Own Good: 150 Years of Experts' Advice to Women*, Pluto, London.

Etienne, M. and Leacock, E. (1980) *Women and Colonization: Anthropological Perspectives*, Praeger, New York.

Fabb, N. ed. (1987) *The Linguistics of Writing: Arguments Between Language and Literature*, Manchester University Press, Manchester.

Fabian, J. (1983) *Time and the Other: How Anthropology Makes Its Object*, Columbia University Press, New York.

Fletcher, A. (1976) *The Literature of Fact: Selected Papers from the English Institute*, Columbia University Press, New York.

Foster, S. (1988) 'Women travellers', a paper to Network feminist theorists, Lancaster, May.

——(1990) *Across New Worlds: Nineteenth Century Women Travellers and their Writings*, Harvester, Hemel Hempstead.

Foucault, M. (1972a) *The Archæology of Knowledge*, trans. A. Sheridan Smith, Harper Colophon, New York (f.pub in French 1969).

——(1972b) 'History, discourse – discontinuity', pp. 225–48, in *Salmagundi*, summer/fall 20.

——(1973a) *Birth of the Clinic: An Archæology of Medical Perception*, trans. A. M. Sheridan, Tavistock, London.

——(1973b) *The Order of Things: An Archæology of the Human Sciences*, Vintage/Random, New York. (f.pub in French 1966).

——(1977a) *Language, Counter-Memory, Practice*, ed. D. Bouchard, Cornell University Press, New York.

——(1977b) 'The political function of the intellectual', pp. 12–24, in *Radical Philosophy*, summer, 17.

——(1979) *Discipline and Punish*, trans. A.M. Sheridan, Vintage/Random, New York.

——(1980a) *Power/Knowledge: Selected Interviews*, ed. C. Gordon, Harvester, Brighton.

——(1980b) 'What is an author', pp. 141–60 in J.V. Harari (ed.) *Textual Strategies: Perspectives in Poststructuralist Criticism*, Methuen, London.

——(1981a) *The History of Sexuality*, vol. I, Pelican, Harmondsworth.

——(1981b) 'The order of discourse', pp. 48–79 in R. Young (ed.) *Untying the Text: A Post-Structuralist Reader*, Routledge & Kegan Paul, London.

——(1982) 'The subject and power', pp. 208–226 in H. Dreyfus and P. Rabinow (eds) *Michel Foucault: Beyond Structuralism & Hermeneutics*, Harvester, Brighton.

Fowler, R., Kress, G., Hodge, R. and Trew, T. (1979) *Language and Control*, Routledge & Kegan Paul, London.

Frétard, A. (1985) 'Alexandra David-Néel: L'Ultime étape', pp. 58–63 in *Grands Reportages*, July/August, 52.

Frow, J. (1985) 'Discourse and power', pp. 193–213 in *Economy and Society*, May, 14: 2.

Fussell, P. (1963) 'Patrick Brydone: the eighteenth century traveller as representative man', pp. 53–67, in W.G. Rice (ed.) *Literature as a Mode of Travel*, New York Public Library, New York.

——(1980): *Abroad; British Literary Travelling Between the Wars*, Oxford University Press, Oxford.

Gallop, J. (1980) in S. McConnell-Ginet (ed.) *Women and Language in Literature and Society*, pp. 274–83, Praeger, New York.

Gates, H.L. (1985) 'Writing, "race" and the difference it makes', pp. 1–20 in *Critical Inquiry*, autumn, 12: 1.

Gattey, C. N. (1967) *The Bloomer Girls*, Femina, London.

Gerrard, N. (1987) 'Travel Books', p. 22 in *Women's Review*, May, 19.

Gilbert, S. and Gubar, S. (1988) *The War of the Words*, vol. 1, Yale University Press, New Haven.

Goodman, S. (1985) *Gertrude Bell*, Berg, Leamington Spa.

Gordon, C. (1977) 'Birth of the subject', pp. 15–25 in *Radical Philosophy*, summer, 17.

——(1979) 'Other inquisitions', pp. 23–46 in *Ideology and Consciousness*, 6.

Gordon, D. (1988) 'Writing culture, writing feminism: the poetics and politics of experimental ethnography', pp. 7–26 in *Inscriptions*, 3/4.

Gove, P. (1941) *The Imaginary Voyage in Prose Fiction: A History of Its Criticism and a Guide to its Study*, Columbia University Press, New York.

Graham, E. Hinds, H., Hobby, H. and Wilcox, H. eds (1989) *Her Own Life*, Routledge, London.

Green, M. (1980) *Dreams of Adventure – Deeds of Empire*, Routledge & Kegan Paul, London.

Gunew, S. (1983a) 'Feminist criticism; positions and questions', pp. 151–61 in *Southern Review*, 16, part 1.

——(1983b) 'What does woman mean?', pp. 111–22 in *Hecate*, 9, part 1–2.

——(1985a) 'Framing marginalities', pp. 142–56 in *Southern Review*, 18, part 2.

——(1985b) 'Migrant women writers: who's on whose margins?', pp. 163–78 in C. Ferrier (ed.) *Gender Politics and Fiction: Twentieth Century Women's Novels*, University of Queensland Press, St Lucia, Queensland.

——(1989) 'PMT (post-modernist tensions) reading for (multi) cultural difference', paper given to the Association of Commonwealth Literature and Language, Canterbury University, Kent.

Haggis, J. (1988) *Women and Colonialism: Untold Stories and Conceptual Absences*, Studies in Sexual Politics, no. 25, University of Manchester.

Hall, H.G. (1984) 'Observation and imagination in French seventeenth century travel literature', pp. 117–39 in *Journal of European Studies*, June 14, part 2, no.54.

Hamalian, L. (1981) *Ladies on the Loose: Women Travellers of the 18th and 19th Centuries*, John Curley and Associates, South Yarmouth, Mass.

Hamon, P. (1982) 'What is a description', pp. 147–78 in T. Todorov (ed.) *French Literary Theory Today: A Reader*, Cambridge University Press, Cambridge.

Harasym, S. ed. (1990) *Gayatri Spivak: The Post-colonial Critic: Interviews, Strategies, Dialogues*, Routledge, London.

Harbsmeier, M. (1984) 'Early travel to Europe: some remarks on the magic of writing' pp. 72–88 in F. Barker (ed.) *Europe and its Others*, vol. I, Proceedings of the Essex Sociology of Literature Conference, July 1984, University of Essex, Colchester.

Harrer, H. (1983) *Seven Years in Tibet*, Granada, London (f.pub 1953).

——(1984) *Return to Tibet*, Penguin, Harmondsworth.

Harvey, A. (1983) *A Journey in Ladakh*, Jonathan Cape, London.

Haug, F. ed. (1987) *Female Sexualisation*, Verso, London.

Hennessy, R. and Mohan, R. (1989) 'The construction of woman in three popular texts of empire: towards a critique of materialist feminism', pp. 323–59, *Textual Practice*, Winter, 3. 3.

Hilton, J. (1947) *Lost Horizon*, Macmillan/Pan, London (f.pub.1933).

Hobby, E. (1988) *Virtue of Necessity*, Virago, London.

Hobsbawm, E. J. (1987) *The Age of Empire 1875–1914*, Weidenfeld & Nicolson, London.

Hobson, S. (1973): *Through Persia in Disguise*, John Murray, London.

Hopkirk, P. (1982) *Trespassers on the Roof of the World: The Race for Lhasa*, John Murray, London.

——(1983) 'Introduction', pp. ix-xvi, in A. David-Neel *My Journey to Lhasa*, Virago, London (orig. pub. 1927).

Hulme, P. (1986) *Colonial Encounters: Europe and the Native Caribbean 1492–1797*, Methuen, London.

Humm, M. (1989) 'Subjects in English: autobiography, women and education', pp. 39–49 in A. Thomson and H. Wilcox (eds) *Teaching Women: Feminism and English Studies*, Manchester University Press, Manchester.

Hutchins, F.G. (1967) *The Illusion of Permanence: British Imperialism in India*, Princeton University Press, New Jersey.

Hyam, R. (1990) *Empire and Sexuality: The British Experience*, Manchester University Press, Manchester.

Jacobus, M. ed. (1979) *Women Writing and Writing about Women*, Croom Helm, London.

Jewkes, W.T. (1963) 'The literature of travel and the mode of romance in the Renaissance', pp. 13–30 in W.G. Rice (ed.) *Literature as a Mode of Travel*, New York Public Library, New York.

Jones, K. (1988) 'On authority; or, why women are not entitled to speak', pp. 119–33 in I. Diamond and L. Quinby (eds) *Feminism and Foucault: Reflections on resistance*, North Eastern University Press, Boston.

Joyce, E. (1984) 'White man's burden: white woman's lark: Mary Kingsley and the myth of the explorer hero', pp. 99–117 in *Trent Papers in Communication*, 2: Power and Communication – Feminist Perspectives.

Judowitz, D. (1978) Review of 'Language, Counter-Memory, Practice', pp. 89–91 in *Modern Language Notes*, May, 93: 4.

Kabbani, R. (1986) *Europe's Myths of Orient: Devise and Rule*, Macmillan, London.

Kamuf, P. (1980) 'Writing like a woman', pp. 284–99, in S. McConnell-Ginet (ed.), *Women and Language in Literature and Society*, Praeger, New York.

Kaplan, C. (1987) *Sea Changes: Culture and Feminism*, Verso, London.

Keay, J. (1982) *Eccentric Travellers*, John Murray, London.

Kempe, M. (1985) *The Book of Margery Kempe*, Penguin, Harmondsworth (f.pub. 1436–8).

Kiernan, V.G. (1969) *The Lords of Humankind*, Wiedenfeld & Nicolson, London.

Kincaid, J. (1988) *A Small Place*, Virago, London.

Kinglake, A. (1982) *Eothen*, Oxford University Press, Oxford (f.pub 1906).

Kingsley, M. (1965) *Travels in West Africa*, Virago, London (f.pub. 1897).

Kipling, R. (1987) *Kim*, Penguin, Harmondsworth (f.pub 1901).

Kirton, J.W. (1882) *Happy Homes and How to Make Them*, John Kempster and Sonnenschein, London.

Kristeva, J. (1986) 'Women's time', pp. 188–211 in T. Moi (ed.) *The Kristeva Reader*, Blackwell, Oxford.

Lakoff, R. (1975) *Language and Woman's Place*, Harper Colophon, New York.

Lapping, B. (1989) *End of Empire*, Paladin, London.

Lévi-Strauss, C. (1973) *Tristes Tropiques*, Jonathan Cape, London.

Lewis, B. (1982) 'The question of orientalism', pp. 49–56 in *New York Review of Books*, 24 June.

Lloyd, G. (1986) 'The mind on sex' (review), pp. 24–7, in *New York Review of Books*, 13 May.

Lugones, M. C. and Spelman, E. V. (1983) 'Have we got a theory for you! Feminist theory, cultural imperialism and the demand for "the woman's voice"', pp. 573–81 in *Women's Studies in Forum*, 6: 6.

Macaulay, R. (1956) *The Towers of Trebizond*, Fontana, London.

McBratney, J. (1988) 'Images of Indian women in Rudyard Kipling: a case of doubling discourse', pp. 47–57 in *Inscriptions*, 3/4.

McConnell-Ginet, S. ed. (1980) *Women and Language in Literature and Society*, Praeger, New York.

Macdonald, D. (1932) *Twenty Years in Tibet*, Seeley, Service and Co., London.

Macdonell, D. (1986): *Theories of Discourse*, Blackwell, Oxford.

Mackay, J. and Thane, P. (1986) 'The Englishwoman', pp. 191–229 in R. Colls and P. Dodd (eds) *Englishness: Politics and Culture 1880–1920*, Croom Helm, London.

Mackenzie, J.M. ed. (1986) *Imperialism and Popular Culture*, Manchester University Press, Manchester.

Maclulich, L. (1979) 'Canadian exploration as literature', pp. 62–79, in *Canadian Literature*, summer, 81.

Maillart, E. (1983) *Forbidden Journey*, Heinemann, London (f.pub. 1937).

——(1986) *The Cruel Way*, Virago, London (f.pub.1947).

Mani, L. and Frankenberg, R. (1985) 'The challenge of Orientalism', pp. 175–91, in *Economy and Society*, May, 14: 2.

Markham, B. (1984) *West with the Night*, Virago, London (f.pub.1936).

Marks, E. and de Courtivron, I. eds (1981) *New French Feminisms*, Harvester, Brighton.

Marxist Feminist Literature Collective (MFLC) (1978) 'Women's writing: Jane Eyre, Shirley, Villette, Aurora Leigh', pp. 27–48 in *Ideology and Consciousness*, spring, 1, part 3.

Mazuchelli, N. (1876) *The Indian Alps and How we Crossed them: being a narrative of two years residence in the Eastern Himalayas and a two months tour into the interior by a Lady Pioneer, illustrated by herself*, Longmans, Green and Co. London.

Mezciems, J. (1982) '"Tis not to Divert the Reader": moral and literary determinants in some early travel narratives', pp. 1–20, in P. Dodd (eds) *The Art of Travel: Essays on Travel Writing*, Cass, London.

Middleton, D. (1982) *Victorian Lady Travellers*, Academy, Chicago (f.pub.1965).

Migot, A. (1955) *Tibetan Marches*, Hart Davis, London.

Miles, P. (1982): 'A semi-mental journey: structure and illusion in Smollett's "Travels"', pp. 40–59 in P. Dodd (ed.) *The Art of Travel: Essays on Travel Writing*, Cass, London.

Miller, L. (1976) *On Top of the World: Five Women Explorers in Tibet*, Paddington Press, London.

Miller, N. (1980) 'Women's autobiography in France: for a dialectics of identification', pp. 258–73, in S. McConnell-Ginet (ed) *Women and Language in Literature and Society*, Praeger, New York.

Millett, K. (1977) *Sexual Politics*, Virago, London.

Mills, S. (1986) 'Alternative voices to Orientalism', pp. 78–91 in *Literature Teaching Politics*, 5.

——(1987) 'The male sentence', pp. 189–98 in *Language and Communication*, 7.

——(1988a) 'British travel writers in India', paper to the ACLALS conference, Kent.

——(1988b) 'A Foucauldian perspective on literariness and fictionality in travel writing', unpublished Ph.D thesis.

——(1990a) 'Discourses of difference', pp. 128–40 in *Cultural Studies*, May, 4: 2.

——(1990b) 'Problems in the analysis of working class women's autobiography', in Conference Proceedings from Humboldt University's Conference on Working Class Writing, East Berlin, 1989.

——(1991) 'Knowing/your place', in Michael Toolan (ed.) *Contextualised Stylistics*, Routledge, London.

Mills, S., Pearce, L., Spaull, S. and Millard, G. (1989) *Feminist Readings/ Feminists Reading*, Harvester, Hemel Hempstead.

Minh-ha, T.T. (1989) *Woman, Native, Other: Writing Postcoloniality and Feminism*, Indiana University Press, Bloomington.

Mitchell, W. ed. (1980) *On Narrative*, University of Chicago Press, Chicago.

Mitchison, N. (1981) *Mucking Around: Five Continents Over Fifty Years*, Gollancz, London.

Mitford, J. (1984) 'The travail of travel', p. 40 in *New Statesman*, 30 November.

Moers, E. (1976) *Literary Women*, Doubleday and Co., New York.

Moi, T. (1985) *Sexual/Textual Politics*, Methuen, London.

——(1986) *The Kristeva Reader*, Blackwell, Oxford.

——(1987) *French Feminist Thought*, Blackwell, Oxford.

——(1989) 'Feminist, female, feminine', pp. 117–33 in C. Belsey and J. Moore (eds) *The Feminist Reader*, Macmillan, Basingstoke.

Monteith, M. (1986) *Women's Writing: A Challenge to Theory*, Harvester, Brighton.

Moore, H. (1988) *Feminism and Anthropology*, Polity, London.

Moorehead, C. (1985) *Freya Stark*, Penguin, Harmondsworth.

Morris, C. ed. (1982) *The Illustrated Journeys of Celia Fiennes*, Macdonald, London.

Morris, J. (1979b) *Heaven's Command: an Imperial Progress*, Penguin, Harmondsworth.

——(1979c) *Pax Britannica: the Climax of an Empire*, Penguin, Harmondsworth.

——(1979a) *Farewell the Trumpets: An Imperial Retreat*, Penguin, Harmondsworth.

——(1984) *Journeys*, Oxford University Press, Oxford.

Morris, M. and Patton, P. eds. (1979) *Foucault, Power Truth and Strategy*, Feral Publications, Sydney.

Murphy, D. (1965) *Full Tilt*, John Murray, London.

——(1983) 'Introduction', pp. i–vi in E. Maillart *Forbidden Journey*, Heinemann, London (f.pub. 1937).

Naipaul, V.S. (1964) *An Area of Darkness*, André Deutsch, London.

——(1979) *India: A Wounded Civilization*, Penguin, Harmondsworth.

——(1981) *Among the Believers*, André Deutsch, London.

Neumark, V. (1985) 'Review' of Bettina Selby's *Riding the Mountain Down*, p. 33 in *New Statesman*, 11 January.

Newby, E. (1985) *A Book of Travellers' Tales*, Picador, London.

BIBLIOGRAPHY

Ngugi, T, wa. (1986) *Decolonising the Mind*, Heinemann, London.
Nochlin, L. (1971) 'Why are there no great women artists?', pp. 344–66 in V. Gornick (ed.) *Women in Sexist Society*, Basic Books, New York.
Norbu, T. (1960) *Tibet is My Country*, Hart Davis, London.
Norwick, B. (1976) 'Alexandra David-Neel's adventures in Tibet, fact or fiction', pp. 70–4 in *Tibet Journal*, 1: 2–3.
O'Barr, W.M. and Atkins, B.K. (1980) ' "Women's language" or "powerless language"?', pp. 93–110 in S. McConnell-Ginet (ed.) *Women and Language in Literature and Society*, Praeger, New York.
O'Brien, K. (1985) *Farewell to Spain*, Virago, London (f.pub. 1937).
O'Hanlan, R. (1986) 'Amazon adventure', in B. Buford (ed.) *In Trouble Again: A Special Issue of Travel Writing*, Granta 20, Penguin, Harmondsworth.
Oliver, C. (1982) *Western Women in Colonial Africa*, Greenwood Press, Westport, Connecticut.
Osborn, J.M. (1963) 'Travel literature and the rise of Neo-Hellenism in England', pp. 31–52, in W.G. Rice (ed.) *Literature as Mode of Travel*, New York Public Library, New York.
Ostriker, A. (1987) *Stealing the Language: the Emergence of Women's Poetry in America*, Women's Press, London.
Owusu, M. (1978) 'Ethnography of Africa', pp. 310–34 in *American Anthropologist*, 80.
Pallis, M. (1948) *Peaks and Lamas*, Readers Union/Cassell, London.
Palmer, P. (1989): *Contemporary Women's Fiction: Narrative Practice and Feminist Theory*, Harvester, Hemel Hempstead.
Parks, F. (1850) *Wanderings of a Pilgrim in Search of the Picturesque: during 24 years in the East, with revelations of life in the Zenana*, 2 vols, Pelham Richardson, London.
Pearson, C. and Pope, K. (1981) *The Female Hero in American and British Literature*, Bowker and Co., New York.
Pecheux, M. (1982) *Language, Semantics and Ideology*, Macmillan, London.
Pfeiffer, I. (1988) *A Lady's Voyage Round the World*, Century Hutchinson, London (f.pub, 1851).
Poetry Review (1986) *Fortunate Travellers: A Special Issue on Travel Poetry*, 76: 3.
Porter, B. (1985) *The Lion's Share: A Short History of British Imperialism 1850–1983*, 2nd edn, Longman, London and New York.
Porter, D. (1982) 'Orientalism and its problems', pp. 179–93 in F. Barker (ed.) *The Politics of Theory*, Proceedings of the Essex Sociology of Literature conference, July 1982, University of Essex, Colchester.
——(1983) 'Reinventing travel: Stendhal's Roman Journey', pp. 467–76 in *Genre*, winter, XVI.
Poster, M. (1984) *Foucault, Marxism and History: Mode of Production vs. Mode of Information*, Polity, London.
Pratt, M.L. (1985) 'Scratches on the face of the country; or what Mr. Barrows saw in the land of the Bushmen', pp. 119–43 in *Critical Inquiry*, autumn, 12: 1.
——(1987) 'Linguistic utopias', pp. 48–66 in N. Fabb (ed.) *The*

Linguistics of Writing: Arguments Between Language and Literature, Manchester University Press, Manchester.

Rabinow, P. (1984) *The Foucault Reader,* Penguin, Harmondsworth.

Rice, W.G. ed. (1963) *Literature as a Mode of Travel,* New York Public Library, New York.

Rice, W.G. (1963b) 'Travellers and travel books', pp. 1–12 in W.G. Rice (ed.) *Literature as a Mode of Travel,* New York Public Library, New York.

Robinson, J. (1990) *Wayward Women: A Guide to Women Travellers,* Oxford University Press, Oxford.

Rochefort, C. (1981) 'Are women writers still monsters?', pp. 183–7, in E. Marks and I. de Courtivron (eds) *New French Feminisms,* Harvester, Brighton.

Rochère, J. (1954) 'Ces femmes ont étonné le Monde', p. 25 in *Voix du Nord,* 23 September.

Rogers, F.R. (1963) 'The road to reality: Burlesque travel literature and Mark Twain's "Roughing It"', pp. 85–98, in W.G. Rice (ed.) *Literature as a Mode of Travel,* New York Public Library, New York.

Root, J. (1984) *Pictures of Women,* Pandora, London.

Rosenberg, S. (1971) 'Travel literature and the picaresque novel', pp. 40–7 in *Enlightenment Essays,* 2.

Russ, J. (1984) *How to Suppress Women's Writing,* Women's Press, London.

Russell, M. (1986) *The Blessings of a Good Thick Skirt: Women Travellers and their World,* Collins, London.

Ruthven, M. (1986) *Traveller Through Time: Freya Stark,* Viking, Harmondsworth.

Sabin, M. (1982) 'The spectacle of reality in "Sea and Sardinia"', pp. 85–100 in P. Dodd (ed.) *The Art of Travel, Essays on Travel Writing,* Cass, London.

Said, E. (1976) 'Interview', pp. 33–45, in *Diacritics,* Fall, 6: 3.

——(1978) *Orientalism,* Routledge & Kegan Paul, London.

——(1978) 'The problem of textuality: two exemplary positions', pp. 673–714 in *Critical Inquiry,* summer, 4.

—(1983) *The World, the Text, the Critic,* Harvard University Press, Massachusetts.

——(1984) 'Orientalism reconsidered', pp. 14–27 in F. Barker (ed.) *Europe and Its Others,* vol. 1, Proceedings of the Essex Sociology of Literature Conference, July 1984, University of Essex, Colchester.

Schaffer, K. (1989) *Women and the Bush: Forces of Desire in the Australian Cultural Tradition,* Cambridge University Press, Cambridge.

Shaw, P. K. (1986) *The Explorer in English Fiction,* Macmillan, Basingstoke.

Sheridan, A. (1980) *Michel Foucault: The Will to Truth,* Tavistock, London.

Showalter, E. (1971) 'Women writers and the double standard', pp. 323–42, in V. Gornick (ed.) *Women in Sexist Society,* Basic Books, New York.

——(1977) *A Literature of Their Own,* Virago, London.

——(1982) 'Feminist criticism in the wilderness', pp. 9–35 in E. Abel (ed.) *Writing and Sexual Difference*, Harvester, Brighton.

Smart, B. (1985) *Michel Foucault*, Tavistock, London.

Smith, B.H. (1980) 'Narrative versions, narrative theories', pp. 209–32 in W. Mitchell (ed.) *On Narrative*, University of Chicago Press, Chicago.

Spencer, J. (1986) *The Rise of the Woman Novelist*, Blackwell, Oxford.

Spender, D. (1980) *Man Made Language*, Routledge & Kegan Paul, London.

——(1982) *Women of Ideas and What Men Have Done to Them: From Aphra Behn to Adrienne Rich*, Routledge & Kegan Paul, London.

——(1986) *Mothers of the Novel*, Pandora, London.

Spivak, G.C. (1986) 'Imperialism and sexual difference', pp. 225–240 in *Sexual Difference: Conference Proceedings*, Oxford Literary Review, Southampton.

——(1987) *In Other Worlds: Essays in Cultural Politics*, Methuen, London.

——(1989) 'Three women's texts and a critique of imperialism', pp. 175–96, in C. Belsey and J. Moore (eds) *The Feminist Reader*, Macmillan, Basingstoke.

Stannard, M. (1982) 'Debunking the jungle: the context of Evelyn Waugh's travel books 1930–9', pp. 100–25, in P. Dodd (ed.) *The Art of Travel: Essays on Travel Writing*, Cass, London.

Stark, F. (1937) *Baghdad Sketches*, John Murray, London.

——(1940) *A Winter in Arabia*, John Murray, London.

——(1945) *East is West*, John Murray, London.

Steedman, C. (1986) *Landscape for a Good Woman*, Virago, London.

Stevenson, C.B. (1982): *Victorian Women Travel Writers in Africa*, Twayne Publishers, Boston.

——(1985) 'Female anger and African politics', pp. 7–17 in *Turn of the Century Women*, 2, part 1.

Stott, R. (1989) 'The Dark Continent: Africa as female body in Haggard's adventure fiction', pp. 69–89 in *Feminist Review*, summer, 32.

Suleiman, S. ed. (1980) *The Reader in the Text*, Princeton University Press, New Jersey.

Theroux, P. (1984) *The Kingdom by the Sea*, Penguin, Harmondsworth.

Thesiger, W. (1967) *The Marsh Arabs*, Penguin Travel Library, London, (f.pub. 1964).

Thieme, J. (1982) 'Authorial voice in V.S. Naipaul's "The Middle Passage"', pp. 137–50, in P. Dodd (ed.) *The Art of Travel: Essays on Travel Writing*, Cass, London.

Thompson, A. and Wilcox, H. (1989) *Teaching Women: Feminism and English Studies*, Manchester University Press, Manchester.

Thomson, P. (1956) *The Victorian Heroine: A Changing Ideal 1837–1873*, Oxford University Press, London.

Thubten, N. (1961) *Tibet is My Country*, Hart Davis, London.

Tristan, F. (1986) *Peregrinations of a Pariah*, Virago, London (f.pub. 1838).

Trollope, J. (1983) *Britannia's Daughters: Women of the British Empire*, Hutchinson, London.

Trungpa, C. (1966) *Born in Tibet*, Mandala/Unwin, London.

Velter, A. (1985) 'Alexandra La Grande: Alexandra David-Neel', pp. 11–18 in *Le Monde*, 5 April.

Vicinus, M. ed. (1972) *Suffer and Be Still – Women in the Victorian Age*, Methuen, London.

——(1980) *The Widening Sphere: Changing Roles of Victorian Women*, Methuen, London.

Visweswaran, K. (1988) 'Defining feminist ethnography', pp. 27–46 in *Inscriptions*, special issue, *Feminism and the Critique of Colonial Discourse*, 3/4.

Vogel, D. (1974) 'A lexicon rhetoricæ for journey literature', pp. 185–9 in *College English*, October, 36: 2.

Walby, S. (1990) *Theorizing Patriarchy*, Blackwell, Oxford.

Waugh, E. (1985) *Ninety-Two Days: A Journey in Guiana and Brazil*, Penguin Travel Library, Harmondsworth (f.pub. 1934).

Weedon, C. (1987) *Feminist Practice and Post-Structuralist Thought*, Blackwell, Oxford.

Wharton, E. (1984) *In Morocco*, Century Hutchinson, London, (f.pub 1920).

Wheelwright, J. (1989): *Amazons and Military Maids*, Pandora, London.

White, H. (1974) 'The historical text as literary artefact', pp. 277–304 in *Clio*, 3, part 3.

——(1976) 'The fictions of factual representation', pp. 21–44 in A. Fletcher (ed.) *The Literature of Fact: Selected Papers from the English Institute*, Columbia University Press, New York.

——(1980a) 'The narrativisation of real events, critical response III', pp. 248–9 in W. Mitchell (ed.) *On Narrative*, University of Chicago Press, Chicago.

——(1980b) 'The value of narrativity in the representation of reality', pp. 1–23, in W. Mitchell (ed.) *On Narrative*, University of Chicago Press, Chicago.

Williams, P. (1986) 'Colonial literature and the notion of Britishness', pp. 92–107, in *Literature Teaching Politics*, 5.

——(forthcoming) *Writing the Raj: Politics of Race and Nation in Colonial Fiction*, Harvester, Hemel Hempstead.

Williams, R. (1976) *Keywords*, Fontana, London.

——(1977) *Marxism and Literature*, Oxford University Press, Oxford.

Wilson, E.J. (1981) 'Orientalism: a black perspective', pp. 56–69 in *Journal of Palestinian Studies*, X, part 2.

Windt, M. de (1984) *Good Morning and Good Night*, Century Travellers, London (f.pub. 1934).

Winstone, H.V.F. (1980) *Gertrude Bell*, Quartet, London.

Wood, H.J. (1951) *Exploration and Discovery*, Arrow Books, London.

Woodcock, G. (1971) *Into Tibet: The Early British Explorers*, Faber, London.

Workman, F. B. (1895) *Algerian Memories: A Bicycle Tour Over the Atlas to the Sahara*, T. Fisher Unwin, London.

BIBLIOGRAPHY

Worley, L.K. (1986) 'Through others' eyes; narratives of German women travelling in nineteenth century America', pp. 39–50 in *Yearbook of German–American Studies*, 21.

Wright, A. (1986) *Fictional Discourse and Historical Space*, Macmillan, Basingstoke.

Wülfing, W. (1986) 'On travel literature by women in the nineteenth century; Malwida von Meysenburg', pp. 289–304 in R.B. Joeres and M.J. Maynes (eds) *German Women in the Eighteenth and Nineteenth Centuries: A Serial and Literary History*, Indiana University Press, Bloomington.

Wykes, A. (1973) *Abroad: Miscellany of English Travel Writing 1700–1914*, Macdonald, London.

INDEX

228

truth-value 53–7, 114–15, 116–22,
125–52
Tweedie, Mrs Alec 81

Vicinus, Martha 27
vraisemblance 117–18, 119

Ward, Harriet 39
Weedon, Chris 15, 17, 18, 195
White, Hayden 74, 84

Williams, Patrick 58–9
women's writing 40–2
Woodcock, George 116
working class 70
Workman, Fanny Bullock 81, 105
Worley, L.K. 62, 70–1, 93, 120

Younghusband expedition 135

Zweig, Paul 77